On the Road & Off the Record with
LEONARD BERNSTEIN

My Years with the Exasperating Genius

CHARLIE HARMON
FOREWORD BY Harold Prince

imagine!

Photograph and other credits are listed on page 259, which constitutes an extension
of this copyright page.

All writings by Leonard Bernstein, whether in the form of verse or prose quotations
from previously printed sources (books, scores, recordings and program notes), or
from unpublished miscellaneous jottings, correspondence and talks are © Amberson
Holdings LLC and are reproduced with the kind permission of The Leonard Bernstein
Office, Inc.

Unless otherwise noted, all music or lyrics by Leonard Bernstein are © Amberson
Holdings LLC and are reproduced with the kind permission of the Leonard Bernstein
Music Publishing Company LLC.

At the time of publication, all URLs printed in this book were accurate and active.
Charlesbridge and the author are not responsible for the content or accessibility of
any website.

An Imagine Book
Published by Charlesbridge
85 Main Street
Watertown, MA 02472
(617) 926-0329
www.imaginebooks.net

LIBRARY OF CONGRESS CATALOGING-IN-PUBLICATION DATA
Names: Harmon, Charlie, author.
Title: On the road & off the record with Leonard Bernstein : my years with
   the exasperating genius / by Charlie Harmon ; foreword by Harold Prince.
Other titles: On the road and off the record with Leonard Bernstein
Description: Watertown, MA : Charlesbridge, [2018]
Identifiers: LCCN 2017059790| ISBN 9781623545277 (reinforced for library use)
   | ISBN 9781632892195 (ebook)
Subjects: LCSH: Bernstein, Leonard, 1918-1990. | Musicians—United
   States—Biography.
Classification: LCC ML410.B566 H37 2018 | DDC 780.92 [B] —dc23
LC record available at https://lccn.loc.gov/2017059790

Printed in the United States of America
10 9 8 7 6 5 4 3 2 1

FOR *Ann,*

FOR *Patti,*

AND TO THE MEMORY OF *Julia Vega*

Acknowledgments

IT IS A TRUTH universally acknowledged, that every writer dreams of an ideal reader. Two very real readers volunteered for that role, relieving me of my daydreams: Henry Adams, who knew nothing of my four years as Bernstein's assistant, and David Thomas, who knew plenty, though from a tangential slant. My thanks to Henry and David for steering me toward the better word, the consistent voice, and the honest examination of these four peculiar years.

Though he wrote the definitive Bernstein biography, Humphrey Burton said what every memoirist wants to hear: "All this is new to me." Humphrey's candor gives me hope that this memoir fills a niche. Thank you, Humphrey and Christina Burton.

Cage Ames is so well-read and articulate, she must have been born speaking in complete sentences. Thank you, Cage, for your tireless assistance and encouragement, pots of tea, freshly baked cookies, and diversionary chat about the Yankees.

Elaine Wang Meyerhoffer offered word choices and grammatical fixes that eluded this first-time author, for which I am very grateful. Thank you Elaine, and thank you, Richard Bentley, for introducing us.

To my final reader, Beth Hughes, thank you for saying, "Put it away. You're done."

My thanks to all who read sample chapters and begged for more: Alison Ames; Alexander Bernstein, Jamie Bernstein Thomas, and Nina Bernstein Simmons, whose joy and kindness are the finest tributes to their remarkable parents; Helene Blue; John Clingerman and Douglas Myhra, Colin Dunn and Bruce MacRae, my adopted siblings on two continents; Paul Epstein, who should have a late-night TV show explaining legal terms; Ella Fredrickson; Roger and Linda James; Liz Lear and Deems Webster; Laurence McCulloch and Bill Hayton; Mike Miller and Tim Weedlun, for housing and humoring me during my Library of Congress immersions; Lee and Tony Pirrotti; Rene Reder and Dan Keys; stalwart Tony Rickard; life-saver Marilyn Steiner; Aaron Stern; Tom Takaro; Mark Adams Taylor; my personal laugh-therapy group, Leslie Tomkins and Michael Barrett; Alina Voicu and Daniel Szasz; my dear friend and mentor, Charles Webb, witness to my long journey from the start; and Mark Wilson.

Affectionate thanks to the friends, family, and colleagues of Leonard Bernstein, living and departed, who consistently encouraged me as I batted my way through the years in this memoir. Starting with those I think of every day: Jennie Bernstein and her sisters, Dorothy Goldstein and Bertha Resnick; Adrienne Barth; Justin and Elaine Brown; Margaret Carson; Schuyler Chapin; Betty Comden; Valentina Cortese; Ann Dedman; Martha Gellhorn; Adolph Green and Phyllis Newman; Dési Halban; Irma Lazarus and Elsa Kaim; Ruth Mense; Patti Pulliam; Sid and Gloria Ramin; Halina Rodzinski; Stephen Sondheim; Michael Tilson Thomas and Joshua Robison; Wally Toscanini; Fritz and Sigrid Willheim; Harriet Wingreen; and the indispensable Julia Vega.

Gratitude also to: Kazuko Amano, John Malcolm Brinnin, Marshall Burlingame, Helen Coates, Bruce Coughlin, Jobst Eberhardt, Jack Gottlieb, Kuni Hashimoto, Gail Jacobs, Gilbert Kaplan, Dorothee Koehler, Harry Kraut (for hiring me), Dale Kugel, Robert Lantz, Arthur Laurents, James Levine, Christa Ludwig, Pali Meller Marcovicz, John and Betty Mauceri, Erich and Jutta Mauermann, Carlos Moseley, Kurt Ollmann, Richard Ortner, Eiji Oue, Vivian Perlis, Todd and Helen Perry, Hanno Rinke, Jerome Robbins, Ned Rorem, Asadour Santourian, Jonathan Sheffer, Avi Shoshani, Roger and Christine Stevens, Auro Varani, Hans Weber, Richard Wilbur, and Stephen Wadsworth Zinsser.

Thanks to the many people I met through working for Bernstein and who remain friends to this day: David Abell and Seann Alderking, Phillip Allen, Marin Alsop, Franco Amurri, Robert Arbuckle, Betty Auman and Chris Pino, David Bachman, Ellen and Ian Ball, Susann Baumgärtel, Johnny Bayless, Burton Bernstein, Karen Bernstein, Stephen Blier, Daryl Bornstein, Serge Boyce, Garnett Bruce, Amy Burton and John Musto, Finn Byrhard, Flavio Chamis, Steve Clar, Ned Davies, Robert Dawson, Emil DeCou, Clare Dibble, Gail Dubinbaum, Roger Englander, Marcia Farabee, Eliot Feld, Martin Fleischmann, Joel Friedman and Jenny Bilfield, Carlo and Giovanni Gavazzeni, Domiziana Giordano, Linda Golding, John Grande, Sara Griffin, Emily Grishman, David Gruender, Paul Gunther, Dan Gustin, Erik Haagensen and Joe McConnell, Connie Haumann, Barbara Haws and William Josephson, Marilyn Herring, David Israel, Diane Kesling, Sue Klein, Frank Korach, Eric Latzky, Holly Mentzer, Linda Indian, Gail Jacobs, Wolf-Dieter and Amalia Karwatky, Peter Kazaras and Armin Baier, Jim Kendrick, Steve Masterson, Larry Moore, Kent Nagano, Richard Nelson, Clint Nieweg, David Pack, Kevin Patterson, Gideon Paz, Sandra Pearson, John Perkel, Shirley Rhoades Perl, Charley Prince, Philip von Raabe, Gottfried Rabl, Madina Ricordi, Paul Sadowski, Karen Schnackenberg, George Steel and both his Sarahs, Mimsy Gill Stirn, Steve Sturk, Robert

Sutherland, Larry Tarlow, Alessio Vlad, Johnny Walker, Ray White, John Van Winkle, George Wolfe, Paul Woodiel, and Patrick Zwick.

Of my post-Bernstein friends, no less encouraging than those listed above, I must thank Yaniv and Meredith Attar, Christopher Confessore and Bethany Barnhorst, Barry and Deirdre Cullen, Barron and Mary Melton, Mark and Laura Patrick, and David and Anne Pandolfi.

Craig Urquhart gets a thank-you all his own; he held the fort to the end.

Thanks to the photographers whose quick eyes preserved LB as we knew him: Ann Dedman, Robert Millard, Joe McNally (and his studio manager Lynn DelMastro), Patti Pulliam, and Thomas Seiler. Special thanks to Arthur Elgort and Grethe Holby, Andrew French, and Henry Grossman, whose work gives these pages a soul.

To Mark Horowitz at the Library of Congress, keeper of the Bernstein flame for the nation, my sincerest gratitude for your assistance, insights, and conviviality.

To Sallie Randolph, who assisted me with legal matters: this is the beginning of a beautiful friendship.

Thanks to Larry Leech, for pointing out the difference between a journal and a memoir at the June 2015, Florida Writers Association workshop.

To Ann Hood, instructor of the memoir workshop at the January 2017 Writers in Paradise conference at Eckerd College: I pledge eternal vigilance at the shrine of literature where you reign as goddess. There has been no more knowledgeable guide since Virgil accompanied Dante, though Ann traverses a happier terrain. Hosannas to my fellow acolytes from Writers in Paradise: James Anderson, Mary K. Conner, Colleen Herlihy, Molly Howes, Karen Kravit, Antonia Lewandowksi, Joan McKee, Meredith Myers, Carlie Ramer, Honey Rand, and Donna Walker. Your perceptions continue to inspire me.

Gratitude beyond measure goes to my agent, Eric Myers, the first to call and the firmest believer in the story I had to tell.

To my editor, Don Weise, and to the dedicated team at Imagine, Mary Ann Sabia, Lauren Barrett, Connie Brown, and Brian Walker: thanks compounded with admiration for turning that most ephemeral of human abstractions, memories, into a tangible book. You know your business!

A last bow goes to Harold Prince for writing a foreword with grace, polish, and admirable alacrity. Mr. Prince energetically burnishes the Bernstein legacy, year after year. I'm his fan forever and am forever in his debt.

Contents

Foreword

WE ARE ENTERING A PERIOD of celebration of Leonard Bernstein's centenary and there will be concerts, opera productions, lectures, reminiscences, books, and memoirs, of which Charlie Harmon's is among the first. Charlie is well positioned to write about Lenny, as he worked with him for the last nine years of his life. It's an informal, affectionate, and not idolatrous account of the life of an astonishingly talented composer, conductor, and teacher.

When Lenny died, I was asked by the *New York Times* why he hadn't written more musicals and operas. And I replied that had Lenny written more music, his conducting, his lectures, and his obsessive desire to teach young musicians and young audiences would have been curtailed. No one was more generous with his gifts than Leonard Bernstein.

I first met him when I was assistant stage manager on *Wonderful Town*, the second musical he wrote with Betty Comden and Adolph Green (the first being the watershed *On the Town*). It was a huge success. The year was 1953. By 1957, I was a producer of *West Side Story*, and by 1974 at the urging of the Chelsea Theatre Center at the Brooklyn Academy of Music, Hugh Wheeler and I tackled *Candide*—a light opera with a major score of Lenny's and a flawed book. Wheeler re-imagined it in one act and we mounted it in an environmental production with a cast of twenty-year-olds. In the intervening years it made its way to the New York City Opera. We added choice musical material and expanded the book into a two-act opera. In the interim forty years since I first started working on it, though it was a great success from the beginning, I believe I finally got it right in 2017 for the new New York City Opera. Finally we achieved the balance between opéra comique and Lillian Hellman's desire to be political.

In the year that Lenny died, he and I met to discuss an opera he had always wanted to write about the Holocaust and of course I was interested. But he got sick and it never happened. Given the scope and passion of his artistry, it represents a potent loss.

In his memoir, Charlie Harmon shares with us a conversation with Lenny from the day he died, but that awaits your reading of this book.

Hal Prince, May, 2017

1 | The Ad under "M"

BEFORE I ENTERED HIS LIFE, Leonard Bernstein's assistants came and went like the change of seasons in New York. I can only conjecture why none of them stayed long. One assistant showed up for four days and then dropped out of sight. Nobody ever said what scared him off. Another started out energetically, sticking labels on clothes-closet shelves—"shirst" remained the butt of jokes for years—but a month later, he was gone. Did he object to the teasing about his dyslexia? One notorious assistant drove the Philharmonic's limo to Georgia, where the FBI apprehended him a few days later. Did he really think a big black car would be inconspicuous? Another assistant quit and tried to return, but in those weeks away, he discovered other priorities: preserving his sanity and pride. I ran into him when I was ready to quit as Bernstein's assistant, and he warned me, "Once you leave, you can't go back." That helped me a lot less than he imagined.

Even more ephemeral were the assistants—if that's what they were—who had hitched a ride on the bandwagon of glamor and fame. They were the perks—often sexual—of notorious celebrity, culled from a salacious entourage. When I'm asked about that category of Bernstein's assistants, I demur. "Hard to say." Actually, I know very well what to say.

I was none of those. Even though I wasn't any more durable physically, I stuck with the position longer than any of my predecessors. Yes, I had to put my life on hold, but working alongside a creative genius gave me the strongest sense of purpose I'd ever had. Serving Bernstein's creativity kept music central in my life, and nothing could make me happier than that. And yet I came to the job with almost no knowledge about this famous man, other than his stature as a serious musician, a major orchestral conductor, a famous composer, a *maestro*.

He had a wife and three kids? He smoked four packs a day? Delivered the celebrated Norton lectures at Harvard in 1973? Couldn't abide elevator music, or champagne, or public transportation? I had no idea. Once I was hired, he let me know what he wanted with no hesitation. "The stereo speakers quit last night," he'd say. Or, "Get me tickets to *Idomeneo* at the Met this Thursday," or, "See if Jackie Onassis can come for dinner tonight." Some of Bernstein's directives were blunt and personal, such as "Stop being so distracted." He was the priest in a theology of celebrity, and I was the novice, baptized by fire for four scorching years.

Bernstein's manager, Harry Kraut, hired personal assistants for the Maestro, regularly replenishing what was once referred to as "the toilet paper job." The musician who said that to me meant it to sting. It did. It still does, thirty-five years later. A rude assessment of an assistant's anonymous personality, *my* personality, as disposable as toilet paper.

After a rapid climb from the Boston Symphony Orchestra's administration, not a bad place to start, Harry Kraut relished the power that came with managing the world's most famous musician, Maestro Leonard Bernstein. Harry sometimes hosted cocktail parties to spot new talent, perhaps an assistant for the Maestro—though some of these parties degenerated into a beauty contest, with the red-haired candidate always crowned the winner. As a Boy Scout, Harry had been so besotted with his red-haired troop leader that he worked his way up to Eagle Scout just to be near the guy. But his troop leader never acknowledged Harry's infatuation, so red hair remained a beacon for the rest of Harry's life, a personal foible Harry confided to me—and the *only* foible he ever confided to me.

Amidst the gathering of beauties—uh, job candidates—at one of those cocktail parties, someone might show off a few superficial social skills, but any talents that could actually help the Maestro? An in-depth knowledge of notating, editing, or performing music? Never. Still, one candidate usually took charge, answering the door, picking up the phone when it rang, calling a taxi to spirit away an inebriated contender. Harry hired his own assistant this way for the summer of 1982, employing a personable and remarkably resourceful man my own age, whose hair looked a lot more blond than red. So the cocktail party routine worked, once.

Harry also had a more sober and time-honored way to hire an assistant for the Maestro: an ad posted in the classified section of the Sunday *New York Times*. Under "M" for "Musician," the ad sought an assistant for a "world-class" musician. The applicant must read music, be free to travel, sport a bit of European languages, and possess finely-honed organizational abilities. Nothing more specific.

For two years I'd toiled as a menial clerk at the Tams-Witmark Music Library, a music theater agency and rental library in Midtown Manhattan, while I daydreamed about how to put my musical skills—a degree in composition from Carnegie-Mellon University—and my life experiences to better use. I'd lived six formative years overseas, when my father's Army career stationed us in Germany and Italy. Germany opened my eyes and ears to music and culture. Italy bestowed its rich history and a sense of life's elusive sweetness. I missed those qualities on our returns to the States. Overseas travel wasn't in my budget, and I'd let my German and Italian lapse. But my proficiency at the piano ranged through the Bach-Beethoven-Brahms literature and the shorter works of Chopin. I'd written songs and chamber works and nursed them through performances. I'd met many professional performers and a few composers, but now, nearly thirty-one years old, I knew I wasn't a performer, nor was I cut out to be a composer. Filling page after page with my own musical thoughts every day? No thanks.

That *Times* ad under "M" in September 1981 seemed tailored expressly for me. I photocopied my half-page resume, typed a breezy cover letter, and sent them off, but I continued to sift through the *Times'* classified section each Sunday, just in case.

Nothing grabbed me like that ad under "M."

It seemed too good to be true when I got a reply and an appointment for an interview. My best friend, John, then an incipient psychiatrist, advised, "Act as though you are already working there. Answer a random question or even jump in on a discussion." I leaned heavily on John for his advice over the years. He possessed social skills more advanced than mine. "Take your personality with you and put it to work," John said.

Mine is a problem-solving mentality. I'm bothered when something is broken—things should function as they were designed. That's how I view an office hierarchy, too. Among close-working colleagues, why not share information?

Immediately after I sat down opposite Harry Kraut's desk, his secretary, Mimsy Gill, burst in with an urgent message from the director of the Hamburg State Opera about the Bernstein, Comden, and Green musical *Wonderful Town*. Mimsy wasn't sure whether the director's name was Friedrich Götz or Götz Friedrich (she got it right the second time). I knew his name because I'd come across it where I worked: Tams-Witmark licensed *Wonderful Town*. I said I'd relay the message at work the next day, and thus slipped myself into a new workplace scenario exactly as my friend John had suggested.

That was the start of the interview, but it went on for three more hours. Harry Kraut nonchalantly explained right off that the "world-class" musician in the newspaper ad was Leonard Bernstein. *Leonard Bernstein?* I combed through the musical part of my brain. At age ten, I'd seen a few televised Young People's Concerts while my father was stationed in the States. In college I almost wore out two of Bernstein's New York Philharmonic recordings: Bartók's *Concerto for Orchestra* and the ebullient third symphony of Robert Schumann (the album cover featured a Leonard Bernstein portrait next to a same-size image of the monumental cathedral of Cologne, a pairing that should have told me something). Of Bernstein's own music, I had a hazy familiarity with *Chichester Psalms*; if you dropped the needle on the LP, I could recognize it. How many snappy twentieth-century choral works in Hebrew are there? Of course I knew the *Overture to "Candide"*—it played over the rolling credits of the late-night *Dick Cavett Show*. But I'd never seen Bernstein perform except on television. I hadn't read a single one of his books, but I'd slogged through one by his mentor Aaron Copland. What about the symphonies of Gustav Mahler, which Bernstein the conductor had mortared into the symphonic repertoire? I'd heard only one Mahler symphony in performance, not conducted by Bernstein nor awakening me to Mahler's genius. During the first two movements, I'd indulged in a profound snooze.

I'd never seen *West Side Story*, because my mother feared I would mimic those juvenile delinquents. Maybe so, but not for the reasons she thought. When I caught the film some years after working for Bernstein, it was George Chakiris— tall, dark, and handsome Bernardo, captain of the Sharks—who stole my heart. I'd have gladly tagged after *him* into the most degenerate delinquency, a proclivity probably true for thousands of other gay boys in the 1960s. But the Sharks and the Jets didn't interest me all that much. My heroes were the authors of that transcendent work of music theater. I owned an LP of 1950s Broadway highlights, and the three selections from *West Side Story* grabbed me with their clever lyrics and punchy Latin rhythms mixed up with 1950s rock-and-roll. The "Jet Song" didn't even sound like show music. It had been pretty nervy of me at age twelve to buy that LP. I usually purchased staid albums by the pianists Brailowsky, Richter, and Rubinstein.

During my job interview, Mr. Kraut spoke persuasively, but his portly appearance put me off. His shirt buttons strained across his midriff. He obviously lived a little too well. A fringe of meticulously trimmed beard edged his bulldog jowls, as if to compensate for his nearly complete baldness. Those peripheral whiskers lent him a late-1800s look, like a New England philosopher. His precise, polysyllabic but leisurely speech put me at ease during the interview, but it also made him sound calculating and slightly pompous.

After Mr. Kraut skimmed over the basic duties of Bernstein's assistant— phones, luggage, mail, appointments—I asked about the schedule for the coming year. He swiveled a bit in his chair and occasionally put a hand to his forehead, as though in his fleshy cranium he could riffle through the files for 1982.

"In March, there are two weeks with the National Symphony in Washington, D.C., followed by two weeks with the New York Philharmonic. Then a week in London with the BBC Symphony Orchestra, and two weeks of recordings and concerts in Israel with the Israel Philharmonic, taking them on a tour to Mexico and Texas," he said.

I'd never been to Mexico or Texas, and I'd already lost count of the orchestras. Four?

He continued. "In June, there's a commemorative concert for Igor Stravinsky's centenary with the orchestra of La Scala in Milano."

I knew he meant the opera house in Italy.

"Then a follow-up performance in Venice, and a live broadcast of a Stravinsky program with the National Symphony at the National Cathedral in Washington, D.C.," he said.

Mentally I tried to add up all those trips across the Atlantic—I'd crossed it only six times in thirty-one years.

"The entire summer is in Los Angeles, to inaugurate the Los Angeles Philharmonic Institute. Lenny calls it 'the Tanglewood of the West,'" Mr. Kraut said.

Though I'd never been to western Massachusetts, I knew about Tanglewood, the posh summer home of the Boston Symphony Orchestra. Next summer in California? Nice.

He went on. "For Lenny's sixty-fourth birthday in August, there will be a big party in Salzburg. Then he goes to Vienna for two weeks to finish a Brahms cycle with the Vienna Philharmonic, after which he'll take that orchestra on a little tour of Germany."

I gathered that took the schedule up through late September.

"Oh, yes," Mr. Kraut said, almost as an afterthought. "The most important project is a three-part commission for an opera, to be premiered in 1983 at Houston Grand Opera, with performances a year later at La Scala and the Kennedy Center." He looked down as if reading a memo on his desktop. "For the first six weeks of 1982, Mr. Bernstein will be a visiting fellow at the Indiana University Jacobs School of Music. While there, his only task will be to begin writing the opera." Finally, Mr. Kraut paused and looked at me directly. "The new assistant's principal duty is to ensure that Mr. Bernstein meets the opera commission's deadline: June 17, 1983."

Did I hear a slightly ominous tone in his voice? Maybe I should inscribe that date on a stone and wear it around my neck.

After Mr. Kraut's *bravura solo*, I took a deep breath. "Mr. Bernstein needs someone with a lot more stamina than I have," I said. High energy wasn't my strong suit, and my thirty-first birthday was only a month away. Whatever youthfulness I still had was ebbing. "Maybe someone half my age?" I ventured, half-jokingly. I'd never heard of such an insane workload as that 1982 schedule, but what frame of reference did I have for the agenda of a maestro? Those orchestras were the best in the world; the music-making would be inspired. What other chance would I have to hear the Vienna Philharmonic or work at La Scala? Or to travel again? But I couldn't imagine keeping up with that overloaded schedule.

Mr. Kraut benignly allowed me to talk a little about myself, but I left his office after politely putting my application on hold.

Though I had other interviews that fall, none of them interested me half as much as those three hours with Harry Kraut. Could I keep up with that insane schedule? I wouldn't know unless I tried. In December I called Mimsy Gill and asked her to keep my name in the mix. But I never expected to hear from her or Harry Kraut again.

2 | Indiana Bound

RIGHT AFTER THE NEW YEAR IN 1982, Harry Kraut called me at work, but Tams-Witmark didn't permit personal calls, so I said I'd be at his office after 5 P.M. I put on a tie as I walked across Midtown Manhattan for what I thought would be a follow-up interview at the penthouse offices of Amberson Enterprises. (The German word for "amber" is *Bernstein*, so Bernstein's management office—i.e., the "son of Bernstein"—would be "Amberson." Many people assumed a mystic connection with *The Magnificent Ambersons*, but no.) Magnificence was in short supply in the Amberson office suite on Sixth Avenue. Once upon a time, Gloria Swanson had resided in that penthouse, but any hint of movie-star glamor evaporated with her departure, leaving a warren of drab rooms.

I heard Harry Kraut talking, evidently on the phone with the student union at the university in Bloomington, Indiana. How absurd that he would arrange for my room in Indiana. As head honcho for Leonard Bernstein, Harry Kraut negotiated contracts with top-tier orchestras and recording companies, not staff hotel rooms. Besides, he hadn't even offered me the job, yet. That phone call had to be a deliberate ploy.

I walked into his office and said lightheartedly, "If you feel I'm up to the job, I'll give it my best."

"I just made your room reservation at Indiana University's student union," Harry said. "You'll fly there with me on Friday."

As I took a seat, I remembered Harry's recitation of the insane schedule for 1982. "Let's make the first six weeks a trial run," I said, figuring I might be able to stick with it that long. "I'll go to Indiana and meet Mr. Bernstein, and on the return to New York, you can decide whether I should continue as the Maestro's assistant."

Harry nodded.

We hadn't discussed a salary until Harry mentioned a figure fifteen percent higher than my current income. Nice, but shouldn't I ask for more? After all, the schedule he'd outlined in our first meeting would require more skills and demand a greater commitment than anything I'd ever tackled. I paused too long, gulped, and accepted his offer.

I regretted that moment four years later, when the assistant after me craftily commanded a salary that was triple the figure Harry Kraut had offered me. Ouch.

Friends in Brooklyn made me dinner that night and presented me with the most useful tool imaginable: a 1982 datebook, one page for every day. I leafed through the blank pages, an apt analogy for my empty life thus far. How would I ever fill up an entire datebook? My friends had a better grip on the reality ahead than I did.

The next day at Tams-Witmark, I told the owner I was leaving to become Leonard Bernstein's assistant. In his genial and astute way, Louis Aborn advised me to "remember this side of the business" after I got to know the principal figures on the other—the creative—side. The business of music theater, in fact the business of all serious "classical" music, marries those who create and those who license. Leonard Bernstein and his collaborators were the creators, whereas Tams-Witmark is a licensing agency. The union of those two sides of the business of music can be prodigiously lucrative or financially disastrous—like any marriage, sometimes serene, sometimes rocky.

On Friday evening, I met Harry Kraut at La Guardia airport for the flight to Indianapolis. As we settled into our seats in first class, Harry promised that during the flight he'd share all the information I needed for what lay ahead. But as the plane lifted off the runway, Harry fell into a profound sleep and snored placidly all the way to Indianapolis.

For two hours I vacillated between panic and deliberation. What had I gotten myself into? I'm meeting Leonard Bernstein, but I know so little about him. Is he a tyrant, a lecher? What if he doesn't like me? How do I get out of this? In the worst case, how would I get back to New York?

I resolved to do my best to stay observant, and reminded myself that, no matter what, I was now on an adventure. Why not enjoy it? Later, if I needed an energy boost, I'd put this panic to better use. By the time the plane landed, I'd calmed myself down.

At the luggage claim in Indianapolis, Harry did show me one piece of business: how to tip the airport porters. They came running as soon as Harry pulled a wad of bills from his pocket. Monolithic pieces of luggage trundled onto the carrousel, each colossus stamped "L. B." but so scuffed it might have been kicked all the way from New York. Harry cautioned me not to touch anything but to let the porters cart all the bags to the rental car. Grateful that Harry offered to drive, I guided him through the signage to Route 37 towards Bloomington. Before leaving New York, I'd bought a map of Indiana and memorized the lower half of it. That impressed Harry exactly as I'd hoped.

We stopped at a cheap roadside diner, and over sandwiches Harry opened up a bit about his own career.

"Management, that's the route to success," he said, a maxim that would haunt me two years later when he boasted that he'd train me to become an orchestra manager. Wait a minute, I knew something about music but nothing about administration. Was he saying I could sell pianos because I knew how to play one?

About Leonard Bernstein, Harry shared only one thing, "Mississippi Mud." On a Midwestern tour years earlier, Mr. Bernstein had relaxed one day on an old-fashioned Mississippi riverboat. At the first stop, he leapt into the water and slathered handfuls of mud on his face. Then, in a raunchy, blackface imitation of Al Jolson, he belted out the old swing number "Mississippi Mud." Oh, the irrepressible Maestro.

Onlookers took photographs left and right. One photo sold to *Life* magazine for tens of thousands of dollars, Harry said. It appeared on the last page of the magazine, that issue's "parting shot," often a photo of outlandish celebrity behavior. But a black-faced Maestro wasn't the publicity that Bernstein's management team wanted.

"If only Mr. Bernstein's assistant had done something," said Harry. "I came up with a plan. If it looks like Lenny's about to embarrass himself, I say, 'Mississippi Mud.'" Harry looked at me more seriously. "Then you go into action. Do something!"

What? I wondered. This plan seemed laughably vague. "Mississippi Mud" was a lot of syllables. Plenty could happen during those seconds.

"At all costs, avoid negative publicity," Harry said, ending his lesson.

THE NEXT MORNING in the lobby of the student union, I met Bernstein's chef and on-the-road housekeeper, Ann Dedman. Pert and attractive with a winning smile, she took one look at me and said, "He's too cute. He'll have to shave off that moustache." Ann sounded like a smart and opinionated New Yorker. I'd never have guessed she came from east Texas.

Harry said, "No, Lenny doesn't like moustaches, so Charlie has to keep his."

I'd never been told I was too cute before, but the wispy growth on my upper lip didn't seem to be the real topic of this conversation. Cuteness was a liability? Had prior assistants been up for grabs in some kind of sexual free-for-all? Was I reading too much into this?

We drove several miles outside Bloomington to a condo where Ann had unloaded an enormous, diesel-fueled Buick station wagon she'd driven from New York with a previous Bernstein assistant—whom Harry had wished really had been up for grabs, according to Harry's tattling later on. Ann had packed into that station wagon every kitchen gadget she owned: an enormous professional mixer with a dozen attachments, a coffee grinder, an electric juicer, a blender, heavy-duty pots and pans of all sizes, massive bowls and serving platters, whisks, spoons, forks, several spatulas, plus Ann's personal set of impressive knives. She had also drawn up a yard-long shopping list while scoping out the condo's shortcomings, upstairs and down.

There weren't many shortcomings. Downstairs, a massive stone fireplace presided over a spacious living area, overlooked by a mid-level platform with a large dining table and an open kitchen. Off the front hall were two cozy bedrooms and a bath. A master suite took up the entire upstairs, as capacious as the living room below. A wall of floor-to-ceiling windows looked out on wintry woods and a frozen lake. Every lake in Indiana probably sported such sumptuous weekend condos, but I'd never seen anything like it. The main drawback: its distance from town. From my modest room in the student union, the drive to the lakeside condo took forty-five minutes over meandering country roads. My terrific sense of direction had better not fail me.

Somehow we had time for lunch at Charles Webb's house. Dean Webb headed the Jacobs School of Music at Indiana University, which made him the administrative mentor for generations of serious musicians. The Jacobs School of Music is the largest music department in the United States—in 1982, it enrolled the biggest population of student musicians in the world. As a music student at Carnegie-Mellon, I'd heard of the Jacob School of Music's legendary teachers, illustrious graduates, and vast library. To meet the man in charge of all that bowled me over.

Only a day earlier, I'd subsisted in a lowly position on the periphery of the music business. Now Indiana's dean was making me a sandwich in his own kitchen. "Charlie, do you want lettuce and mustard?" he asked. "How about a pickle?" Entirely down-home and unpretentious, Dean Webb possessed a solidly good soul. The balm of his reassurance got me through those six winter weeks in Indiana.

On the way back to the condo, I drove through a stop sign at a deserted intersection. Of course, Harry Kraut noticed. I hadn't driven in more than a year, but the last thing I wanted was to be stopped by a state trooper, get my name in the Bloomington newspaper, and blotch Leonard Bernstein's residency with negative publicity. *Mississippi Mud!* I resolved: no matter how preoccupied, I'd drive more carefully than ever in Indiana, a resolution put to the test a month later.

3 | The Rebbe in Wolf's Clothing

BACK AT THE LAKESIDE CONDO, I had no idea how to make myself useful. Should I ask when Mr. Bernstein would show up? Why hadn't Harry or Ann said anything about the Maestro's arrival?

Harry sauntered around with no sense of urgency, so I traipsed after him up the stairs. The Baldwin piano company had delivered a concert grand to the master bedroom—a courtesy, Harry said, that the company extended to Bernstein anywhere on the planet. In return, Bernstein endorsed Baldwin exclusively, a hard-and-fast rule, until some years later when he spotted an advertisement featuring a luxury watch on Plácido Domingo's arm. Envy—that's all it was—of Domingo's princely timepiece induced Bernstein into endorsing a watch company in return for its sponsoring a music festival. But Bernstein wouldn't consent to appear in any watch-company ad.

In the upstairs bedroom, Harry fingered the thin draperies drawn across the wall of windows overlooking Lake Monroe. "Attend to these right away. Lenny requires his bedroom to be pitch black," Harry said. "Find some black plastic bags and pin them to the outside of the drapes." Simple enough. Then Harry collected Ann with her three-foot-long shopping list and drove off to the biggest supermarket in town.

How much time did I have? I found a box of heavy black plastic bags and some straight pins, slit one bag open to make a large sheet, and standing unsteadily on a stool, held the plastic against the flimsy drapes. The plastic wouldn't lie flat unless it fit the hang of the curtains and I was no expert with straight pins. I felt like the hapless maiden in the fairy tale "Rumpelstiltskin," commanded to spin straw into gold before the troll returned. My fix-everything obsession seemed doomed to failure.

Two hours passed. I'd blacked out only a third of the draperies when Ann dashed into the bedroom and urged me to unpack the luggage right away. Then she ran back downstairs to make dinner.

Each suitcase approximated an armoire, but all were nearly empty: a few thin black socks, scandalously flimsy underpants, some sport shirts, a couple pair of tailored jeans, and two blazers. No flannel, no thermal cotton, no woolens. The housekeeper in New York had packed Mr. Bernstein's clothes, but evidently no one had told her about winter in Indiana.

I had no idea how Mr. Bernstein organized his things, so I had to guess. I filled the drawers of a tall dresser with upper-body clothes at the top, socks at the bottom. As I stashed the last empty suitcase into a utility closet, the front door opened downstairs and a boisterous crowd of people burst into the condo. Ann certainly knew about timing.

I could hear Charles Webb with his wife, Kenda, coming through the door. As I descended the stairs, Harry entered the foyer and introduced me to Stephen Wadsworth, Bernstein's librettist for the new opera, and Richard Nelson, a film and television actor serving as Bernstein's interim assistant. A few other university people spilled out of a sizable van in the driveway—and then there was the Maestro.

A cocktail party already in progress inched through the door, the noise at peak volume, as though somebody had just delivered one hilarious punch line. Over the hubbub, Harry said the van's stock of scotch had flowed freely on the short ride from the Bloomington airport. "Lenny raved about the van's cup holders because they lit up," Harry said with a chuckle.

From my spot at the foot of the stairs, I took in this diminutive, decidedly derelict geriatric cocooned in an enormous white parka. Mr. Bernstein made an inordinate amount of noise. "It's the pelt of a real wolf," he said several times, indicating the lining of his parka. *Good, one piece of winter clothing*, I thought. All his energy was going into his jabbering and joking, so he barely moved into the foyer, forcing the crowd behind him into a semi-circle. He looked like a priestly leader shepherding a worshipful flock. The procession shuffled to a standstill but remained on high volume.

Despite the deep tan on his face, Mr. Bernstein looked terrible: shriveled and wizened and wildly unkempt. He looked like he hadn't slept in ages. Nor had he shaved or showered that day. He reeked of rancid suntan lotion, strong cologne, and a damp-dog rankness that wafted from his parka's wolf fur.

I had discreetly poured myself a tablespoon of gin to steady my nerves, but I hadn't yet taken a sip. After Harry Kraut said my name, which was all the introduction I was going to get, I took the wolf off Mr. Bernstein's shoulders and asked him if he'd like a drink.

"What are you drinking?" he asked. I picked up the small glass of gin. He grabbed it out of my hand and drained it in one swig.

"That's *my* drink!" I said.

Mr. Bernstein tilted back his head and roared like a wild beast ready to kill. "You don't talk that way to the *rebbe!*"

My mouth fell open. He's a rabbi? I'd never heard anyone refer so vehemently to himself as a rabbi—while snatching a glass of gin, no less. In the brief pause, I saw not a biblical scholar but a weary and drunk elderly man, genuinely angry, ready to toss me out on my ear into the snowy fields of Indiana.

Everyone else stood around grinning. Somebody suggested scotch on the rocks, so I poured a little Ballantine's on ice and handed it to Mr. Bernstein, who then swept into the condo for an inspection.

I had no idea what was going on. Was I already out of a job? Had I been rude? I stood by with the rest of the flock and watched the Maestro-Rabbi as he talked first to one university official, then another. When Mr. Bernstein spoke to anyone, he placed one hand on the listener's shoulder, oddly reminding me of a dog steadying itself on its hind legs. As Mr. Bernstein gazed directly into his listener's eyes, he gave the impression that he was devoting his exclusive, utterly rapt attention.

I noticed Mr. Bernstein squinting and screwing up his eyes, and figured they had dried out on the airplanes that day. Later he told me he had herpes on his eyeballs (not exactly the correct medical description) for which he'd been prescribed eye drops that required constant refrigeration. In the months ahead, I nurtured an international network of eye doctors who delivered those eye drops to his hotel suites, and I took great pains to keep those drops refrigerated. His herpes affliction slowly receded, though strong sunlight brought it back. Given that tan on his face, Mr. Bernstein had overindulged in sun exposure and his eyes suffered.

Mr. Bernstein asked to see his bedroom, so I led him upstairs while everyone else stayed below. Now I could find out if this room met his needs and what he expected of me. He'd spend six weeks in that room, so it had to be a place away from all cares except the as-yet-unwritten opera, which, if I still had a job, might be my duty to see through to completion.

I pointed to the plastic bags pinned to the draperies.

"I'll finish this later," I said.

"Don't bother," he replied kindly. "I always wear a sleep mask."

I almost followed up with "*But Harry said—*" as Mr. Bernstein continued: "I have this white noise machine," as he pulled a squat appliance the size of a mixing bowl out of his carry-on bag.

"See, it has two settings, but I always set it on high, and it covers up any outside noise." A sleep mask? A white-noise machine? So I could drop the pin-on-the-plastic bag project, thank goodness. I surmised that Harry's instructions might not always align with the Maestro's reality.

I showed him the dresser drawers. He laughed and rearranged the contents to match his dresser at home. Top drawer: handkerchiefs on one side, socks on the other. Next drawer: underwear. His jovial tone told me that the roaring *rebbe* of fifteen minutes earlier might have been an act, now abandoned downstairs.

I hadn't unpacked the book bags yet. He offered to go through them with me. The Chambers English dictionary, the standard for aficionados of the cryptic anagrams in British crossword puzzles, went on the shelf most easily reached from the bed. Dictionaries in Italian, German, and Spanish; a single-volume edition of the complete works of Lewis Carroll; the Oxford compilation of English verse; and several current fiction and nonfiction works—these had to be within an arm's length of the bed.

There was also a small Hebrew Bible, as I called it then because I wasn't sure it was the *Torah*, bound in silver and studded with semi-precious stones.

"This travels with me everywhere," he said. "At sunset every Friday, I phone my mother. This is an inviolable rule." It didn't matter what else was in his schedule, or where in the world he was. One Friday, he called his mother after visiting Tchaikovsky's grave. She responded with memories of her Russian childhood. He said he didn't celebrate Shabbat, but this particular weekly observance was sacred to him.

Then he showed me how to unpack a hefty leather valise he had brought on the flights that day. "This is the medicine bag," he said. It contained everything under the sun: an electric toothbrush, Tums and other antacids, toothpaste, hair gel, combs, collar stays, scissors, an expensive electric razor ("Let's plug it in now or the battery will die," he said), three big bottles of cologne, more Tums, more hair gel, Aquafilters—plastic cigarette holders each containing a tiny water-saturated sponge—safety pins, dental floss, buttons, a sewing kit, more Aquafilters, yet more Tums—and prescription canisters of pills he said helped him to sleep, wake up, get over indigestion and diarrhea and just about any other conceivable ailment. I'd never seen Bronkotabs before; those dilated his lungs. I'd never seen inhalers, either. There were several, yellow and blue, for Mr. Bernstein's periodic bouts with emphysema.

I could scarcely make sense of the medicine-bag mishmash.

A small compartment in the bag held collar stays and safety pins mixed up with assorted cufflinks, including a pair shaped like miniature tennis racquets. "Stephen Sondheim gave me these," he said, handling them delicately.

All about playing games, I thought.

He showed me a pair of elegant lion head cufflinks with tiny diamond eyes that were a gift from President Jimmy Carter. Then Mr. Bernstein held up a pair of gold squares. "Koussy gave me these."

I knew he meant Dr. Serge Koussevitzky, music director of the Boston Symphony Orchestra and founder of Tanglewood, the orchestra's summer home.

"They were his, and I wear them for every concert. If my shirt doesn't have French cuffs, I carry them in my pocket."

I took a breath. Here's Mr. Bernstein standing next to me, telling me that before he walked onto a stage, he brought each cufflink to his lips for an affectionate ritual kiss. These small golden squares were more than a talisman. They represented a first-hand connection to the ancient and exalted history of serious music.

Almost ready to go onstage, Leonard Bernstein kisses the Koussevitzky cufflinks while holding a cigarette and a baton. Standing to his left, the late Carl Schiebler, personnel manager of the New York Philharmonic.

As we stood in front of this disorganized valise, I made a mental note to find a pillbox so I could carry the Koussevitzky cufflinks in my pocket rather than risk losing them in the medicine bag's unholy mess. I was taking stock of things I could improve. Looking back now on what I saw in that valise that afternoon, I realize how Mr. Bernstein's complex life was reflected right there in that chaos.

He showed me two plastic tooth guards, which I'd heard about from my dentist but never seen before. One of them Mr. Bernstein called his "morpho-Max," a combination of Morpheus, the Greek god of dreams, with Max Widrow, the name of Mr. Bernstein's orthodontist. The other tooth guard was the "conducto-Max." One for the upper jaw, worn while sleeping, and the other for the lower jaw, for conducting. When sleeping or conducting, Mr. Bernstein uncontrollably ground his teeth, so he took these two prophylactics seriously.

"Now, the critical thing about the morpho-Max," he said confidentially, "is that I sometimes hurl it across the room. Unconsciously, of course." It would be up to me to find the morpho-Max, rinse it, and nestle it on a clean, damp tissue in its little blue case. A previous assistant had balked at doing this, but a piece of plastic dripping with gooey saliva didn't bother me.

We spent nearly an hour sorting through his books and medicine bag, but it seemed as though no time had elapsed at all. There was a lot for me to remember, but Mr. Bernstein confided his personal details with such appealing trust that I felt completely at ease. He looked the part of the wild and exhaustingly intense God the Father on the Sistine Chapel's ceiling, but he really wasn't so threatening. His mixing up of words and languages, the names of people and classical references—thank goodness I'd had four years of Latin—sparkled with fun. Yet I detected an underpinning of vulnerability in the chaos of his belongings.

And those cufflinks!

They represented deep personal esteem from some mighty exalted personages—a former president, for one. And a Broadway icon, the lyricist of *West Side Story*—imagine, a present from Stephen Sondheim. Realizing that I worked for a man who led such a fascinating life, I felt a little thrill run through me.

We trundled downstairs to join the Webbs et al., and to find out what Ann had made for dinner. She apologized for serving meatloaf but said it was the best she could do, given the unfamiliar kitchen, the last-minute food shopping, and not knowing the number of guests—or the actual dinner hour. I quickly set the table for everyone, including Ann. Mr. Bernstein paused before taking his seat and counted the place settings. He declared haughtily, "I don't eat with my cook." In dead silence, I removed a placemat to the kitchen counter top a few feet from the far end of the dining table. Mr. Bernstein seated himself at the table's other end, where he could see Ann hunched over her plate by herself in the kitchen. In the months ahead, Ann and I got Mr. Bernstein to come down from his high horse, but it took a lot of coaxing.

Mrs. Webb charitably tried to include Ann in the conversation, but Mr. Bernstein took over, running at full tilt. He began anagramming the names of everyone present and turned to me with undisguised condescension.

"You don't know what we're doing, do you?" he said.

"I haven't played anagrams since I was nine years old," I responded weakly. Better not add that at age nine, I knew nobody with any interest in anagrams. I was not in Mr. Bernstein's league.

Richard Nelson challenged a word Mr. Bernstein had come up with, so the Maestro turned to me again. In his grandest Bostonian intonation, a voice heard on many a Young People's Concert—dropped *r*'s and vowels as broad as the Charles River—he commanded, "Fetch me my Chambers."

What? Was this imperious tone a joke? I ran upstairs, grabbed the crimson English-language dictionary, and laid it before him. I wondered if henceforth I'd be addressed like an obedient dog.

"Fetch!"

I had a lot to ruminate on and was glad the evening came to an early end. On my drive back to the student union, I thought about the ease I felt with some of my new colleagues: Ann, Harry, Stephen Wadsworth, Dean Webb. Beneath, I felt distinctly uneasy. What was expected of me? Was I up to this job? What about a dividing line between the Maestro's grand demands and the refuge of a personal life?

In Indiana, far from my friends in New York, I soon found I wouldn't have any personal life.

4 | The Cabin Fever Ward

THE WEATHER IN BLOOMINGTON turned stormy and brought a fresh snowfall every day. The station wagon that Ann had driven from New York wasn't winterized—on day two its battery died. My automotive expertise didn't even encompass how to pump gas, but I soon learned that a diesel has a built-in heater under the hood. Plug it in when the temperature drops below freezing, and the car will start.

Not this car. On day three I called for a tow truck. Hauling the station wagon twenty miles cost a couple hundred dollars, garnished by the bill for a winter tune-up. I had no idea what that involved, and I had no way to pay for it. I used Bernstein's own credit card after calling his accountant in New York. Then I took Ann to the car rental in town to get her another vehicle. This business with the car took up two entire days. Why hadn't this been attended to in New York? I was learning fast: the assistant does the menial tasks no one else can be bothered with.

Every morning I arrived at the condo around 11 A.M., greeted by two men in bathrobes: librettist Stephen Wadsworth, unwashed and unshaven as he rubbed his eyes over a cup of coffee, and Mr. Bernstein, disheveled but bright-eyed after a productive night of writing music at his piano. One guy barely awake, the other ready to go to bed. Ann Dedman, up since 6 A.M., had cleaned the entire condo except for Mr. Bernstein's bedroom and she was itching to escape the confines of that remote condo on the frozen lake.

Ann was lively, fit, and attractive. She was used to having a social life. What a trial it was for her to leave New York with all her food sources and contacts for this Midwestern, mid-winter isolation. Now she had to deal with me, the none-too-swift novice. I had to write down every little detail and was thrown by the most basic demands, whereas Ann fielded phone calls while stirring three saucepans. Both of her hands were always busy and she remembered everything.

The university provided Stephen with an IBM Selectric typewriter, but its font didn't satisfy him. The type was on a removable ball, so Stephen proposed that I get him a variety of these font balls, each font in assorted sizes. Stephen was collaborating with LB on the opera, so I should do whatever he asked. He seemed to be about my age, but he boasted an upbringing far more intellectual than mine. As well, his was an ambition-driven personality. Stephen had a lot at stake with this opera, as would anyone collaborating with Leonard Bernstein. But I sensed a barrier between us. I could have worn a uniform of denim overalls, for all the credit he gave me.

I dutifully wrote down every one of Stephen's commandments, not suspecting anything was afoot. But every flock has its pecking order. A year later, he and Ann confessed that each morning before my arrival at the condo, they dreamt up something for me to do, the more picayune the better. Stephen specified odd varieties of paper, Bernstein demanded a particular brand of soft-lead pencils, they both required more reference books: a thesaurus or two, *Bartlett's Quotations*, an unabridged dictionary. I wondered why hadn't those things been shipped from New York? There wasn't anyone to do that—that was the assistant's responsibility, I guess, and the assistant was stuck in Indiana.

Doggedly, I fetched winter clothes for Mr. Bernstein. I also started calling him "LB," as everyone else around him did. He even referred to himself as "LB," in the hand-written notes he left me on the dining table if I arrived after he'd gone to bed. In the years ahead, I discovered that LB was decidedly "the Maestro" when on tour; in Vienna, *der Meister*. In Bloomington, he was just LB. I bought him flannel shirts, heavy wool socks, sweaters, and gloves. It was part of the job: fetching for the Maestro, but he seemed pleased, cooing with delight over the shearling gloves.

I also had to buy the *New York Times* every day. In 1982, the newspaper was printed in Chicago and trucked to Bloomington. Snow and ice often closed the roads so that only part of the *Times* made it to the Indiana newsstands. But if I brought only two sections of the newspaper instead of the normal six, I faced the Spanish Inquisition. LB, abetted by Ann and Stephen, accused me—seriously—of withholding the Sunday magazine, the section with those holiest of holies, the crossword puzzle and double acrostic.

"Are you hiding the Sunday magazine in your room?" Stephen inquired in his pointedly accusatory voice.

"Did you leave it behind?" asked LB.

"Where is it?" they cried in unison. If I were put in that predicament today, I'd roll my eyes and say, "*You guys need to get out more*," but instead I blamed myself. The missing Sunday magazine was my problem, and I couldn't solve it.

I didn't know that I could call the Bernstein office in New York and demand that they mail the entire newspaper every Sunday. But my true failure was not recognizing the symptoms of cabin fever, the irritability that comes from being cooped up indoors for too long. It was making LB, Stephen, and Ann hypercritical. Ann escaped to the supermarket now and then, but LB and Stephen never stepped beyond the front door.

Wackiness took over. LB impersonated Katisha in *Mikado*: "My right elbow . . . is on view Tuesdays and Fridays." So I borrowed a *Mikado* vocal score from the university library and played from it when I had to wait for LB to emerge from his bath. Stephen repeatedly rattled through a bizarre ragtime number, "Who Put the Snatch on the Lindberg Baby," sometimes mimicking Billie Holiday. It was amusing the first time.

Fortunately, I had the unwavering support of Dean Charles Webb and his unflappable executive assistant, Pam Duncan. In short order, they supplemented the fonts for Stephen's typewriter. When segments of the new opera were ready for a trial hearing, they corralled two pianists and a raft of young vocal students, all vetted by Stephen. To supply this cast with music, Pam granted me use of the photocopier in her office. LB's first notation in his 1982 datebook is a coaching session for the Act I Trio, "Dear Daddy," sung by the characters Dede, Junior, and François.

The birth of an opera!

One morning at the condo, as I stuffed dirty clothes from LB's closet into a laundry bag, LB asked me why I was doing his laundry.

"Don't you have a degree in music?" he asked.

"Yes," I said, "A BFA in composition, from Carnegie-Mellon University." I looked at him. "You're not, say, an oil executive who could hire anybody to do his laundry. You're writing an opera, and I might learn something." I hadn't put much thought into what I said. "In the meantime," I added, "there's dirty laundry and somebody has to pick it up."

He sat at the piano in his bedroom, not really listening to me, I thought. He shuffled some pages on the piano's music rack. "Here, see what you can do with this," he said. "Make a piano reduction of these pages." He handed me a scene he had completed that morning. "Make sure you lay out the vocal lines clearly."

I put the laundry bag down.

LB wrote in short score, which can be any number of instrumental or vocal lines of music ("staves"). It can almost look like an orchestra score, though with less vertical space. But a piano reduction is on only two staves. It looks like it was written for the piano. LB asked me to condense his short score onto two piano staves, a considerable skill. I also had to make the music playable by a single pianist. I'd done this before, but not for anyone on Bernstein's level, and never with a score as complex as this opera. I welcomed the challenge and got to work.

We didn't have the right paper, and my music manuscript looked spindly, but each day I reduced several pages of LB's short score. He looked over what I'd done and made changes. Bit by bit, I figured out what he wanted. I also tried to improve my manuscript. LB was an excellent teacher: to the point, charitable, and encouraging. He teased me about my thinly-drawn lines. The stems I drew, attaching notes to beams, were so lightweight that they disappeared in a photocopy. "Be more forceful," he said. I aimed for accuracy, but there was more than that to strive for. He wanted the music to look solid, even bold. A steady presence across the page.

On campus, I made photocopies that I then distributed to the singers and pianists for the workshops. Except for the photocopier, that's how operas have been prepared for centuries.

I also added the copyright notice, supplied by Bernstein's in-house lawyer. I figured that the singers in those Indiana workshops would keep their photocopies as souvenirs of this brief association with the Maestro. The copyright notice reminded them of the music's strict limitations. It also made the subtle point that I grasped the business of serious music.

LB's genius for collaboration kindled his success in music theater, where the authors of the book, the lyrics, and the music, together with the choreographer and stage director, all work side by side. I came to see how this collaborative spirit pervaded all LB's projects, from his Young People's Concerts to his Broadway shows, and even to his symphonic programs. The musicians, the composer—living or dead—even the audience—all turned a concert into a collaborative event.

For most of his projects, LB corralled a team. He usually hired whatever help he needed. Hired to assist in the completion of his new opera, I was now part of his team. In my first months on the job, I learned that LB's professional dedication—a level of intensity normal for him—was what he expected from everyone around him. But he was a genius, right? If I applied myself, could I step up to that level? My head spun. Was I ready for this?

CH
No need to Xerox on one side of sheet only.
Save time, money, effort, punch-holes!
Love LB

I noted the precise placement of the word "only" at the end of the first sentence in this Post-it. That "only" refers to "one side of [a] sheet" of paper. I understood that to place the word *only* elsewhere would change the sentence's meaning. It's not an "only need" or an "only Xerox." It's one side of a sheet *only*. Clarity in thought and writing consumed LB. He lectured anyone who made a grammatical error, because he was certain that a spoken error indicated a more harrowing error in thinking.

A split infinitive? Regrettable, but understandably idiomatic. But a pronoun in the wrong case—*for you and I*—inevitably derailed any conversation. As for a misplaced *only*? Inexcusable. Luckily, I remembered a 1960s CBS broadcast on English grammar, in which the sentence "I punched Walter Cronkite in the nose" served to show how to place the word *only*. *I only punched Walter Cronkite in the nose*; that is, I did not flay him as well. *I punched only Walter Cronkite in the nose*; I did not punch his dog also. *I punched Walter Cronkite only in the nose*; I did not punch him elsewhere, say, in his gut.

LB spared me his "misplaced only" lecture.

In their opera, LB and Stephen intended to bring the American vernacular to the operatic stage: the actual speech of Americans, with its mix of rhythms and tempi, its contractions, slang, and slipshod idioms. Stephen's libretto in the first act is peppered with interruptions, apologies, apologies for the interruptions, people speaking at cross purposes, and absent-minded woolgathering—all in ordinary, loose language.

One morning at the condo, Stephen read me an entire monologue, probably the second act breakdown by the character Junior. At that point, Stephen was forging onward, though LB was still writing the music for Act I.

I felt flattered that Stephen had asked for my opinion. He sat across from me in his bathrobe. He was deathly pale, unshaven, and as unappetizing as an unearthed but highly caffeinated corpse. I'd had plenty of experience reading plays and opera libretti. As an undergraduate, I'd attended lectures and superbly staged plays at Carnegie-Mellon, and I'd gained some insight on the mechanics of drama. But I wasn't ready for an intimidating face-to-face with Stephen. As he read Junior's free-associative going-to-pieces monologue, I leaned back in my chair, as though trying to distance myself.

All creators put pressure on the people around them. *Isn't this the best thing you ever heard? Are you on this bandwagon or not?* That morning, I evaded giving

Stephen my opinion. I coughed up a lame excuse that the principal characters in what became *A Quiet Place* weren't fully fleshed out for me, and without the music they lacked depth. Stephen wrote me off as utterly clueless and never again asked for my opinion.

At least I got those damn font balls for his typewriter.

5 | Composers, Conductors, a Celebrated Cellist, and a Charred Cork

BERNSTEIN'S RESIDENCY at Indiana University had no "official" responsibilities, but Dean Webb hinted that LB should feel free to drop by the Jacobs School of Music at any time, sort of like lobbing a tennis ball at an off-duty pro.

It was just the two of us when I drove LB to the campus. We gabbed about ourselves as if we were on a first date. I told LB about my first piano lessons in Germany at age six with Herr Falke. With his beard and girth, black frock and cigars, Herr Falke could have staged a convincing one-man show: *Johannes Brahms Tonight!*

Shortly after my mother rented a piano, Herr Falke strode into our living room and set a book on the keyboard rack. He explained, "This black note below the staff is 'C,' here, on the keyboard, and we have four notes every bar. Now we play!" Together we hammered out "Mädchen, warum weinest du?," the tune fitting easily beneath my fingers and Herr Falke's accompaniment making the rhythm obvious. I had no other memory of learning to read music and played through the entire book in a few weeks, especially smitten with an excerpt from something called *Die Zauberflöte*, or *The Magic Flute*.

LB talked about himself with a casual openness that gave me the feeling of being trusted. Because he liked me? Or was I just the new face in his retinue? I couldn't tell.

He said his first teachers put music in front of him and he played it without hesitation. Hearing an orchestra was the big revelation. "My father could buy tickets for something called 'a concert'—and that changed my life," LB said. I'd felt a similar jolt when my father got tickets for the San Carlo opera house while we were stationed in Naples. The sound of an orchestra and the complexity of staging grabbed me viscerally. I begged to go to every production.

On one of our drives into Bloomington, LB and I talked about Mozart's piano concertos, and I asked if he played the concerto in E flat, K. 271, "Jeunehomme." The opening is notable for two statements by the solo piano, each played after a phrase from the orchestra: orchestra, solo piano, orchestra, piano—unusual for a concerto in 1777. Normally the solo piano enters after the orchestra has played through a third of the first movement.

LB said the first time he played this concerto, he forgot to play the piano's initial solo statement, so there was dead silence for two bars (orchestra; then silence). When the orchestra played its phrase again, as written, LB came in with the piano statement correctly, and the concerto continued without mishap. He said he felt like an idiot through the entire performance, certain that the critics would comment only on his memory lapse. "But nobody mentioned it," he said. "Not even the most erudite critics."

So LB wasn't infallible, I thought to myself. That grandiose employer who bade me fetch his dictionary was human after all.

I asked him if the conductor of that Mozart performance noticed his memory lapse, and a hauteur suffused LB's voice.

"When I play a concerto, I always conduct from the keyboard," he said.

Did he have to sound so pretentious? How was I supposed to know that when he played a piano concerto, he conducted, too? Suddenly, I was no longer chatting amicably with LB, I was in conversational intercourse with the Maestro. There are limits. He doesn't eat with his cook.

One afternoon, I drove LB to the campus to meet the composition students. I knew what to expect, given the school's music-factory reputation. When the door to the lecture hall opened and LB faced seventy young men—I'm sure there weren't any women—he actually reeled backwards.

"How is it possible that every one of you will end up a composer?" he asked the tiers of faces. "How could there be room in the world of serious music for seventy guys to earn a living, writing music?"

The students laughed, but something made them uneasy. They hesitantly placed their scores on a table before LB and played taped performances. As a student, I'd had a session like this, though not with anyone as exalted as Bernstein. Yet I had never been as reluctant as these undergrads.

After three mind-numbing twelve-tone works that rigorously shied away from any emotional attachment, LB had had enough of academic assignments. He leaned back and challenged the students directly. "What do you write for yourselves? Where's the music that you most want to share?"

Dead silence. After an awkward squirminess, LB shouted, "What? *What*?!"

Two guys bashfully admitted to their passion for improvising together at a piano—but only at parties, and only if no faculty were present.

"C'mon, let's hear something," LB said.

The two tentatively approached the piano. After a bout of giggles, they launched into a selection of Romantic riffs, catchy rhythms, and bits of melodic cheese. As they found their nerve, they turned the lecture hall into a party. For the moment, they were stars.

Captivated, LB asked, "So what's wrong with that?" He pressed the group with questions: what sort of instruction did they get? What were the opportunities for performance? What did they want to write? And the opposite question: what was expected of them?

"Our professors require us to produce twelve-tone music," they said, almost in unison. Neither minimalist nor post-modern music existed in academia in 1982. To be a composer meant giving up one's personality. None of those composing students contacted LB after that afternoon, so whether their imaginations caught fire from his questions remained a mystery.

Other afternoons, an orchestra assembled at the Jacobs School of Music, and LB held master classes for the conducting students. LB's teaching fascinated me. Of course, I received a dose of his tutelage every day as I copied his opera manuscript. As with me, LB supported and encouraged the students on the podium, but he stopped them as soon as he saw something questionable.

One student conductor, George Hanson, led the orchestra with his eyes closed, in the manner of Herbert von Karajan—heresy to LB, who insisted on maintaining full visual communication with the entire orchestra, while at the same time continually scanning the score on the podium. Rather than scold George, LB turned to the orchestra.

"Are you missing something?" he asked the musicians.

"Yes," a couple musicians said. "We want George to look at us."

"Right!" LB exclaimed as he turned to George.

George opened his eyes and became a conductor, glancing at the music and encouraging the musicians by looking directly at them. How simple.

LB stopped other student conductors, too, and asked them what happens "between the beats." How do you show those inner beats? About a particular page in one score, LB asked, "What's important on this page? Where is the music going?" If the woodwinds didn't enter together as they should have, what could the conductor do? And, by the way, what was the second clarinet playing in bar twelve?

"Don't look, tell me!" LB commanded, and sometimes the befuddled young conductor skimmed the correct answer off the top of his head.

LB often said that a conductor hadn't actually learned a score until he could write from memory any instrumental part, from start to finish, a depth of study one of my college professors had tried to instill in me. My professor had copied an entire Brahms symphony, as assigned by Fritz Reiner, the legendary Hungarian émigré who taught conducting for a decade at the Curtis Institute. It was there that Reiner became one of LB's mentors. I never tackled a feat as weighty as a hundred pages of Brahms, but I filled notebooks with the works of Bach and Mozart in my spindly manuscript.

OFF-CAMPUS EVENTS began to fill LB's schedule, with faculty gatherings far more elevated than any I'd experienced. Musicians I'd heard about all my life collegially greeted one another, but of course no one wanted to greet *me*. I dutifully delivered the star of the evening to the right house and waited until it was time to leave, careful to stay sober so that I could drive LB back to the condo on roads slick with snow.

Cellist János Starker, who had been teaching for over fifty years and who also counted Fritz Reiner as a mentor, hosted a gathering at his house for fifty illustrious faculty members. LB mingled easily but quickly got very drunk. I sensed a Mississippi Mud moment in the making, or was I being too protective? Someone asked Starker to play a Beethoven cello sonata. He agreed, provided Bernstein accompanied him.

Everyone found seats and got deathly quiet. No one came forward to turn pages for LB, so I volunteered. Starker played magnificently, the sound of his cello filling the room, but LB played as though he'd never touched a piano in his life. He swatted recklessly at the keys. He was even drunker than I thought. He couldn't manage the simplest scale passages. At the end of the first movement, I tried to save LB from further embarrassment. I leaned toward him and mumbled that he didn't have to continue.

In a rage, LB yelled, "Don't tell me what to do!" He had turned into the same drunken *rebbe* who had grabbed a glass of gin out of my hand. In a fury, LB hashed through the rest of the Beethoven sonata. My face burned with humiliation and I could barely follow the music as I tried to focus on the page turns. What did I look like to that roomful of world-class musicians? The Maestro's whipping boy?

After the performance, I haltingly made my way towards Stephen Wadsworth and Ann Dedman, off in a corner telling one another jokes saved up for a dead moment. "What's invisible and smells like carrots? Bunny farts," said Stephen as I got within earshot. I didn't feel like laughing, but they wouldn't look in my direction anyway. Their snug club of two couldn't accommodate me. I found a chair, stared into space, and wondered if this was now my life. Fetch and watch out for the Mississippi Mud. When LB got abusive, I was out of my depth. Should I get the next bus back to New York? I could pack and be ready to go before dawn.

That night in my solitary room at the student union, I gave in to that feeling of humiliation and cried quietly. I couldn't remember the last time I'd cried, and I couldn't explain to myself with much conviction why I was crying now. Driving a celebrity around wintry Indiana, hearing János Starker play Beethoven: how bad was that? My confusion only added to an overwhelming feeling of worthlessness. I didn't have the backbone to stand up to LB's abusive behavior. No wonder his assistants didn't last long. Though the first six weeks of this job were on a trial basis, somehow I was the one on trial. I wanted this trial to be over.

If I left, what would I go back to? I'd never get to work for another musician like Bernstein. What about the opera? What about my musical skills? I had a difficult time thinking coherently, but when I woke up the next morning, I resigned myself to stick it out for the whole six weeks.

———

ANOTHER NIGHT Dean Webb and his wife, Kenda, took LB and me—Ann and Stephen wanted a night off—to Bloomington's swankiest restaurant. We sat smack in the middle of the room, surrounded by tables packed with Bloomington's elite. Everybody there knew the Webbs and recognized their distinguished guest, Leonard Bernstein.

After the waiter opened a bottle of wine, LB picked up the cork and fastidiously rotated one end of it in the flame of a candle. Carbonizing the cork, he turned it into a charcoal wedge as wide as his thumb.

Then LB turned to Kenda and before she could flinch, he drew sweeping patterns in blackest charcoal on her forehead. He picked up her chin in his left hand and deftly turned her head a little left and right as he swiped symmetrical sooty smudges on her cheeks. He spoke in a low undertone about facial symmetry. His seriousness obliged Kenda to stay calm. Then LB leaned across the table and applied the cork to Dean Webb's face with much more bravado: a big "X" on his forehead, a swooping D'Artagnan-like moustache. LB handed the cork to Kenda, who did her best on LB's face, which took some time, and finally she leaned across the table and marked me up while I closed my eyes and relaxed.

The Webbs managed to stomach their horror throughout this ordeal. None of us laughed. Out of the corners of my eyes, I saw that all other eyes in the room were fixed on the four of us. Not a single utensil clinked. Nobody so much as lifted a napkin. Then the waiter brought our plates, and we four ate a splendid gourmet dinner, looking like tribal initiates in a prehistoric ritual. After a half hour, I excused myself to use the men's room. I looked in the mirror, and decided to wash my face, quickly obliterating Kenda's artwork. When I returned to the table, there

My corked face in Key West, Florida, December, 1988. At the fancy restaurant in Bloomington, LB didn't sing.

were sighs of disapproval all around. Later, LB lectured me about spoiling a party. I got the point: as uncomfortable as I'd been with the greasy carbon on my face, washing it off had disassociated me from the tribe.

As we walked out of the restaurant, the Webbs holding their besmirched heads high, the entire place stood and applauded. There's no record of that evening—digital cameras didn't exist in 1982—but charred cork remained LB's preferred pre-prandial ice-breaker. He never deployed it more dramatically than that evening in Bloomington.

A week later, after a much less formal Chinese New Year feast, LB got as far as the parking lot of the student housing before singing tipsily, at the top of his lungs, a personalized version of "A Bicycle Built for Two" in lyrics expressing his complicated affection for Dean Webb—who fortunately wasn't present.

Deanie Weenie,
Show me your peenie, do.
I'm all steamy
Over the length of you.
I won't show you mine, it's teenie,
But that's 'cuz I'm a sheenie,

But you're a goy,
And boy oh boy
I just betcha it's built for two!

Scores of people leaned from their apartment windows to catch LB's impromptu performance. At the song's last line, they raised a raucous cheer.

I was beginning to grasp how much LB relished performing. Whether he understood the limits of decorum was another matter. In fact, were there any limits? Was shamelessness part of being a celebrity, or was that simply the way Leonard Bernstein behaved? "Mississippi Mud" or the irrepressible Maestro? People loved LB at his most outrageous, and he wasn't about to disappoint them.

That evening at János Starker's, I learned the hard way not to interfere. And a week later in a public parking lot, I stood back and let the Maestro sing his heart out. If he wanted to wallow in the mud, let him.

Actually, his personalized lyrics were pretty funny.

6 | "Chich" and a Concussion

THE SCHEDULE IN THE FIRST WEEK of February 1982 took Leonard Bernstein to Cleveland, where amid a hoopla of receptions and performances he'd receive an honorary doctorate from Cleveland State University. LB said he'd lost count of his honorary degrees, but this would be his nineteenth. After an easy flight from Bloomington, Indiana, LB and I were to be met in Cleveland by LB's manager, Harry Kraut, and press agent, Maggie Carson. In my first try at the tricky mechanics of Maestro travel, I was concerned most of all about my stamina. After four weeks in the "on" mode—"off" being an option only when alone in the car or asleep in my room— I was running on empty. That wasn't a problem in Bloomington, where I knew the stops I had to make en route to the condo every morning: the dry cleaners, the newsstand, Dean Webb's office. Cleveland loomed like an uncharted territory. What about LB as a celebrity? I'd need a big boost of energy to keep up with that.

Gaps in the Cleveland schedule worried me. A year later, Maggie Carson divulged Harry Kraut's modus operandi. "Harry always withholds some information," she said in her laying-down-the-law voice, "so that only Harry knows what's going on. Then he steps in and saves the day." A simple way to garner plaudits for his suave salvaging skills. As Maggie pointed out, "He gets better at this with each success." By "better," I guess she meant "more devious."

We were to depart for Cleveland on a Monday, so I had all day Sunday to think about packing luggage, which I planned to do after I'd taken LB to church. Dean Webb not only managed the largest school of music in the country but also served as organist and choir director for Bloomington's most imposing Methodist sanctuary. He and his choir had prepared Bernstein's *Chichester Psalms* for that Sunday, in the composer's honor.

But when I arrived at the condo, I found LB perched on the edge of his bed, his sleep mask on top of his head and the white-noise machine already whirring. Church was no longer in LB's plans. He begged me to go in his place and let him sleep; my assignment was to ask Dean Webb's forgiveness. LB had already taken a sleeping pill and he could barely sign his note of apology. I patiently held the paper for him, put his note in my shirt pocket, and drove off to the church by myself.

It was a dark and stormy day, a wintry cliché in Indiana. Freezing rain turned to slush on the roads and severely challenged my driving skills. Tire chains? I knew absolutely nothing about them.

Kenda Webb met me at the church door, graciously accepted LB's apology, and led me upstairs to seats in the loft. From there, we saw that the place was packed, with not a spare pew cushion anywhere.

So many years had passed since I'd last heard *Chichester Psalms* that this performance seemed as if I'd come across the music for the first time. Plus, after a month of immersion in *A Quiet Place*, I listened with a new aural sensibility, a sort of Bernstein filter. I heard certain similarities in melodic contour and rhythmic pulse and sensed a long compositional line running throughout all LB's works.

A couple weeks earlier on campus, I'd caught the film *On the Waterfront*, and although LB didn't attend, he had a lot to say about his only film score. "I had to fight for that horn solo over the credits," he said. "The producers wanted a big orchestra, right from the start." Bernstein had argued for a stark contrast instead. Begin with a simple, noble melody—that solo horn—and switch, under the opening shot, to a bombardment of percussion. A percussion fugue, no less.

For that film, LB got what he wanted. Now, I heard an echo of that fugue in the middle of *Chichester*—though I didn't yet know that LB had borrowed that music from himself; he had repurposed a discarded number from *West Side Story*.

LB also described wrangling with a Moviola, a contraption for frame-by-frame film playback. Moviolas were still in use when I took a film course in the 1960s, so I understood the tricky coordination of two film spools and a wacky speed-control mechanism. For LB, even a simple on-off switch tested his technological skills.

LB said that in Hollywood he was shown to a room with a desk and a Moviola, and told he had a specific number of hours to fit his music to the frames in the film. Figuring things out on his own in that room must have been lonely work for a natural-born collaborator, far from the camaraderie of *On the Town* and *Fancy Free*.

In LB's essay "Notes Struck at 'Upper Dubbing,' California," written in 1954 for *The New York Times*, he recounted his disillusionment over the massive cuts made to his score for *On the Waterfront*. But as I watched the movie in Bloomington, I wondered about LB's musical thinking—it didn't seem intuitively filmic. He wrote distinct musical numbers. After the love theme's first three notes, the entire romantic tune was sure to follow—beautiful music, but there was too much of it and it was too loud to serve as underscoring for Marlon Brando and Eva Marie Saint's subtle acting. LB's score called attention to itself like a symphonic opus.

MEANWHILE, seated at the Methodist church's magnificent organ and unaware if LB was present, Dean Webb led his choir through *Chichester Psalms,* giving a polished, lively performance. The concluding unaccompanied chorale satisfied me emotionally in a new way. I heard inner voices resolve slightly at odds with the rules I'd learned in counterpoint class. *So that's how a real composer writes.* That morning, I heard for the first time "the note that costs"—a witticism LB borrowed from Aaron Copland to describe an inevitably "right" sound, achieved after diligent deliberation. (Copland might have meant that "the note that costs" allowed him to command the big Hollywood tunesmith fees.)

Freezing rain came down more relentlessly as I drove to the brunch afterwards. Ice formed on the streets alongside the slush left over from that morning. How bad would the roads be on my drive back to LB's condo?

On my first solo social outing since tackling the job of assistant to the Maestro, I discreetly said nothing about the opera-in-progress, but I gamely fielded questions about what it was like to see Bernstein every day. The word games: Mental Jotto and add-a-letter, cryptic British crossword puzzles in *The Listener* and *The Guardian*. I described LB's hilarious impersonation of Katisha in *Mikado* and his dinnertime recitations of entire Shakespeare soliloquies.

Talking about LB triggered my jitters about the impending trip to Cleveland. I hadn't packed for the trip and the flight was less than twenty-four hours away. I kept pulling slips of paper from my shirt pocket to jot memos: *pack the crossword puzzles, stash extra pencils in the carry-on bag, don't forget music manuscript paper.* A chorus of "write that down" rang around the table whenever I reached into my shirt pocket. Later, somebody gave me a miniscule notepad and pencil. The size of a teabag, it nestled in my shirt pocket for years.

As I drove to the lakeside condo after the brunch, the dim winter light faded to black and the dark, icy roads demanded total concentration. The free day had revived me a little, but deep down I was exhausted.

While Ann prepared dinner, I told LB about Dean Webb's performance of *Chichester Psalms.* As a student, I'd spoken with composers about their works but never with a composer so famous or a piece so well-known.

LB admitted, "In 'Chich,' I didn't plan my setting of the text, and I ran out of words." Toward the end, the chorus sings "Ah."

"I thought that was deliberate," I said, "as if words were inadequate."

"Rapture," LB said, with a hint of irony.

He insisted I stay for dinner, but I wanted to go back to the student union and get some sleep, mindful of the next day's trip to Cleveland.

To return to the campus quickly, I opted for the limited-access highway instead of the back roads, but as I maneuvered onto the highway, I nearly panicked. It was solid ice. I'd never driven on ice. My car got no traction at all as it slid forward.

I let the car slow to a crawl and looked for the first exit. I could just make out the off-ramp and gently gave the steering wheel a nudge. The car spun around once, then spun around a second time. I put my foot on the brake and the car slid sideways. I'd lost all control. There were no guardrails at the highway's edge, and the car pitched headfirst down a steep embankment.

Even with my seatbelt buckled, my face smashed into the rearview mirror. The glass shattered. Shards rammed into my forehead. I opened the car door and climbed up the embankment to see if anyone was on the highway. I made a mental note of what was in the trunk: no Bernstein manuscripts, of that I was sure. I could abandon the car and whatever was in it without much worry, but I forgot to turn off the car's engine. When the state police came by later, they found the lights on and the motor still running.

I heard ice crunching not far off, so I waved my arms. Without coming to a complete stop, a car slowed enough for me to get in back. Of course, this car had tire chains. Any sensible driver in Indiana had chains in this weather. The driver said he'd seen me spin around and dive off the road. He was relieved when he saw me standing upright. His girlfriend handed me tissues to stanch my bleeding, while I apologized for the blood I dripped on the back seat of their car. But I was cushioned by mounds of debris from McDonald's: Styrofoam boxes, paper napkins, hamburger wrappers, paper cups, and paper bags. My bleeding dribbled onto only the topmost layer.

The driver said his mother was a nurse at the Bloomington hospital, so he knew exactly where to go. In no time, I was lying on a gurney in a brightly-lit room as I gave a deposition to a state trooper. He said breezily, "We lost three people at that exit last year," when I asked why there were no guardrails at such a precarious ramp. Then he explained that Indiana doesn't plow or salt the main highways, since everyone knows to use back roads in severe winter weather. *Gee, thanks, I wish I'd known that.*

After picking the shards out of my face and stitching up the largest cut, the doctor in charge made an appointment to reset my nose. It had fractured when my head hit the rearview mirror. The doctor stressed that I had a serious concussion and shouldn't spend the night on my own. I'd need to be awakened throughout the night. The trooper called the condo after I gave him the number. Ann and Stephen were on their way.

When we got back to the condo, Stephen cleared out his room—I don't know where he put himself the next few days, but it was exceedingly considerate of him—and Ann fed me something. As I sat at the dining table, LB looked gravely at me.

"Call your mother," he said.

That hadn't occurred to me. I wanted to explain to LB that when I communicated with my parents, I wrote a letter. I almost never made a phone call. Why would they be interested? Their support had never existed, so why should I turn to them now? I couldn't manage to say all that, but LB never took his eyes off me, as though he were reading my thoughts. Ann brought the phone to the table, and LB watched closely as I told my mother that I'd hit some ice and banged up my nose but was generally all right. After I hung up, LB badgered me further.

"How do you feel?" he asked, not referring to my physical aches and pains—this was a therapist's question. LB considered himself not only the Chief Rabbi of the Universe but therapist to the entire planet. For once, I took him seriously.

"I feel like a failure," I said. "I won't be able to make the trip to Cleveland. I was looking forward to it." I was also truly exhausted, banged-up, and miserable. "I'm letting you down," I said.

"Go to bed," LB said decisively.

There must have been morphine in my system, because I fell asleep instantly. Now Stephen was talking me into wakefulness, and I thanked him: yes, I was awake. This concussion business was new to me, but Stephen let me go back to sleep. Just as suddenly, LB was pushing my shoulders, growling, "Wake up, wake up." I hoped this was it for shoving me into consciousness. I'd have preferred slipping into a coma.

"OK, I'm awake," I said with some irritation.

This time the morphine had worn off, and adrenaline coursed through me like an electric current.

"How am I going to get back to sleep?" I asked LB. "Could you tell me a boring story?" What did I have in mind? "Something dull and uneventful."

He hesitated but sat down.

"There were two women living in a cottage in Wales," he began. "The cottage was perched on a hillside where the wind blew so fiercely that the two women could barely open the door, but every morning they shouldered it open just enough to pick up the newspaper on the doorstep."

LB paused.

"*The Daily Leek*," he said dryly.

The play on the Welsh national emblem perked me up. I knew LB had received a letter from Martha Gellhorn that week, posted from a village in Wales. Years later I read that letter: she described a wind so fierce that she struggled to open her front door. She was a famous journalist, but she didn't mention any newspaper, much less the fictional *Daily Leek*.

"What was in the newspaper?" I asked, now wide awake.

"Oh, the local gossip," LB said, veering off into his imaginary village. "It's all in Welsh," he said, "which sounds like baby talk. Richard Burton tried to teach me a few phrases," and LB made gurgling noises like an infant sucking on a pacifier. "There's a lot of sheep news, and of course the police blotter. Who got robbed, who got drunk, and whose horse got loose."

"What sort of news about sheep?" I asked, sitting up in bed. LB could not tell a boring story.

"The two women had some sheep themselves," LB said, "up on the hillside above their cottage." He paused. "But it's time you went back to sleep."

He stood to leave and said goodnight.

The next day, LB flew to Cleveland, and I stayed three days in the condo with Ann and Stephen, both of them now full of solicitous concern. They drove me back to the hospital for my appointment with the surgeon, a young man with a confident way about him. He'd played football at Bloomington High School and could tackle anything that came his way. After he coated the interior of my nose with cocaine to dull the pain of setting the fracture, he waited a minute, said that wasn't enough for a fracture like mine, and gave my nasal passages another coat. Then he stood behind my head, and with a thumb on either side of my nose, snapped it back into place.

Cocaine was new to me. Whoa, no pain. I'll always remember the snap, and being at the mercy of a hulking blond football hero. As Ann drove back to the condo, she giggled at my cocaine-induced monologue, even as I panicked at a curve in the icy road.

One evening at the condo, Stephen entertained the student participants from the opera-in-progress workshops. Ann turned out fantastic things to eat and I sat on the sofa in a daze, accepting condolences. What else could I do, fogged on painkillers and no longer anything close to "too cute"?

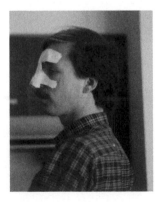

7 | What Universe Is This?

AFTER LB RETURNED to Bloomington from Cleveland, Dean Webb and his wife, Kenda, invited the Bernstein household—now a social unit not unlike a tribe—to dinner at their house. In lieu of flowers, LB copied the chorale from Act I of *A Quiet Place*, with its lyrics altered to laud the Webbs' devotion to one another, a page that adorns their dining room today. Six years later, in "Mr. and Mrs. Webb Say Goodnight" from *Arias & Barcarolles*, LB named the four singers Charles and Kenda, Malcolm and Kent (the Webbs' two middle sons), another affectionate testimonial to this loving family.

Franco Amurri, an Italian screenwriter living in Los Angeles, arrived a few days before our return flight to New York. Still recuperating, I was excused from attending to Franco's demands, while Ann sharply mimicked Franco's petulance. "Make me a sandwich" became our watchword for a transgressive guest; we didn't even bother to roll our eyes. Ann's patience had thinned even more than mine, but this roadshow was about to head home.

The night before our departure, students invited me to an informal Mardi Gras, hoping I'd bring the Maestro. Of course, LB kept that party going until dawn. To make our midday flight, he planned to stay up all night anyway. *No time for a nap*, I realized, spying the sun above the horizon as we left the party.

My first Maestro travel day couldn't have been simpler: drive LB, Stephen, Franco, and eight pieces of luggage to Indianapolis for a nonstop to La Guardia. After they settled in the back seat of the car, Stephen proposed a game of Mental Jotto and begged to be allowed a six-letter word rather than the usual five. LB and Franco guessed six-letter words—*robins, wrongs*—while Stephen clued them with the number of letters that matched those in his word. For those two specific words, he'd have said "zero." If LB had guessed "prongs," Stephen would have said "one"—one letter in common with his word, but he wouldn't have said which letter. The game is a process of elimination in anagrams, played without pencil and paper. It can take hours, so it's perfect for a boring drive.

Barely out of Bloomington, I had Stephen's word: "yclept." But I kept it to myself, so as not to spoil his game. Besides, they couldn't hear me over their three-way cacophony in the back.

Harry Kraut greeted us at La Guardia airport. He cheerfully embraced LB and then casually scanned the scar on my forehead. "It doesn't look bad at all," he said patronizingly, though I looked like the victim of a lobotomy-by-chisel. I suspected a maneuver to dismiss an insurance claim, my first conscious mistrust of Harry's motive. I felt like tugging at his little chinstrap whiskers to give him a sense of the pain I was still enduring.

Harry waved a hand at the luggage and said, "Take them to the Dakota in a cab," even though his secretary Mimsy had promised a van. No one held a HARMON or BERNSTEIN sign, so I got a taxi, hoping I knew the address. Um, West 72nd Street?

I'd had little experience with New York taxi drivers. This one was hostile, and I had no patience after being awake thirty hours. In the Dakota driveway, I scolded the driver and didn't give him a tip. While the porters took everything up to the apartment, I introduced myself to the building's receptionist, who directed me to the northeast corner staircase. Inside the celebrated century-old Dakota for the first time, I found the door to Apartment 23 unlocked and stepped across the threshold.

In one corner of the foyer, a fireplace radiated welcoming warmth. In another corner, a bartender poured drinks at a small bar. Straight ahead, an impressive library overlooked Central Park. Golly. My entire two-bedroom apartment in Brooklyn—plus the apartment next to it—could be shoehorned into that space.

Over the conversational hubbub of fifty of LB's nearest and dearest friends, none of whom I would meet that evening, I heard a telephone ringing, constant but distant. Where the heck was the phone? It was my job to answer it, but I didn't see a phone anywhere.

Harry spotted me and took me to the assistant's office, where the luggage sat waiting. I opened a few bags, but the housekeeper, Julia Vega (pronounced HOO-lyah, befitting her proud Chilean spirit), interrupted me and said she'd unpack the clothes herself. I was too worn out to absorb much, but Julia's grandmotherly calm reassured me and I was grateful to have one less thing to do. She pointed me to LB's study down a corridor, where I spread the opera manuscripts on a vast table that served as LB's desk.

In that hushed, dimly-lit room, the accumulations of a productive, creative life covered every surface. A dozen framed photos stood like dominoes on the lid of an enormous piano. Orchestra scores filled an entire wall of shelves. A phone rang somewhere but now even more faintly.

Jamie Bernstein, LB's older daughter, the oldest of three siblings, came into the study, complaining about her bad cold and a recent break-up with a boyfriend. Nearly my age, she seemed agreeably sociable despite her not-very-fresh sweat-pants and a baggy sweatshirt. She hadn't run a brush through her hair in a while,

LB's studio in Apartment 23, the Dakota. That mammoth wall of shelves is all music.

but then, she had a cold. Nice of her to introduce herself to the current assistant, something she must have done on an annual basis.

The damned phone continued ringing, if only I knew where. Jamie gave me a look as if to shove me off a cliff and said, "Aren't you gonna get that?"

"Um," I said. If only I knew where the phone was.

Jamie's eyes looked sideways at a low table, and that's when I saw a phone. One button in the row across the phone's base blinked away, but how did I deal with a multi-button unit? Julia entered, saying she had picked up the call in the kitchen. The taxi driver downstairs wouldn't leave until he got a tip.

I exploded. "He doesn't deserve a tip!"

Jamie's brother, Alexander, whom I hadn't met yet, looked in his wallet and went downstairs to give the guy some cash. Harry appeared, telling me to go home. I was obviously frazzled. I took my single suitcase to the driveway, the doorman hailed a cab, and within two blocks I was sound asleep.

ON MY WAY TO THE Dakota the next morning, I bought the *New York Times* and handed it to LB at his breakfast table. He gave me a puzzled look. "The papers are delivered to the back door every morning," he said. "Don't you know that?"

"Um," I said, now my standard reply to a question from a Bernstein.

No, I didn't know anything. Home delivery of the *Times*? Beyond my means, true for everything else about LB's New York life. I'd returned to a city I thought I knew, but now I had to pay attention, negotiate, participate. No passivity allowed in this up-tempo parallel universe.

The Bernstein assistant's office—my office—had been Nina's bedroom until she decamped for Harvard. Nina was the youngest of the three siblings, and her cheery yellow-flowered wallpaper perked me up. Otherwise, the Dakota was a somber pile, its interiors weighted with imposing moldings and substantial oak doors, the floors blackened beneath a century of polish. The furnishings in LB's apartment had a comfy, slightly-worn charm, but the scale? Palatial. Apartment 23 extended half a city block along Central Park West. There were seven fireplaces.

My office was the one room, other than the kitchen, without a fireplace. A large window next to my desk overlooked Central Park. Creaking wooden shutters helped block the blinding morning sun. A two-seat couch unfolded to a single bed, but most of the room was taken up by two mammoth storage units, their deep shelves painted Harvard crimson. One unit reached to the ceiling, seventeen feet up, every cubicle filled to capacity. I asked LB about a block of wood sticking out of one cubicle. It looked like an organ pipe. "It's from Anton Bruckner's—pardon the expression—organ," he said, which I knew to be the most celebrated church organ in Austria. What was it doing here? I blew on it and recognized the dry, fluty sound of the *Rohrflöte*. Then I stuck it back on the shelf. It took me two years to sort out all that clutter.

Exactly three things sat on the desk: two wagon-wheel Rolodexes holding more than three hundred handwritten cards, and a telephone. No typewriter. The desk, a piece of the late Mrs. Bernstein's favorite wicker, had seen better days. As I struggled to open a warped drawer, I gouged my hand on a protruding nail. Dripping blood, I ran to the kitchen, where Julia gave me some bandages. The next day with pliers and a hammer, I extracted several nails. They stuck out like porcupine quills.

Finding a drawer stuffed with credit card receipts, I called Charlotte Harris, the accountant at the office where I'd had my interview with Harry Kraut six weeks earlier. In her exasperated gratitude—many expenses had gone unaccountable—she said, "Send the whole sheaf" along with my handwritten ledger from Indiana. It took me twenty minutes to find an envelope.

Harry's secretary, Mimsy Gill, called to ask why I hadn't used the luggage van at La Guardia. Oh? So I might have been spared that obnoxious taxi driver. Riffling through the Rolodexes for the DAVE-L limo account, I called and introduced

At my desk, March 1985. Bruckner's organ pipe is in a cubicle out of view, high up on the left. I demanded the typewriter in late 1982: an IBM Selectric with font balls. Central Park is visible through the window. A prime seat for the Macy's parade!

myself. On my first day in New York as LB's assistant, I had to establish contacts and ask basic questions, not so different from re-inventing the wheel.

LB was gratifyingly helpful. He urged me to check his datebook first thing each day, where he meticulously logged his appointments: a roster of dentists; visits from his barber or from his secretary, Helen Coates; the names of anyone stopping by for drinks; and dinner invitations after the word "*chez*," a useful affectation.

Only a few names in his datebook looked familiar. One evening at five o'clock, Dr. Lewis Thomas came for drinks. I'd read his book of essays on biology, *The Lives of a Cell*, which had won two National Book Awards. LB was still in the shower, so I took Dr. Thomas's coat and kept him occupied with questions I'd always wanted to ask. Why did he view extra-terrestrial microbes as generally benign? He didn't seem to mind.

Another evening I opened the door to Elie Wiesel and his wife, Marion. The intensity in Mr. Wiesel's face startled me, but shaking his hand thrilled me deeply. LB was nearly ready for his guests, for a change, so I got only a few minutes to speak with this remarkable activist, survivor and chronicler of the Holocaust— possibly the noblest soul of the twentieth century. I regretted not sitting in on his discussion with LB that evening.

In front of the photographs on the piano, is that a soup bowl? No, it's an ashtray.

For a preliminary rehearsal for William Walton's Concerto for Viola and Orchestra, the Philharmonic's principal violist, Sol Greitzer, came to the Dakota with a pianist. As I opened the door, LB—prompt this time—greeted Mr. Greitzer warmly, then crushed the accompanist, petite Harriet Wingreen, in a smothering hug supplemented by a dog-sloppy kiss. As the Philharmonic's pianist, Harriet was very special, most memorably in LB's concert performances of *Fancy Free*. She smoked nonstop, so a rehearsal at LB's piano was a treat for her. Ashtrays waited to be filled at both ends of the keyboard. The keys themselves had already been branded with cigarette burns.

Another evening, I opened the door to Adolph Green—Broadway legend, life-long collaborator with Betty Comden, and friends with LB since their teenage years—and his wife, Phyllis Newman—likewise legendary—plus LB's brother, Burton Bernstein, an editor and writer at the *New Yorker* magazine; and Burton's son, Michael, all joining LB to see a new Woody Allen film. LB asked me the location of the theater where I'd reserved seats. Um, reserve seats at a movie theater? Could anybody actually do that?

Adolph Green jumped in, looked in the *Times* for the theater, called, and asked for the manager. Without disguising his voice—which any theater-savvy New Yorker would have recognized—Adolph said, "I'm the Maestro's secretary. Yes, that Maestro, Leonard Bernstein. We'd like five seats for the 7:35 screening."

It worked! Adolph's demonstration of this fundamental celebrity gambit earned my undying gratitude. I had a lot to learn.

On Friday, LB decamped to his house in Connecticut, driving his Mercedes convertible. Julia took the train from Grand Central. I called her the next day for directions, listening carefully through her rich Chilean accent.

"Jou look for Dannon Road," she said over the phone.

"Spelled like the yogurt?" I asked.

She hesitated. "*Jess*."

After aimless driving on country roads, I spotted "Dunham Road." My brain got a funny tickle. *Oh, I get it. The Chilean accent.* I resolved never again to ask Julia to spell anything. Even now, years later, I still say "Dannon" when I see that street sign. A little prayer of gratitude to Julia.

The property didn't catch my eye from the road, but up the driveway it was pure Norman Rockwell. Beyond a white clapboard house sat a smaller red house—LB's studio—and beyond that, a big red barn and a caretaker's cottage. The spacious studio had two large desks, a long, rumpled sofa, a fireplace, a bar (of course), and a grand piano. From the upper end of the driveway, I noticed a swimming pool behind the house. Quite a comfy suburban retreat.

Mindful that LB didn't eat with his cook, and hoping to get to know Julia better, I had dinner in the kitchen with Julia, Ann, and Gigi Cantera, the household maid who roomed upstairs in the Dakota and also helped out in Connecticut. LB and Alexander sat at a round table in a far corner of the living room. That lasted one night. The next night, Alexander said LB wanted me to join them in the living room, so Julia picked up my plate and utensils, and I traipsed after her. Ann let out a big sigh. (She'd never be invited to eat with the Maestro in the living room of his own house.)

The mysterious dividing line between family and hired help might never be erased, but smudged? *Jess*.

Three nights later we were back in the city. For the fortieth anniversary gala of City Center, LB had agreed to play the piano, but he hadn't yet decided on the piece. While a barber gave him a haircut in the bathroom, I offered to play through the Chopin mazurkas at the piano in LB's study, maybe twenty feet away. I hadn't practiced in a while, so I started with Chopin's fairly easy opus 63. After I played op. 68, no. 2, LB asked me to play it again—he might remember that one if he heard it a couple times. We talked about the difficulty of memorizing Chopin, a composer who rarely repeats a phrase exactly. LB had played that same mazurka on Chopin's own piano in Warsaw a few years back, so the music was securely in his memory. At the gala, LB introduced his performance with that Warsaw reminiscence.

The next night, I saw some friends for the first time since becoming LB's assistant, and they asked what my working days were like.

"I played Chopin while LB got a haircut," I said.

My friends were incredulous. "Weren't you nervous?"

"No," I said, "It wasn't an audition, so why would I be nervous? I made myself useful, that's all." Besides, LB's concert grand was like flying first class compared to my upright piano out of steerage.

⌇

FOR JULIA VEGA'S birthday at the end of February, an event she resolutely refused to celebrate because her father had died on the very day she turned six, LB threw a party that she couldn't avoid. Forty people came to the Dakota, including three former assistants: Jack Gottlieb, the Maestro's first assistant during LB's invigorating years as music director of the New York Philharmonic; Daryl Bornstein, who'd preceded me as assistant before *interim* Richard Nelson; and Johnny Walker, who had served through the death of Felicia, the late Mrs. Bernstein. That had been an overwhelming trauma for the family and the entire staff.

Lined up in my office like the Fates, these three former assistants insisted: *maintain your own life! Don't take the job too seriously!* Johnny emphasized, "Take some free time"—a concept new to me. Wouldn't it be obvious when I needed a break? Why were these three guys warning me so sternly? The boisterous party prevented me from pestering them that night, and months went by before I saw them again.

Later that same night, I thought about those former assistants, their observant and articulate skills versus my fixation on petty details and how tongue-tied I was. Those three engaged with the wider world. It was a vast landscape that filled me with apprehension. How could I fit in alongside such professionals? *Ambition?* Not sure I had any. *Pride?* A foreign concept.

If only I'd had a therapist's tools to examine the engraved die of my dysfunctional past: an alcoholic mother; a dismissive father; and a resentful, belligerent older sister. I didn't realize that I'd become proficient at propping up the illusion of a functioning family. I'd cleaned up other people's messes, pouring down the drain the drinks that my mother left around the house, doing the laundry, washing the dishes, taking out the garbage. I was nearly twenty-six when I left that scenario for good. So I thought.

And now this other family and its patriarch, Leonard Bernstein. What messes could there possibly be? The short tenures of those prior assistants puzzled me.

Julia's birthday party was capped with a *cueca, una canción rústica,* music from the Chilean countryside, though the version LB had written was more raucous than the norm. Everyone crowded into LB's study, Julia at the center, a colorful shawl wrapped over her quotidian black housekeeper's uniform. LB, still in his bathrobe, thumped at the piano and howled as if he were hawking peanuts at a ballpark. Each verse ended with a ribald rhyme for "Vega," but I didn't know enough Spanish to get the jokes.

Julia swayed slightly to the music, looking pleased, and especially happy to see her *chicos queridos,* Jack, Daryl, and Johnny. I was merely the next face in an unending gallery of assistants, and so far, Julia hadn't said more than three words to me. Eventually, we developed a deeply trusting relationship. I grew far closer to Julia than to my own mother. Julia's generosity may have been calculated at times, but from her I learned to appreciate the things people did for me. With her, I stepped into a world where people trusted one another. When Julia died many years later, I had known her for half my life. By far, the better half.

Party animals! Somehow, Julia let me crown her with bunny ears.
Left to right: Gigi Cantera, Ann Dedman, and Julia Vega.

The night of the City Center gala, I attempted for the first time to serve as LB's valet. While he took a shower, I laid his dress clothes on his bed in the reverse order he'd put them on: tuxedo pants with braces (suspenders) already buttoned into place, a dress shirt on top of that—collar stays already inserted, cufflinks positioned in the outside slits—underwear and socks on top of the shirt.

He fumbled with the shirt buttons, annoyed that one was missing. From the shelves of a nearby closet, I brought another shirt, but it lacked two buttons. LB tugged that shirt over his head so violently that it ripped straight up the back. He wasn't the angry *rebbe*, but he was certainly annoyed. There were no more shirts with the right collar for black tie, so I brought a dress shirt with a stand-up collar for white tie, after checking all the buttons first.

"I can't wear that. It's the wrong collar," LB said.

Harry Kraut entered the bedroom just then and said, "I've seen that combination of black tie with stand-up collar. It's a new look."

LB would never have gotten dressed if Harry hadn't said that. I was grateful.

LB's life should have revolved around music, family, and friends, but many unattended details wasted his time. Julia tried valiantly to keep LB's shirt buttons sewn on, but that was something his wife, Felicia, used to do. Like the interior of his medicine bag, the people around LB were a jumble of seemingly random helpers.

I resolved that night to stick with the assistant position beyond the trial period I'd asked for. Could I organize the minutiae of LB's daily life, try nudging him beyond the anger of his grief over the loss of Felicia? It was naïve of me to think so; I should have sought the guidance of a psychiatrist.

But something crucial had been taken from LB's life, and those missing buttons broke my heart.

8 | On Your Mark

IN 1980, A REVIVAL OF *West Side Story* had a good run on Broadway. As director, Jerome Robbins had instructed the cast to think of themselves as two rival gangs, offstage as well as on, and that meant that they dressed like gangs. The Sharks wore purple satin jackets, flashy and sexy, with "Sharks" emblazoned across the back. During rehearsals, LB bonded with the cast more deeply than usual, even for him, and as a token of affection the cast gave him a Shark jacket. He wore it with great pride everywhere he went.

In 1981, LB wore the Shark jacket to a concert at Tanglewood. That attracted a lot of attention. Normal dress for that crowd is khakis and a button-down shirt sporting a microscopic logo. Nobody at Tanglewood would wear a shirt advertising a bowling team, much less a garish jacket that broadcasted membership in a street gang.

But it was more than the jacket that got everyone's attention that evening. LB had arrived late with a boisterous entourage and insisted on being seated even though the music had already started. The ushers balked and threatened to eject him and his whole group.

As punishment for his disruptive behavior, Harry Kraut took the Shark jacket away. LB had no idea what had happened to it, and he desperately wanted it back.

LB was still deeply grieving over Felicia, acting out his loss with bouts of fury and bratty behavior, and, as far as I could tell, he hadn't put his life back together yet. Drinking every day didn't help. He usually had two glasses of scotch around 5 P.M., though his stomach was empty by that hour so those sips of Ballantine's had an acute effect. He turned even more talkative, ready to find fault in those around him, and defensive about his own behavior. No one spoke to him about his behavior or about his drinking, at least not while I was around. To me it looked like he didn't get much encouragement to pull himself together, just disapproval whenever he acted out.

LB never told me the whole story of the Shark Jacket Incident at Tanglewood. But he said I would do him an enormous favor—and add to my value as his assistant—if I could find out where the Shark jacket was and get it back.

It didn't take long to discover that Margaret Carson had the jacket in her apartment. As LB's press agent, she carefully monitored how he presented himself to the public, and the jacket was safe with her because LB rarely went to her apartment. When I called Maggie (as she was called by everyone in the business), she wasn't keen to give up the Shark jacket without some statement of contrition from LB. "Where is he going to wear it this time?" she asked, as though the jacket was a Halloween costume he should have outgrown.

But one afternoon a shopping bag arrived at the Dakota apartment with the Shark jacket bunched up inside. LB was overjoyed when I brought it into his study. He rhapsodized about his intimate bond with the *West Side Story* cast during that Broadway revival and how good they were in their roles. As soon as he put the jacket on, he slouched into a tough-guy pout. He looked ghastly in it. The purple color reflected off his bronzed face like a diffused bruise. He swaggered around his studio for a bit, and said, "Make sure you pack this jacket for the trip to Washington." I hung the jacket in his closet and "forgot" to take it on the first two trips.

As I'D LEARNED in my first interview when Harry Kraut recited the overwhelming schedule for 1982, LB tackled several projects simultaneously: writing an opera, recording symphonic works by Brahms with the Vienna Philharmonic, co-founding a "Tanglewood of the West" in Los Angeles, and publishing a book— an assemblage of his writings starting with a 1935 essay he'd written as a Boston Latin School student.

Richard Nelson had acted as interim assistant to LB but was now in charge of putting this new book together. He stopped by the Dakota with sheaves of LB's poems, essays, even LB's thesis for his Harvard Bachelor's degree, which on its own filled more than sixty pages in the finished book, *Findings*. I'd met Richard briefly when he flew with LB to Indiana. It was good of Richard to check up on how I was doing when I was back in New York. He often surprised me by placing his hands on the sides of my head and snapping my neck vertebrae. My neck and shoulders had turned to a solid knot after cradling the phone most of every day. I needed a chiropractor and some regular exercise, not easy to fit into the upcoming months on the road.

For the stint with the National Symphony Orchestra in Washington, D.C., Richard offered to show me how to pack and suggested we drive together in the station wagon to the Watergate Hotel. We got to work one afternoon when LB was out seeing his doctors. I hadn't yet explored the huge closet in LB's study, where the suits and concert frocks hung five rods deep. An identical closet above that, tall enough for me to stand up in, stored empty suitcases. I handed Richard seven big ones and we started to fill them.

After consulting the schedule—five rehearsals and three performances in each of two weeks—Richard selected three conducting suits. He checked each item for wear and tear while I looked over all the buttons. Pants, braces, vests, shirts, white ties, and tail coats—a maestro's uniform. Then he added two more complete outfits for good measure. He pointed out that for television or film, there were shirts, vests, and ties dyed in tea, which turned the fabric a soft beige that appeared white on camera. LB's wife, Felicia, had taken care of that. But none of the concerts in Washington would be televised or filmed, so we packed only the plain white shirts, vests, and ties. For afternoon concerts, press conferences, and formal dinners, Richard picked two sober, dark suits, a few blazers—including the one in crimson sporting the Harvard seal on the breast pocket—and tuxedo jackets. For rehearsals: blue jeans, pullover shirts, cotton sweaters, and several *guayaberas*, roomy oversize shirts with cargo pockets stitched across the front. Suits and jackets stayed on their hangers, which locked onto built-in clothes rods in luggage like small armoires, the same beat-up pieces I'd first seen at the Indianapolis airport a few weeks back.

One heavy-duty square suitcase held eight pairs of shoes inserted into plush pockets stitched to its inside edges: the patent leather boots LB wore when conducting, track shoes for rehearsals, loafers, and fuzzy bedroom slippers. Trunks the size of packing crates held as many as ten folded shirts in a stack, along with a few sublimely soft cashmere pullovers, a couple dozen silk pocket squares—red ones for the breast pocket of LB's conducting tails—boxes of new white handkerchiefs, a couple of silk dressing gowns and a wool bathrobe, underwear, ties, socks, winter scarves, and gloves. Several pairs of reading glasses fit into the trunks' inside pockets.

Two hefty book bags carried reference books and LB's current reading, plus music paper, erasers, and a gross of Alpheus Music Writer pencils in their blue cardboard box, plus a few red-blue pencils (LB called them "reddy-bluies"), and LB's conducting scores: three works by Brahms, Elgar's *Enigma Variations*, Walton's Concerto for Viola and Orchestra, and *Halil,* written by LB in 1981. A long leather box held several handcrafted batons, made by the timpanist at the Metropolitan Opera, Dick Horowitz.

As an Army brat on the move every two years, I'd lived out of suitcases all my life, so I understood the basics: heavy books go in small bags, and lightweight things—shirts and sweaters—go in large suitcases. But I'd never packed like this. In went family photos in their silver frames, cartons of cigarettes, packets of Aquafilters and Tums, extra inhalers, a stuffed white monkey called Moneto—all right, I'd carried a teddy bear around Europe once upon a time—an electric pencil sharpener, and the white-noise sleep machine retrieved from LB's bedside in Connecticut. The kitchen sink? Why not.

Halfway through the afternoon, Richard veered into a riff about trying on LB's clothes. "When the Maestro isn't around, wear his bathrobe and sleep in his bed. Pretend you're the Maestro," he said casually.

I didn't know what to say. Was this a grown-up version of pretending to be royalty? Playing dress-up made me queasy, and it sounded like the opposite of the advice I'd heard from the three former assistants: *Maintain your own life.* Maybe Richard had harmless illusions of grandeur, but had previous assistants been caught in LB's bed at the wrong time?

We had a carefree drive to Washington, singing along to Karl Böhm's recording of *Le Nozze di Figaro*, of all things. Richard allayed my concerns about the concert schedule ahead with easy-going confidence that I'd do well. It was the opposite of the panic I'd experienced on the plane to Indiana two months earlier, when Harry Kraut promised to clue me in to my responsibilities but instead spent the flight snoring. At the Watergate Hotel, Richard greeted the staff by name and Betty Bradley, the concierge, took us up to the suite. I'd never met a concierge before, and as Betty demonstrated with grace and thoughtfulness what a talented concierge could do, I learned how to depend on an adept hotel staff. Betty was as warm and personable as though we'd dropped in at her own home.

The expansive Suite 916 felt like a one-level suburban house. A wall of windows overlooked the Potomac River, from the National Cathedral in the west to the nearby Lincoln Memorial, and right next door, the big, boxy Kennedy Center. A limo could ferry LB to the stage door in less than three minutes.

I unpacked the luggage fairly quickly and placed framed photos and sharpened pencils on the Baldwin grand piano, on the desk, in the bedroom. There were plenty of drinking glasses in the suite's kitchen; the short ones made perfect pencil holders, including one batch in the bathroom for LB's crossword puzzles.

The empty luggage I trundled down the hall to my room, then I returned to the lobby with a typed list of names for the hotel phone operators. Calls only from those on the list—a sprinkling of Kennedys and senators, several *Washington Post* journalists—were put through to the Bernstein suite. All other calls went to my room. A big box of chocolates for the phone operators accompanied the phone list. On overseas jaunts in the years ahead, I left space in the carry-on luggage for exotic chocolates picked up in duty-free shops, and presented the gift—with a detailed phone list—immediately on checking into the next hotel. Even before our arrival, phone operators fielded calls for Bernstein, and the chocolates let them know: *The Maestro's here.*

Then Richard took me on a shopping spree in the liquor store on the lower level of the Watergate complex. What an extravagance. We piled bottles of scotch, gin, vodka, tonics, mixers, wines, and beers into a shopping cart, including labels I'd never noticed before. Pisco from South America—"A good present for Julia," Richard said—and Bushmill's Irish Whiskey, Humphrey Burton's favorite. As film director for most of LB's concerts, Mr. Burton would have dinner with LB that weekend to plan the broadcast of the Igor Stravinsky centenary-birthday concert coming up in June. "See who's on the schedule," Richard said. "Stock the bar with the right labels." I'd grown up with an alcoholic, so I knew about the good stuff.

Where could I stash four dozen bottles in the hotel suite? The only open space was the top of a dresser in LB's bedroom, and that was the first thing LB noticed when he arrived the next day. "Liquor in the bedroom reminds me of a bad Susan Hayward movie," he said with a laugh. Um, I got it—a B-movie scenario: sloshing booze while entertaining on the sheets. I called Betty Bradley, who quickly sent up a table that fit against a living room wall and was big enough for a complete bar.

That evening, I took the Metro out to Virginia to have dinner with the parents of a college friend. They peppered me with questions about the life of a celebrity, while understanding that to have a quiet meal in their home was a big escape for me, a dip into normalcy. The next day, I was relaxed, cheerful, and ready for the new challenge of assisting Leonard Bernstein the conductor. It was time to pay attention to the music, the central focus of LB's life and work. I hoped my own musical training was up to the task.

AT THE FIRST REHEARSAL in Washington, LB barely got the music under way when Mstislav Rostropovich rushed noisily onstage. As a celebrated cellist and human rights advocate, known to all as "Slava," Rostropovich occupied his own special category of celebrity. After Rostropovich reached the United States in 1977, Bernstein wrote him an orchestral overture, *Slava! A Political Overture for Orchestra*, premiered by Slava himself as music director of the National Symphony Orchestra.

Now in front of that orchestra, the two *Maestri* embraced like long-lost brothers as the National Symphony Orchestra musicians burst into cheers and laughter. Amidst the music stands in front of the podium, Bernstein and Rostropovich exchanged two or three jokes and another hug, and then Slava waved goodbye, running off to catch a flight to some other part of the world where music and imperiled freedom beckoned for his attention.

After another rehearsal, a cheerful blond kid trotted up to the podium: George Steel, a student at St. Albans, the prestigious prep school on the grounds of the National Cathedral. George also sang in the cathedral's choir. He'd met LB in 1981 while singing in Bernstein's Symphony No. 3, "Kaddish." Bright, good-humored, and exceptionally musical, George took notes that year for LB during rehearsals of the revival of *Mass* at the Kennedy Center, writing down everything LB said. Not as easy as it sounds. LB retained every detail of the score in his head. Taking notes required a similar grasp of every word, every note, every stage direction, plus the dynamics, articulation, and instrumentation. To nail every reference uttered by the Maestro demanded total recall, and George was pretty good at it. A year later, I passed a similar test during rehearsals of *A Quiet Place* in Houston.

George and a couple of schoolmates from St. Albans jocularly inducted LB into their private circle, "The Amorphous Wombat Society," with a presentation of Smurf stickers, a tribe of animated elves that appealed to kids in the 1980s. LB readily pasted the stickers all over the cover of his *Halil* score, where they remain today, possibly the only Smurfs cavorting in the music division of the Library of Congress.

At first there wasn't much to do musically, but in case LB needed fixes in the orchestra material, I asked the librarian, Vernon Kirkpatrick, if he could help me. Instead, he handed me the library key, and in the hours between rehearsals I worked in a place that I'd long dreamed of: the library of a major orchestra. As it turned out, LB marked up his score of Elgar's *Enigma Variations* as though looking at it for the first time, penciling something on nearly every page. Most of his notations emphasized what was already in Elgar's score: extending a diminuendo one more bar, adding "scherzando" (humorously) to a clarinet line. But in the next to last bar of the first variation, LB wrote "in 8," indicating he'd give the orchestra eight beats in that bar. The musicians needed to see that "in 8," which meant I had to copy it into sixty orchestra parts. I called up the trusty Amorphous Wombats to help me out.

The one free night that week, Leo Tonkin—formerly a legislative assistant and educational consultant—hosted a party in his apartment. LB decided to bring Lee, a preppy young man at loose ends. LB never said where or how they had met, but he was trying to help Lee in whatever way he could. Most of that year, Lee hovered reticently on the periphery of LB's entourage.

Leo Tonkin's party turned out to be a decorous gathering of conservatively suited gay men, all far more ambitious, socially adept—and prim—than I. When LB walked in, a coterie formed around him, and I was on my own. I never attended gatherings like this, but I knew if I didn't act quickly, I'd turn into a wallflower. I took a seat next to the only woman in the room, unaware she was Leo Tonkin's mother and a very live wire. She talked eagerly about her recent surgical procedure. Fine by me; it's always interesting how intelligent people deal with health issues. Suddenly she stood, dropping her dress to the floor to show the patch on her shoulder that gently fed medication into her system. A modest slip kept her covered up, but she stopped the party for a full minute. I felt like I'd met a star.

LB asked me later what I'd said to prompt Leo's mother's strip act. "I didn't ask her to do that," I said. "That's something you'd do, but not me." I couldn't tell if LB believed me or not, but it didn't matter. In a roomful of strangers, I'd had a good time.

9 | The Maestro Dines Out

THE TWO WEEKS IN WASHINGTON in March 1982 resembled a left-wing variety show. Politicians and members of the press stepped into LB's schedule like actors in and out of the limelight. First up, the journalist and civil rights activist Roger Wilkins, whose autobiography, *A Man's Life*, was published that year, ten years after he'd shared the *Washington Post*'s Pulitzer prize for exposing the Nixon Watergate scandal.

That same newspaper's music critic, Paul Hume, invited LB to his home for off-the-record discussions about contemporary music and overly ambitious critics. LB griped about every music critic in *The New York Times*, underlining every equivocation with a pen. His point: pompous critics pad their columns.

Adrienne Barth, the widow of the author and *Washington Post* editor Alan Barth, invited LB for dinner at her home, as did Roger and Christine Stevens. LB's friendship with Mr. Stevens extended over several decades. Mr. Stevens had helped produce *West Side Story* on Broadway in 1957, commissioned *Mass* for the opening of the Kennedy Center in 1971, and continued to serve into the 1980s as chairman on the Kennedy Center's board.

Most of the time I was invited, too, and if I sat in the limo's back seat, I'd ask LB about these people and their politics. Given his steep political slant to the far, far left, LB's optimistic long view often turned to frustration in the short term. My views were similar, though I'd put political participation aside since leaving college, when I'd trekked door-to-door for Eugene McCarthy in 1968 and for George McGovern in 1972. Fervent and idealistic back then, now I had questions. Was the Democratic Party splintering? What was happening in the South? What about politics and the arts? I could learn plenty from LB's articulate friends.

Assisting LB in his conductor role had a learning curve, too. After the first concert with the National Symphony (NSO), the orchestra's management invited Harry Kraut and LB to a restaurant at the Watergate. I was invited as well, but it took me a while to deal with that evening's concert wear. During the intermission of a concert, LB changed his shirt, vest, and tie, all soaked through with sweat; most of the time the tails and pants lasted through an entire concert. After the last encore, LB took everything off in the green room. He never took a shower, but rolled on deodorant with abandon and spritzed himself with Eau de Cologne 4711, which LB claimed evaporated sweat instantly. Slinging on a garish silk robe,

LB was ready to socialize with his fans. Back in the hotel, I hung the damp concert clothes in my bathroom to dry out before the laundry pickup the next morning.

In the restaurant that night, my chair sat empty as LB, Harry Kraut, and the NSO management talked idly, when suddenly LB mused aloud, "Charlie must be upstairs, trying on the wet clothes." Harry reported that a disturbed look bordering on revulsion passed around the table, which LB deigned not to notice.

Harry took me aside later. "Is this a secret fetish of yours?" he asked. "Trying on wet conducting outfits?"

Was he serious? I couldn't decide which was funnier: a fetish that peculiar or Harry's prurient concern. He gave me the best laugh I'd had in a long time, though I was careful not to mention Richard Nelson's suggestion about dressing up as the Maestro and sleeping in his bed. What bizarre behavior had LB and Harry put up with in the past?

Shortly before St. Patrick's Day, Ethel Kennedy's secretary called to invite LB for dinner on March 17th, the saint's day itself. Relaying the invitation to LB, I asked if I could come along. After so many high-level meals in Washington, I thought I'd be up to mingling with the Kennedys, and when would I have another opportunity? LB surprised me. "Of course," he said. I was never sure of my status as part of his staff—remember, the Maestro didn't eat with his cook. Then, too, sometimes he suggested a free evening would do me a lot of good.

The grand white columns fronting the house at Hickory Hill gave me a twinge of nerves. Was I ready for this level of aristocracy? LB had other concerns. In the driveway, he grabbed my arm and cried out, "If Teddy's here [Senator Edward Kennedy], please don't let me say anything about Chappaquiddick!" In 1969, Senator Kennedy had driven off a bridge on Martha's Vineyard, drowning his car's passenger, Mary Jo Kopechne—a scandal that ended his presidential hopes forever. That much I knew, but how could I stop LB from putting his foot in his mouth? Shout "Mississippi Mud"? Maybe it helped LB to panic out loud, what a shrink might call "acting out."

From the hallway into the dining room, LB spied the journalist Diane Sawyer—dazzlingly blonde—seated at Senator Ted Kennedy's left. "I knew it! There's a blonde right next to him," LB said in a stage whisper, grabbing my arm again. I'd forgotten Mary Jo Kopechne had been blonde.

As LB panicked, I only half-listened, my eyes on the wall behind his head, scanning a framed letter signed by Thomas Jefferson. *Oh my*, I thought, *this place is the real deal. Senator Robert F. Kennedy acquired that letter and put it there, on that very wall. A thinking, problem-solving, compassionate man, whose tenure would have been as noble and erudite as Jefferson's, if only . . .* I felt flooded with warmth, as if an unseen hand extended a welcome into a world more high-minded, optimistic, and gracious than any I had ever imagined.

LB made such a ruckus in the hallway that Ethel Kennedy came in to see what the matter was. LB shifted gears and said he didn't know it was going to be such a formal event—all the men, including me, were in suits. LB had thrown on an old fisherman knit sweater, and he felt underdressed.

Mrs. Kennedy said, "Come on, Lenny, it doesn't matter, it's just us." She pulled him into the dining room as though she were used to shoving her guests around. "Now sit down and join the party."

Two large round tables took up the entire dining room, one table headed by Senator Ted Kennedy, the other by his sister-in-law Ethel. I recognized a couple of senators at each table. LB was seated at Mrs. Kennedy's table, and I was shown a seat between Diane Sawyer and a venerable Kennedy family friend, Dorothy Tubridy. To her left was Senator Mark Hatfield, a Republican from Oregon, the state where I was born.

Diane Sawyer took up Senator Kennedy's attention, so I turned to Mrs. Tubridy, who twinkled with grace, lightly dusted over a pretty earthy Irish humor. Her theatrical Irish accent and low-pitched laugh delighted me no end as she shared her sharp insights on the Kennedys, their glamor, and their fierce competitiveness. Now and then I leaned across to speak with Senator Hatfield, whose political career I'd followed a long time. *So this was dinner in Washington*, I thought: gossip and politics. Nothing I couldn't handle.

Suddenly Ethel Kennedy ran about the room, ringing a spoon in a glass like a little bell, announcing the first round of a competition. Uh-oh. I'd read somewhere how mortifying these contests could be. At a dinner honoring Robert Frost, she had challenged everybody to write a poem, as if tossing off "Stopping by Woods on a Snowy Evening" was child's play. Tonight's competition was tied to St. Patrick's Day: ten points to the table producing the best Irish song.

Senator Kennedy leaned toward me and suggested persuasively that, as a musician, I could probably sing, but did I know any Irish songs? This was an expectation of a high order. I knew that I should go first or I'd never have the nerve to say anything the rest of the evening. Mrs. Tubridy kindly whispered that it didn't matter if my song was Irish or not, as nobody there would know the difference—except her. She was as Irish as could be.

I stood and announced, "Sorry to say, I'm not a singer, so I will recite a poem that is like a song: 'A Coat,' by William Butler Yeats." As a student composer, I'd struggled through five attempts to set these words to music, in the process firmly embedding them in my memory.

I made my song a coat
Covered with embroideries
Out of old mythologies
From heel to throat;
But the fools caught it,
Wore it in the world's eyes
As though they'd wrought it.
Song, let them take it,
For there's more enterprise
In walking naked.

At the applause and appreciative laughter, I smiled and looked around, glancing at LB, who sat open-mouthed in astonishment. Was I his first assistant who could recite a poem off the top of his head? I'd earned more than ten points.

The Kennedy competitiveness was contagious. LB immediately rose and ostentatiously cleared his throat. "I shall recite a poem by John Keats, whose name some people pronounce *kates* to rhyme with Yeats—which *some* people mistakenly pronounce *yeets*," he said, to general giggles. "I dedicate this poem to our hostess this evening," he said, waving his wineglass toward Mrs. Kennedy.

Then LB recited the sonnet "Bright Star," in a steady, carefully calibrated voice. He certainly knew how to hold the attention of a roomful of people, in a quiet and beautifully moving soliloquy. I remembered this moment when I visited the Keats house in Hampstead, north of London, fifteen years after LB died. The manuscript of "Bright Star" used to be on display there, and as my eyes passed over the handwritten lines, LB's voice sounded in my ear: every carefully-enunciated word, his brief pauses, the cultured Bostonian vowels. My tenacious memory for sound summoned up emotions both vivid and soothing. *Another layer of memory*, I thought, *tied forever to this verse*. "Thank you," I said aloud, in that room of the Keats house.

Ethel Kennedy sprang to her feet and again ran between the tables. "Ten extra points for anyone who can define 'Eremite'!" she shouted.

I knew that slightly archaic word, Keats's characterization of the remote loneliness of his bright star. My hand shot up as though I had the winning bingo card. "Hermit!" I called out. Hey, this was fun. Was the competition still on? Our table might be winning.

Diane Sawyer rose demurely. "I don't know anything Irish, but I'll sing something from my family's Scottish heritage," she said. The room quickly hushed and everyone paid close attention to her voice, which was sweet and low.

With Irish references in short supply, Mrs. Kennedy dragged LB to the piano in the next room. He played a lively ragtime number as some of the men danced a jitterbug punctuated with Irish heel-stomping. LB segued into a soulful rendition of "Maria" from *West Side Story*. Over the final chord, Mrs. Kennedy commanded, "That was beautiful, but now play a song about Ethel."

"Ethel?" LB asked, as if he'd never heard the name before. "I'm not sure there is any song about Ethel."

By then most of the politicians had departed, and the youngest Kennedy children came in to say goodnight. LB gave each of them an affectionate hug, and soon we were in the car headed back to the Watergate. I thought the evening had been a lot of fun, and LB agreed as he reminisced about visits to the upstairs living room in the Kennedy White House. He made it sound as casual as dropping in on neighbors. One of those evenings, LB said, he sprawled on the floor to watch one of his television broadcasts, while Caroline Kennedy sat quietly beside him, immersed in the music—or so he thought. When it was over, she turned to LB and stated flatly, "I have my own pony."

"And I thought she was absorbed in 'What Does Music Mean'—or whatever it was," LB chuckled as he retold this in the car.

The next day, I asked Watergate concierge Betty Bradley to send Mrs. Kennedy a big bouquet of flowers in her favorite shades of purple, with LB's name on the card.

10 | At Home in the Parallel Universe

ONLY TWO DAYS AFTER WE LEFT Washington, rehearsals started with the New York Philharmonic. No time to switch gears, but LB didn't need to. Most of the music on the Washington programs overlapped with the upcoming ones in New York, easing LB's workload. Both orchestras played Elgar's *Enigma Variations* and a month later LB recorded it with the BBC Symphony Orchestra in London—an English work with an English orchestra.

In 1982, LB recorded works by Copland, Gershwin, and William Schuman, all Americans, with the Los Angeles Philharmonic; Stravinsky with the Israel Philharmonic, whose string sections were solidly stocked from Russia and East Europe; and Brahms with the Vienna Philharmonic. Many years later, an otherwise well-informed colleague complained to me that LB made one orchestra sound like another. Not at all. LB taught orchestras the sound of the composers: Haydn, Mahler, Stravinsky, Copland. The Philharmonic Orchestras of New York and Vienna might sound similar when they played Mahler under Bernstein's direction, but that was because they had mastered Gustav Mahler's orchestrations. Yet there was still a sense of tradition and an innate style when playing the music of a hometown composer: Brahms in Vienna, Gershwin in Los Angeles or New York.

How exhilarating to be back in New York, with LB in great spirits and his mind focused on music. The two weeks with the Philharmonic focused me as well. I lived in my own apartment and slept in my own bed, which felt like a reward for surviving the past three months. That little bit of time in my own room gave me just the distance I needed from my duties as LB's assistant. It doesn't sound like much, but when I did things for myself, I had a greater appreciation of what I could do for LB.

As a conductor, LB had to stick to a routine, unlike LB the composer. And for his "family," the Philharmonic, LB made an extra effort to be on time. For me, new colleagues I met at the Philharmonic turned into lifelong friends. Even LB's housekeeper, Julia Vega, felt this uplift and started talking to me—because of a broken bottle.

During our shopping spree for booze in Washington, Richard Nelson had pointed out a bottle of pisco, the perfect little gift—a *regalito*—for Julia. A gift would show we'd thought of her and it might make the hectic pace on the Maestro's return a little more bearable for her.

Packing in Washington, I swaddled a bottle of pisco among the clothes in my fiberglass-shell suitcase, hoping this *regalito* would open up a channel to Julia. After three months on the job, I felt she still hadn't accepted me into the household.

At the Dakota, the porters hauled the luggage through the kitchen door and dropped my suitcase on the floor with a thud, even though it wasn't heavy. As I ran over to open it, a clear liquid trickled onto the floor. Julia looked over my shoulder as I opened the suitcase, and she let out a chesty laugh when she saw my sodden clothes and the broken glass.

"Oh, Charlie, I wash those for you," she said between big heaves of laughter as I picked glass out of my suitcase.

"But this is your *regalito*," I said, almost in tears. "I brought you pisco, and I packed it so carefully." My first *regalito* for Julia, now merely a nuisance to be cleaned up, a *lata*. "I will find you another bottle of pisco, and you don't have to do my laundry," I said, but Julia shooed me away as she shook the glass out of my clothes, laughing so hard she had to sit down.

After that, Julia became my best friend. If I arrived at the Dakota early, she served me French toast, trimming the crusts off Pepperidge Farm white bread and whisking extra eggs in the batter. Was a dollop of rum the mystery flavor?

"No, no," she said with mock peevishness. "You are *chinchoso!* I use no *ron*." I never quit bugging her about her secret French toast batter, and she always shot back with "*Chinche!*"—bedbug!

Those weeks with the Philharmonic, LB often roused himself out of bed even before I got to the Dakota. For a 10 A.M. rehearsal, he liked to arrive on the dot, to walk from the car to a waiting elevator and directly onto the stage. I dashed ahead to the podium, placed the open score on the music stand, set a baton on the central fold, and draped a towel over the back of his chair. In later years, the Philharmonic's principal librarian, Larry Tarlow, took the score and baton from my hands and put them onstage, while I scooted upstairs to the green room to hang the shirts LB changed into over the course of the day.

LB's secretary, Helen Coates, received the mail addressed to Bernstein care of the Philharmonic. She warned me to look for a young man who had asked to attend LB's rehearsals. At the rehearsal's first break, a good-looking guy sauntered onto the stage while LB took questions from the musicians.

I extended my hand: "Michael Barrett?"

He said, "How can I meet Lenny?" as if an informal chat with LB were an option available to anyone at a Philharmonic rehearsal.

I didn't care for the way Michael spoke out of the side of his mouth, but his timing was good. As we reached the podium, LB looked up and shook his

LB in his former studio in the Osborne, Apartment 2DD, 205 West 57 Street. Photos of the New York Philharmonic in Russia are on the wall behind him. Upper right: Dmitri Shostakovich takes a bow.

hand. I couldn't have known it then, but this meeting changed both their lives—mine, too, though not for many more years, after I'd quit as LB's assistant.

When rehearsals continued into the afternoon, Ann Dedman delivered a platter of sandwiches and fruit, and LB held court in the green room during the lunch break. Carlos Moseley, the managing director of the Philharmonic, gave LB a mammoth hug before taking a seat on the sofa. Slim and sprightly despite his thirty-year tenure with the orchestra, Mr. Moseley spoke with a Southern lilt that lent an endearing confidentiality to everything he said. He and LB giggled like schoolgirls as they swapped memories of the Philharmonic's 1959 tour to Russia.

"In Moscow, I had to beg Shostakovich to take a bow," LB said. "He didn't want to come to the stage, and he bowed so painfully," after the performance of his Symphony No. 5. "And what happened when I made that analogy between Billy the Kid and their folk hero version of Robin Hood?" LB asked. "The entire panel of Soviet censors stood and shouted '*Nyi pravda!*'—Not true!" LB chuckled. "Hadn't they read my script?"

Carlos Moseley reminded LB of the cups of coffee waiting for them on the runway in Amsterdam, their first real coffee after the bitter brown liquids of the Soviets, and how they all came down with colds, returning to New York very, very sick.

To me it sounded like LB's schedule hadn't changed: still richly entertaining but crazily exhausting.

LB chastised Carlos's one-upmanship at the Philharmonic's press conference in Japan in 1961. Carlos had phonetically memorized his entire speech in flawless Japanese. He swept the newspaper headlines with his diplomatic prowess and relegated LB's speech—merely in English—to chopped liver. On a narrow garden path in Kyoto a week later, Carlos had to step aside for the Maestro. LB muttered, "Smarty-pants," as he passed by without stopping.

Was this a normal music director/orchestra manager relationship? LB and Carlos seemed as familiar with one another as if they'd spent their childhoods together. Later that year, I discovered for myself how the intensity of an orchestra tour forges a bond as durable as "next of kin."

The Philharmonic's artistic administrator and press secretary, Frank Milburn, entered the green room, so I gave him the room's only chair. Famously reticent, Frank added wry comments to every Moseley-Bernstein reminiscence. The three of them had seen a lot together: over a thousand concerts, umpteen world premieres, many tours throughout the United States and around the globe. I tried to absorb as much of this history as I could. Could this be my future? Did I want it? I had no idea.

After one morning rehearsal, LB spent the afternoon talking to Bob Jacobson, editor of *Opera News* magazine, about *Tristan und Isolde*, a recording that LB approached one act at a time in concert performances in Munich. It took nearly three years to complete. Final listening sessions were still to come, but the release date was set for that autumn and LB had a role in generating publicity. Jacobson was relaxed and well-prepared. I liked speaking with him while he waited in LB's library at the Dakota. Would working at an arts journal be a feasible direction for me? But by the time I was ready for the next step, Jacobson had died of AIDS, and my life went in another direction.

Another afternoon, LB got into the hired car for a round of doctor consultations and an hour with his tailor, Otto Perl. Much of what hung in LB's closets no longer fit him. He had the blocky shoulders of a vigorous conductor, but his mid-section had turned into a beer barrel. Blazers and conducting frocks accommodated well, but LB's pants brought him nothing but grief. His favorite hip-huggers, "picked out by Princess Margaret on a London shopping spree," LB said, wouldn't zip up. Without a discernible waist, LB simply shoved his belt beneath his protruding gut.

The Philharmonic performed Wednesday and Thursday evenings, Friday afternoon, and the following Tuesday evening—LB's least favorite day, with a rehearsal of the next program Tuesday morning but a concert of the previous program that same night. Friday afternoons he dubbed "the blue-haired ladies" concerts, when the hall was packed with elderly women, who made a racket with their voluminous shopping bags.

One blue-haired afternoon from way back stuck in LB's memory. Near the end of Tchaikovsky's Symphony No. 5, a famous pause often takes an audience by surprise. The orchestra plays full tilt up to that sudden silence. It's like a cartoon character screeching to a stop at the edge of a chasm.

In that pause, a woman in the front row shouted at her companion, "I always use lard!"

LB said, "Obviously, she went to concerts to talk to her friends, not for the music," and that Tchaikovsky was so darn loud she had to shout to share her crucial tip—which LB hoped was about pie crust. LB said, "The musicians in the front of the orchestra"—the first violins, especially—"cracked up and barely came in on the downbeat of the next bar. I really had to work to hold the orchestra together." No wonder he didn't care for Friday afternoons.

After each concert, the green room filled with people from the top tier in the arts, a way station on the slopes of Mount Parnassus: William Schuman, the first Pulitzer prize-winning composer, the first president of Lincoln Center, and former president of the Juilliard School of Music; Oliver Smith, set designer for several dozen Broadway musicals, including LB's *On the Town, Candide, West Side Story*, and the ballet *Fancy Free*; Jerome Robbins, dancer, choreographer, director, and one of LB's closest collaborators—and according to LB, the most contentious; lyricists Betty Comden and Adolph Green; Adolph's wife, actress Phyllis Newman; actress Lauren Bacall; Mary Rodgers, composer and daughter of Broadway composer Richard Rodgers; David Diamond, composer—whose date was sometimes Greta Garbo, though she never ventured into the green room; Ned Rorem, composer and author; John Guare, playwright, who sometimes brought along French film director Louis Malle; Schuyler Chapin, Dean of the Columbia University School of the Arts and former general manager of the Metropolitan Opera, and his wife, Betty Steinway; and Lukas Foss, composer, pianist, conductor. Other dependable colleagues of LB's might also appear, such as John McClure, record producer; Robert Lantz, literary agent; Paul Epstein, legal counsel; John Mauceri, conductor and principal promoter of LB's musical legacy; and, always, a long queue of many, many fans.

Everyone got LB's hug, and he graciously introduced me when I met someone for the first time—at least in the green room, though LB's graciousness evaporated outside the hall. One night, when Jerome Robbins followed LB into the dressing area, he winked at me. Though initially I was more than a little afraid of him, we had a cordial friendship for the rest of his life.

LB never left the hall before 1 or 2 A.M. Gerry, the security guard for the green room, managed the hordes down to the last kowtowing fan. I handed him a fat envelope after the last concert, though no amount of cash sufficed for his smooth handling of the interminable backstage hours.

An after-concert party popped into the schedule sometimes, like one hosted by Karen Davidson, a friend of LB's who served in an artistic capacity at Lincoln Center. She promised an only-in-New York experience, the other celebrity guest being Mick Jagger. But LB and Jagger merely stood grinning at one another as the rest of us clutched our drinks and gawked. Jagger towered over LB, whose grin took a pasted-on look when he felt he was on display. He probably couldn't recall a single phrase from a Rolling Stones album, with his brain still full of Walton and Elgar from the concert a few hours earlier.

That same week, LB hosted a dinner for Lillian Hellman, aiming to butter her up in advance of *Candide* at New York City Opera that fall. She'd written the book for the original version of *Candide* in 1956, and LB felt obligated to consult her for proposed alterations whenever the musical was revived.

I called Ms. Hellman to ask if she could manage the stairs in the Dakota. If not, she'd have to come through the dreary basement and use the service elevator. Her secretary called back and insisted that Ms. Hellman's car always drove into the Dakota courtyard, and that she'd take the elevator from there. I checked with the manager at the Dakota's front desk, the redoubtable Winifred Bodkin, known as "Miss Winnie." She'd worked at the Dakota for fifty years, exactly half the lifetime of the building itself.

"No cars have ever been permitted in the courtyard," Miss Winnie said. "It's not designed to hold that much weight. There is no way to avoid the stairs in each corner of the building," she continued, "except through the basement entrance and a service elevator."

As I thought.

In my next phone call to Ms. Hellman's secretary, the legend herself took the phone. She gave me an earful as she spat out a string of four-letter words in imaginative combinations, paused only to drag on a cigarette, and climaxed her tirade with an emphatic, "Cocksucker!"

I burst out laughing, but it didn't matter. Ms. Hellman had hung up. LB seemed less amused than I and griped that whenever he tried to do something for Lillian Hellman, she voided his good intentions.

"I'll find a restaurant in her neighborhood," I said, "one with no steps." When I made my final phone call to Ms. Hellman, she seemed placated, but LB had the best idea of all. When the Harvard men's vocal ensemble, the Krokodiloes, serenaded LB following the Friday concert, he invited those adorable undergraduates to sing for Lillian Hellman at the restaurant that evening. I wasn't there—no way would I eat in the same room with her after those phone calls—but she was completely surprised and enchanted, and told LB so. Whew.

When I brought coffee and orange juice into LB's bedroom before the next 10 A.M. rehearsal, another person was in bed with him. This hadn't happened before, but I calmly went back to the kitchen for another coffee, and Julia didn't bat an eyelash. By the time I re-entered the bedroom, the other guy was in the bathroom, and LB had put on his bathrobe. I never did get the guy's full name, but he rode with us in the car to Lincoln Center, sitting silently in the back as LB patted his arm and sang a slow blues:

Over and over. No conversation, only LB singing in his tuneless growl. Did the guy ever get the point? I hoped LB was being careful.

ANOTHER MORNING we stepped into the Dakota courtyard at the same moment as Lauren Bacall—she lived two floors above LB. She was on her way "to save the Morosco," she said, though the battle to preserve that historic theater was won by the wrecking ball. LB greeted Ms. Bacall with an affectionate hug and waved his arm toward me.

"Meet my new assistant," he said, "Charles Manson."

I winced. Manson's parole denial had been in the news, and LB thought my moustache made me resemble that psychopath. Besides, I shared his first name.

"Really," Ms. Bacall said in a dramatically throaty drawl as she inched away from me. Maybe her alarm wasn't so half-hearted. We were walking toward the driveway where John Lennon had been shot only a year earlier.

"Um, no," LB corrected himself. "His name is Harmon."

I'm not sure Ms. Bacall got my name that day, but it didn't matter. LB later came up with a nickname that made up for his unfunny gaffe: "Charlito."

11 | *Princess Margaret Can't Go Shopping*

THE FIRST OVERSEAS TOUR covered a lot of ground—and the water in between: London, Israel, Mexico, Texas, all new territory for me except for London, which I'd visited eighteen years before. I had no qualms about touring with the Israel Philharmonic because I figured those in charge knew what they were doing. Shepherding twenty pieces of luggage through customs gave me enough jitters, thank you.

In the van to JFK airport, I compulsively counted those twenty pieces over and over and put myself so much on edge that a sympathetic British Airways clerk upgraded me to first class. As someone took my jacket and brought me a drink, a comment attributed to Mrs. August Belmont, founder of the Metropolitan Opera Guild, popped into my head. Of her private railway car, she said: *It's not an acquired taste. One gets used to it immediately.* I've never flown coach over an ocean since.

At Heathrow, a uniformed attendant from the Savoy Hotel hailed me and whisked everything into a waiting van, customs be damned. In no time at all, I stood amidst twenty open trunks in a sumptuous hotel suite, smack in the middle of London.

Two Noel Coward comedies could be staged simultaneously in LB's suite at the Savoy, what with a dozen chairs, two sofas, several small tables, a desk, a grand piano—of course—and the three doors requisite for farce: right, left, and center. A faded violet chaise longue angled into the room like a reclining odalisque. LB said later that Maria Callas loved this suite; the sole survivor of her visits was that violet chaise. I opened the draperies: at my right the Houses of Parliament stood at attention; downriver the Tower of London sported fluttering Union Jacks. Nearly beneath my feet, blooming daffodils bordered the Thames. What a long way from Lake Monroe in ice-bound Indiana.

After two hours of unpacking, I fell into a deep sleep while sitting upright. Loud voices and the rattle of a door key suddenly woke me as LB entered the suite, followed by a strikingly beautiful woman, Martha Gellhorn.

LB had told me about his first encounter with Martha Gellhorn in Israel in 1948. He as a young conductor in the first flush of celebrity; she as a war correspondent recently divorced from Ernest Hemingway. Rations and privations ruled at that time; arguably the most annoying was the substandard toilet paper. As

LB entered a bar, he heard someone say "carefully waxed toilet paper," and he swiveled to face the begetter of that phrase, a glamorous blonde: Martha Gellhorn. On the spot, they became fast friends.

As they entered the suite at the Savoy—thirty-four years later—I snapped to attention, to offer drinks and to order room service (I'd already figured out the function of a discreet button by the door, which had long ago replaced a bell pull). "Let's get potted shrimp," LB said, "In fact, two orders." In seconds, the waiter produced washbasins of congealed butter stuck with little pink bits. Shrimp butter! I'd made that once but never attempted polishing off two one-gallon crocks of it, much less at midnight.

Martha Gellhorn clipped LB's penchant for grandiosity and anagrams by trotting out Problems of the World and Perils of Contemporary Literature. He had no choice but to respond on her terms. I tried to keep up, but it was the middle of the night, and the fast-paced conversation accompanied by the fatty shrimp bits was too much for me. I excused myself, floated to my room down the hall, and passed out.

Whenever LB received a letter from Ms. Gellhorn, he shared it with me. She was a fastidious correspondent. When she could no longer find copies of her early novels, I tracked them down and sent them to her. An extension of fetching for the Maestro? Maybe. For someone so engaging and brilliant, I'd do anything.

Rehearsals with the BBC Symphony Orchestra started the next day at the White City complex west of Notting Hill. Our driver advised me to allow forty-five minutes, but LB didn't believe it and continued to putter around the hotel suite, thinking up things for me to do. "Call Princess Margaret," he said. "You'll find the number in my smaller address book."

LB bragged incessantly about his "royal" shopping trip on a previous London visit, when Princess Margaret had found him a pair of pants he adored: houndstooth hip-huggers belted with a five-inch swath of leather, probably a relic from once-fashionable Carnaby Street. These outlandish trousers no longer fit and LB's tailor, Otto Perl, who could make a bath towel look bespoke, threw up his hands. Time for another "royal" shopping spree.

Downstairs, the car and driver waited to take us to the BBC studios, but I gamely dialed the number for Kensington Palace. An equerry with a pained voice answered on the first ring. *Maybe he has a migraine*, I thought.

"Her royal highness is not available at all this week," he said. "No, we will not take a message. No, her highness will not ring back."

Click.

LB came into the room as I put down the receiver.

I said, "Princess Margaret can't go shopping," a line I'd never dreamed of utter-ing. Was LB showing off? He often seemed besotted with the status of royalty, but I suspected a delaying tactic and reminded him, "We really have to get in the car now."

In the hotel lobby, LB dithered by the display cases of perfumes and handbags, but I steered him toward the center of the lobby so he could see the car at the curb. He said grumpily, "It's just a straight shot through Hyde Park," and lit another cigarette. I walked ahead and the doorman sprang into action, but as the car merged into traffic in the Strand, we were already ten minutes late. Many more minutes ticked by as we inched around the park's perimeter. A straight shot? I thought LB surely must have understood that, unlike New York's Central Park, Hyde Park has no transverse roadways.

At White City, Harry Kraut paced at the curb, more agitated than I'd ever seen him. I nudged LB into the building while Harry launched a tirade directly into my ear: the orchestra had sat under baking television lights for forty-five minutes, the musicians were fuming, the BBC crew bristling, and the clock for the three-hour rehearsal was ticking away. Two hours and counting.

LB remained blithely unconcerned. He nodded at some familiar faces in the orchestra and launched into a speech about "Eddie" Elgar—although he knew very well that Elgar is always reverently referred to as "Edward"—and the musico-logical theories surrounding the *Enigma Variations*.

LB read aloud the anagrams he'd jotted in his score, combining the letters in "Elgar" and "enigma." What did this prove? Nothing other than he often stayed up late to futz with anagrams. Then he expounded on his thesis that Elgar's late bloom as a composer indicated an inferiority complex, evidenced by a reluctance to tackle large musical forms. Moreover, Elgar's self-doubt was a manifestation of Britain's self-perception as a musically inferior culture. Isn't that why composers went to Germany to study? The studio lights got hotter the longer this unhinged lecture went on.

But LB couldn't stop himself. "Auld Lang Syne" was the key to Elgar's "enigma," he proclaimed, a notion that Elgar had expressly denied. LB notated the tune above the first two bars in his score, in counterpoint to the palindromic opening of Elgar's theme.

By the time LB picked up his baton, the musicians had lost all patience. When he singled out the three trumpeters, demanding a less brassy quality—more "wraugh" than "wreah"—and chided them as though they'd never played together, the principal trumpeter talked back. Under those broiling lights, those brass instruments must have been scalding.

"Auld Lang Syne" penciled by Bernstein into his score
of the *Enigma Variations*.

In the "Nimrod" variation, LB took an excruciatingly slow tempo, later dubbed "glacial" by critics. As notes trickled from the orchestra like droplets from melting ice, LB requested an intense vibrato from the strings: a "loud" left hand, wildly wobbling the fingers in an enormous triple forte vibrato, while at the same time barely moving the bow across the strings, a "soft" right hand. Was the sound more intense? I couldn't tell. LB said it was exactly what he wanted. Laughter welled up from every section of the orchestra.

No let up the next day, even though it was Easter Sunday: a four-hour rehearsal in LB's hotel suite for the six singers in LB's *Songfest* followed by a *Tristan und Isolde* listening session with the Phillips recording engineer. In my spare time, I'd played through the *Songfest* vocal score, and had noted the careful organization of this work: a solo and a small ensemble for each singer, plus three sextets, all in LB's most accessible vocal style.

At two o'clock on the dot, as the singers arrived, I took their coats, set up music stands, poured glasses of water, and was about to sit at the piano to accompany this ensemble when Michael Tilson Thomas (MTT) walked in, volunteering to play for the entire rehearsal. In 1982, MTT spent much of his time in London, as music director of the London Symphony Orchestra. I offered to turn pages, but MTT said he didn't need a page turner. With no reason to hang around, I lit out for my favorite London institution, the British Museum.

Lo and behold, in the manuscript room, Elgar's manuscript of the *Enigma Variations* lay open to the very page where LB had questioned a tempo marking. Elgar's manuscript showed more notations than the published score, so I copied everything down, making sure I fully understood Elgar's intention. That took a while and left me barely enough time to skim past the marbles from the Parthenon.

LB was disappointed that I hadn't stayed for the rehearsal. "You could have learned something," he griped.

"But look what I found at the British Museum," I said and showed him my notes.

After an intense musicological discussion, comparing my notes against LB's score, he conceded, "You did something good."

The preparation of the music was always my main concern. I'd been hired to help get his opera completed, after all. I even told him once that, although he might have to conduct in his bathrobe, the music would always be ready on the orchestra stands.

On the British holiday of Easter Monday, LB had only an afternoon rehearsal of *Songfest* with the BBC Symphony Orchestra. We were on time, and LB restrained himself from lecturing.

That evening we saw *Noises Off*, a new farce starring Patricia Routledge. Six years earlier, she'd played the female lead—several First Ladies to a roster of U.S. Presidents—in the musical *1600 Pennsylvania Avenue*, the major (and final) collaboration between Bernstein and Alan Jay Lerner. Though a high-profile bicentennial commission, the musical expired after only four Broadway performances.

LB spoke often with pride about the music in *1600 Pennsylvania Avenue*, but he criticized himself for allowing his collaboration with Lerner to fall apart. LB said it alarmed him when Lerner didn't have an ending in mind for *1600 Pennsylvania Avenue*; he should have pressed Lerner for a dramatic resolution, or at least a list of ideas. LB admitted a similar misgiving about the ending of *A Quiet Place*—though collaborating with Stephen Wadsworth was a breeze compared to working with Lerner, who was slogging through his fifth or sixth divorce during *1600*. "He was so unpredictable," LB said. Once, when LB called Lerner's secretary to confirm a scheduled collaborative session, she told him that Lerner had run off to Tahiti.

LB always praised Patricia Routledge for her outsized talent and professional dedication. She had trouped through out-of-town tryouts of *1600* amid a barrage of rewrites and new orchestrations, with friction onstage and off. At one performance, LB said, Ms. Routledge's voice could be heard clearly as she waited in the wings to join her co-star onstage. "That man has liquor on his breath, and I will *not* go onstage with someone who has liquor on his breath," she declaimed. LB never revealed whether she did go on or if the performance ground to a halt then and there.

A young composer who had finagled his way into the *Songfest* rehearsal showed up at the hotel that night. The next morning, I ordered another breakfast for this bearded youth who was writing an opera—maybe for a cast of mice, played by children? I wasn't paying attention. LB seemed fond of the guy and kept up a correspondence for several years. I was surprised that his beard didn't put LB off. Maybe his dislike of facial hair was mutable. At least the conversation that morning was about music, and this young composer seemed to have no agenda.

For the British premiere of *Songfest* at Royal Festival Hall, a live broadcast, the BBC had prepared a banner production, replete with illustrations and narrators. For instance, an actor read Lawrence Ferlinghetti's "The Pennycandystore Beyond the El" in a convincingly slangy American accent while a camera glided over an Ashcan School depiction of a New York City elevated train. The backstage monitor mesmerized me. I've never seen a better presentation of *Songfest*.

The week ended with recording sessions for an entire Elgar LP, including three marches that LB and the BBC Symphony Orchestra had to nail without any rehearsal.

"How is that possible?" I asked LB.

"We did that all the time with the Philharmonic," he said. "Columbia Records called me the 'one-take wonder.' Just watch. The BBC musicians can play these marches blindfolded."

Before LB gave the downbeat for one march, the trumpeter who had talked back earlier in the week held up his hand. He thought he was supposed to play, but his part was blank. "Maestro, am I *tacet* in this march?" he asked. But his part didn't say *tacet*, the musical term for "don't play."

The editor in New York hired to prepare this music hadn't looked through these marches. Editors are supposed to check for errors, fix awkward page turns, and add instructions such as string bowings (the bow goes either up or down and the bows of a string section should be moving as a unit). And if there's a major mistake in the printing, such as a part being blank, the editor writes in the music. That hadn't happened. On future tours, LB assigned the musical preparation to me.

The BBC librarian copied the trumpet part from LB's score while everybody else took a coffee break. Meanwhile, the previous night's bearded composer/bedmate kept LB engaged in a probing conversation about Elgar.

THAT WEEK, I MET THE Deutsche Grammophon (DGG) recording crew, headed by Hans Weber, whom LB always dubbed "the best ears in the business." Mr. Weber's engaging personality inspired profound loyalty over many decades from a roster of technicians. Joachim Niss and Jobst Eberhardt, who usually set up microphones, became close friends of mine. Karl-August Naegler, Klaus Scheibe, and Wolf-Dieter Karwatky appeared regularly at recording sessions in Vienna, Tel Aviv, and New York. LB always greeted the diligent DGG crew with genuine affection.

At listening sessions, LB could pinpoint a "take" and name its exact date, even for performances many months previous. Without referring to his notes, Hans Weber confirmed LB's accuracy. Their musical memory floored me. The DGG crew also recorded Herbert von Karajan and Carlos Kleiber, but after Karajan's death in 1989 and Bernstein's in 1990, Hans Weber retired. For him, no living conductors equaled those two masters.

In London, Harry Kraut introduced me to Hanno Rinke, a producer for DGG. Hanno's sensibility in marketing classical music left me in awe, but as we became better friends, my regard for him shifted to bemusement at how he'd applied his wide-ranging education to a merchandising career. Did Hanno know more than I did about serious music? Only that music could be a commodity, and how to make the most of it.

Four of the best ears in the business: Hans Weber and Leonard Bernstein, circa 1980.

On a completely free day before flying to Israel, I walked up Regent Street to the luxury-goods emporium Liberty where I bought a tie for myself and crimson silk pocket squares for LB. For the filming of upcoming concerts, the color of the silk in LB's breast pocket had to match from one take to the next. An extra half dozen silk squares was a legitimate expense.

A perfect day for a shopping spree, if only Princess Margaret had been available!

12 | Speaking Hebrew in Only One Lesson

PACKING UP IN A HOTEL resembles a treasure hunt combined with a half-marathon: open every drawer, peek in every closet and behind every door, don't stop for a second—it'll all be over in ninety minutes. Then comes the payoff, but in reverse: tips for the porters as they schlep twenty trunks to the lobby, a tip for the concierge, tips for two doormen and the driver of the luggage van. To get out of the Savoy in London, I distributed over a hundred pounds sterling in cash.

Prepared for whatever the Maestro could want on the flight to Israel, I carried seven conducting scores, pads of paper, British crossword puzzle books, and a change of clothes—in case the luggage flew to the other side of the planet. The young El Al stewardess, a *yenta*-in-training, insisted LB had to eat something after he put away several drinks. "Okay, show us what you've got," said LB, as if auditioning her for a role in *On the Town*. She brought appetizers but discreetly turned off the scotch spigot.

As we noshed, LB asked me, "Do you know any Hebrew?"

I said, "When I was twelve and living in Naples, I studied the alphabet with an Israeli girl in my school," but that had been twenty years ago. Of the basics, only "*todáh*"—see the sheet below on the left—stuck in my memory, useful if someone held open a door for me in, say, an Orthodox enclave in Brooklyn.

The rebbe's Hebrew lesson, initialed and dated: LB, 7 Apr '82

"Let's start with the alphabet," LB said as I handed him a pad of paper. At the top of a page—the upper right corner—he drew a number. I'd never grasped Hebrew numerals, nor the mysterious Hebrew vowels, but as LB filled several pages, the letters looked more familiar and their sounds snuck back into my head. When our stewardess relented on the booze, gin dissolved the locks on some of my brain cells—but this visit to Israel wouldn't be an immersion in the language. Everyone there spoke English.

Nothing made LB happier than sharing knowledge, whether in front of an orchestra or one-on-one during a five-hour flight. His joy in teaching stemmed from his earliest school days in Boston, where he "fell in love" with his temple's Hebrew School teacher, Goldie Feinsilver. A lively and enthusiastic pupil, LB loved learning, which went hand in hand with his rabbinical love of teaching.

Having refreshed his colloquial Hebrew by tutoring me, LB admitted it took him ten days to remember conversational phrases, not that it mattered much when speaking to the musicians in the Israel Philharmonic (IPO). "Whatever I say in a rehearsal, the first violins translate it into Russian, the violas into Bulgarian, the cellos into Ukrainian, and then there's Romanian, Latvian—what a hubbub," LB said. "The most important word with this orchestra is 'sheket'—shut up!" He wasn't kidding.

The IPO's executive director, Avi Shoshani, greeted us on the tarmac at Tel Aviv. Tall, energetic, and gregarious, Avi knew his business. I liked him immediately. On the drive to the hotel, Avi reviewed the upcoming schedule without referring to notes and responded to all of LB's observations with a personable mix of jokes and serious asides. Making music in Israel sounded like fun.

LB's suite at the Tel Aviv Hilton occupied the panoramic end of the top floor. Views to the south stretched beyond the old quarter of Jaffa, and to the west into infinity over the placid Mediterranean. The suite's modern décor gave it a comfortable spaciousness, and the grand piano fit nicely along a wall near the kitchen.

In front of the suite's double doors, the hotel's housekeeping staff lined up for Maestro hugs. Their crew leader explained the laundry schedule: on Fridays, Christians picked up the laundry; Saturdays, an Arab company; Sundays, a Jewish laundry service. Everybody observed a Sabbath, but the laundry still got done. (Cunegonde, in the Paris brothel scene in *Candide*, schedules similar weekends for her clients the Archbishop and the Chief Rabbi.)

Not expecting to have a social life on the road, I perked up when Deutsche Grammophon (DGG) technician Jobst Eberhardt came by the hotel to take me out for dinner. He'd already set up the recording equipment in Frederic Mann Auditorium (now the Charles Bronfman Auditorium) with his colleague Joachim Niss. Openly gay and only slightly older than I, Jobst and Joachim commanded great respect within DGG and from the artists they recorded around the world. They spoke English perfectly, though Jobst prodded me to brush up the German I'd learned as an army brat in West Germany. As a five-year-old, I'd translated for my parents on shopping trips, so German grammar had to be lodged somewhere in my brain.

As we walked back to the Hilton after dinner, Jobst insisted we detour into Independence Park, a dusty patch of cactus on the hotel's north side. The lack of lighting there drew throngs of gay men, many engaged in sleazy sex within earshot of Tel Aviv's most luxurious hotel rooms. I had naively expected the Book of Leviticus to rule as Israel's bylaws, but this was a modern country: women wore skimpy bikinis on the beach, and some people ate pork, calling it "white steak." But the furtive activity in the park took me aback. Ten seconds was enough. I said to Jobst, "Let's get out of here."

Waking LB the next morning, I told him about the park, but he knew all about what went on there. Why was I not surprised? When we got to the concert hall, LB greeted the DGG crew, looked down at Jobst's shoes, and exclaimed, "Jobst, your shoes are covered with dust! Did you have a good time in the park last night?" As his colleagues hooted with laughter, Jobst retorted, "And were you watching from your window?" and then turned bright red. First thing every day thereafter, Jobst wiped Tel Aviv's dust off his shoes.

Israel resembled a summer camp for grown-ups, everyone in shorts and T-shirts, everyone on a first-name basis, the IPO one extended family. Ruth Mense, the orchestra's pianist, invited LB for dinner—and put in a request for strings for her piano, if I could get them from the Baldwin piano company (I did). The musicians seemed more personable than those I'd met in Washington and New York, and with no union rules, they determined their rehearsal breaks by simple consensus.

At the end of the first rehearsal, LB excitedly pulled me towards an elegant bright-eyed woman standing with perfect posture in the wings: Halina Rodzinski, widow of the conductor Artur Rodzinski, the man who'd hired LB as assistant conductor of the New York Philharmonic in the 1940s. Maestro Rodzinski got the call on November 14, 1943, when Bruno Walter was too ill to conduct that afternoon at Carnegie Hall. Maestro and Mrs. Rodzinski were away that weekend—probably at their house in Massachusetts, where they kept bee hives—and Rodzinski told the Philharmonic's manager, "Have Bernstein do it [the concert]. That's why we hired him." Bernstein's debut was a live radio broadcast and launched his career. The rest is history.

Talking to Mrs. Rodzinski transported me to another time. With her rich life story, her profound love of music, and her affection for LB, she made an indelible impression. She'd recently published a memoir, so recollections bubbled out of her as though they'd happened that morning. In her eyes, LB was still a twenty-five-year-old kid with outsized talent.

———

MY OUTSIZED ISSUE was a basic health problem. An annoying infection in my urinary tract wouldn't clear up. Probably due to stress, and consistently misdiagnosed by my doctor in New York. The antibiotic wasn't working, and it put me in a woozy stupor. Harry Kraut criticized my look of "grim disapproval"—gee, I was only trying to focus—and decided I needed to smile more.

One morning Harry handed me several small orange tablets. "Take one. Now," he said. They looked identical to the Dexedrine in LB's medicine bag. LB always broke his tablets in half. I broke one of Harry's tablets into quarters, but even that tiny dose thrust me onto a high-speed treadmill. I couldn't sit still. All my responsibilities took on equal importance. I flew around, talking incessantly. Nothing got done. Harry said, "Charlie, this is a big improvement."

Now I understood LB's antic behavior: a drug-induced mania. The Dexedrine made me so uncomfortable that I stopped after two days and secreted the remainder of Harry's largesse into LB's supply. The following nose-dive into depression deepened my insight into this drug: so that's what I was dealing with when LB and Harry seemed so energetic—and then so grim.

I came back to earth when Isaac Stern and LB got into an involved discussion after a piano rehearsal in the green room. LB stretched out on the sofa, leaving no place for Mr. Stern to sit, so I lugged in an armchair. Mr. Stern looked at me with astonished gratitude and whispered, "Thank you." It was only a chair. But from then on, he always remembered my name, a detail that was becoming important to me. We were friends for life.

The discussion: were they still cultural icons or not?

LB said, "Israel has changed. Serious culture here doesn't mean what it used to." He pointed out that one of his concerts would benefit an Israeli Army literacy program. "The Israeli Army is the best-educated fighting force in the world!" LB said ("most enlightened" might have been a better description). "And now recruits are functionally illiterate," LB said, and to clinch his point, added, "My concerts might not sell out."

Mr. Stern said, "It's not that bad. Right now, if we walk down Dizengoff [Tel Aviv's main commercial street], we'll be mobbed."

I broke in with a suggestion: "It's a beautiful evening. Let's walk back to the Hilton, down Dizengoff Street, and see what happens." I asked our driver to take the bag with the scores back to the hotel, and then I led the way as LB and Mr. Stern ambled behind me. At one intersection I stared up at a street sign for a full minute, sounding out the Hebrew letters for "Queen Esther Street." LB sidled up to me. "You look particularly idiotic gaping at that street sign," he said, but as I read the letters aloud, he patted my shoulder approvingly. I'd given myself a quiz from the *rebbe's* lesson and passed.

We arrived at the Hilton after an uninterrupted forty-five-minute stroll. No one had recognized the foremost living violinist nor the most famous conductor on the planet. Mr. Stern admitted, "Lenny, you may be right. Culture here has changed."

On the hour-long drive up the steep climb to Jerusalem for the first concert, LB pointed out the corroded tanks and artillery scattered by the road, rusted memorials to the battles of 1948. The weaponry reminded me of the Army bases where I grew up, where I learned tank classifications, but the vehicles in Israel with their sides punched in and treads violently detached only heightened my life-long pacifism—not a subject to bring up in Israel.

Harry Kraut stressed that if violence erupted, I should be prepared to leave Israel immediately, so I always carried our passports, a supply of LB's pharmaceuticals, and a change of clothes. Readiness felt familiar. During my childhood in Germany, we kept a "bug-out box" under the kitchen sink: canned food, a first aid kit, a map, underwear—and comic books. Preparedness was a fact of life in post-war Europe.

In Jerusalem that night, I listened from the wings to Stravinsky's *Petrouchka*. The IPO performed with precision and verve. *This orchestra "owns" Stravinsky's music*, I thought. I watched LB give cues right and left, but in the boisterous vamp in the "Dance of the Coachmen," LB looked at the first violins one bar too soon. A few musicians entered, making one bar of strangely ragged scratching. In this foot-stomping dance, it sounded like someone had stubbed a toe.

Coming off the stage, LB looked shaken. "I've never done that before, cueing a whole string section in the wrong place," he said. "How could I do that?"

"How did you fix it?" I asked.

"Some of them came in with me, and some of them didn't," he said. "I encouraged the ones who didn't follow my mistake, giving them a look, hoping they'd stick to the printed music, and within two bars they got back together." My experience with Dexedrine that week made me suspect the drug's attention-deficit potential, but could I point that out to LB? No.

After four months on the Maestro-assistant job, I'd learned a little about mingling at post-concert parties. That night I had a good time with Teddy Kollek, then in his seventeenth year as mayor of Jerusalem, and asked him about the headaches of governing that famously divided city. Simple. He grasped all sides of an argument, never allowed self-interest to get the better of him, radiated optimism all the while, and somehow turned his optimism into reality. He smiled! (Without Harry Kraut's admonishment to do so.) That smile must have often softened the hearts of his city's litigants.

Later, LB mused on one personality's power to pave over deep political cracks. "What will Jerusalem be like after Teddy's gone?" LB asked, but he didn't live long enough to find out.

After the next concert in Tel Aviv, LB changed into black tie for the Israeli Army literacy benefit. Ariel Sharon, then Israel's Minister of Defense, greeted people at the door and immediately provoked an argument with LB—hardly surprising, given their lack of common ground.

Whatever Sharon said made LB so angry that he drew his right arm back as if to punch him squarely in the nose, but Isaac Stern—bigger than LB—grabbed his arm and pulled him away. The next day in the newspaper, a photo showed LB and Sharon—both in elegant tuxes—glowering at one another. To his litany of Israel's cultural shifts, LB added rampaging militarism, personified in Minister Sharon.

Rehearsals of Stravinsky's *Rite of Spring* took up our final week in Israel. LB's score and orchestra materials, bequeathed to him by Dr. Serge Koussevitzky, always required some explanation.

"Koussy couldn't learn the tricky rhythms in the 'Danse Sacrale,'" LB said to the IPO, "so he hired Nicolas Slonimsky to play the score on a piano," while Dr. Koussevitzky conducted from a chair. "But he still couldn't get it," LB said. "All these crazy meter changes, two eighths to three sixteenths to five sixteenths. The only solution was to re-bar the music into simple meters," to which Dr. Koussevitzky very reluctantly agreed. Slonimsky, an absolute musical genius, marked up the score and the orchestra parts in red ink for new bar lines and green ink for the new meters, which he drew neatly above the top staff. Of course, the IPO played this passage impeccably.

Igor Stravinsky: "Danse Sacrale" from *The Rite of Spring*. Upper left, Leonard Bernstein's documentation: "Re-barring by Nicholas [sic] Slonimsky (c. 1924) LB" Note the arrow moving Rehearsal 144 one bar left.

To prepare encores for the upcoming tour, LB rehearsed two movements from his *Divertimento for Orchestra,* a Boston Symphony Orchestra centenary commission. New to me, this fun-loving music is sprinkled with quotes from chestnuts that LB had heard as a youth at Boston Pops concerts, but in *Divertimento*, retold slightly askew. Leroy Anderson's *Syncopated Clock* wood blocks in an undecided meter: two? three? And a waltz in seven beats, rather than the usual three.

I tried to say something enthusiastic afterwards but blurted out, "*Divertimento* would be fun arranged for piano four-hands." LB dragged on his cigarette. Utterly offended, he said, "Why don't you make one?" Usually, I always said three positive things before mentioning anything else. This time, I'd forgotten to do that. Six years later, I presented LB with my four-hand arrangement of *Divertimento* as a 70th birthday present, but he didn't show much interest in it.

The "Waltz," possibly the sweetest music LB ever penned, simultaneously served as a birthday song for his daughter Jamie. LB said, "Her language was the foulest imaginable, filled with four-letter words," so under the winsome tune LB sprinkled his lyrics with flecks of smut.

After I shared those lyrics with Marilyn Steiner, the IPO's librarian, we sang along backstage whenever LB added the "Waltz" from *Divertimento* as an encore. Neither of us could keep a straight face.

Yes, making music in Israel was fun.

Allegretto senza rancor (Shit-a-Brick)
Shit-a-brick, time is running out on me,
I must get moving fast undoubtedly.
Suck-a-dick, I am sick in heart and soul,
Got to get moving fast to reach my goal:
Rock 'n' Roll

13 | Souvenirs Picked Up on the Road

THE ISRAEL PHILHARMONIC (IPO) tour began with a concert in the German capital—in 1982, the village of Bonn. Since Isaac Stern understandably never performed publicly in Germany after the war, he flew directly to Mexico, where we met up with him later.

At the airport near Bonn, LB's European press agent, Dorothee Koehler, greeted LB warmly. Matronly but stylish, she worshiped LB but was distressed by his many four-letter words. After all, not many newspapers would print his favorite exclamation: *Un-be-fucking-lievable!* Dorothee often took me aside before LB met with a reporter. "You told LB this is a *serious* interview, I hope?" she'd say, perennially in doubt as to whether LB appreciated her efforts.

Harry Kraut's dismissiveness toward Dorothee looked at first to me like a game of keep-away with the Maestro as the prize, until I recognized Harry's misogyny for what it was. Maggie Carson, LB's American press agent, got the same snide treatment. Both agents worked around Harry by depending on me to prep LB for his press events.

The IPO tour schedule kept performance days and travel days separate, but I was unprepared for the thirteen-hour flight to Mexico City, quite an endurance test after a three-hour flight that morning. After two movies, several meals, a book, and too much to drink, I ran out of ways to amuse myself.

When we finally landed, bright lights and TV cameras threw me off kilter. The press corps shouted questions at the Maestro while I corralled the luggage. A dozen cameras sporting telltale red lights—we were on the air—turned in sync from LB toward the customs inspection for a publicity stunt: live news coverage of Mexico's vaunted anti-drug stance. Dozens of hands picked through the contents of our twenty pieces of luggage—in the blinding lights, all I saw were the hands—as I repeated, "No, no, no, no," to questions barked at me in Spanish.

Brandishing a trophy, one hand held up a white plush monkey by the scruff of its neck: little Moneto, LB's pillow toy. A criminally suspect smuggler? I went ballistic and shouted, "No! No! Not Moneto!" as though the monkey were my only child. I climbed onto the suitcases, shoved them closed, and yelled at the top of my lungs, "We don't have any drugs! There are no drugs!"

Not what the news networks wanted, I guess. The lights quickly went dark and porters materialized. Their carts parted the crowd as I trotted behind to a waiting van. I shook uncontrollably all the way to the hotel.

As I unpacked, Harry Kraut asked me how the customs inspection went. By then I had calmed down but could manage only a wordless grunt.

The penthouse suite in the Hotel Prince Chapultepec desperately aimed for luxury on an oversize scale. Shades of overripe fruit—deep pomegranate, vibrant mango—saturated its walls and triple-wide thrones. Massive black-stained tables and consoles dominated the acreage like onyx boulders, mere platforms for off-putting sculptures. Harry said, "It's a Mexican bordello," but surely a whore-house would be more cheerful.

In a quick survey of the layout, I didn't see a piano. I called the hotel manager, who explained that the hotel's decorator felt a piano would spoil the suite's décor, and besides, a piano wasn't necessary because there was one in the lobby. I had to see this for myself.

Sure enough, amid the splashing fountains in the high-ceilinged lobby, a precious white piano perched on a marble island, where it glittered like sugar-sprinkled marzipan. The manager couldn't contain his pride as he gushed that Liberace—yes, really, Liberace!—had played that very piano during his stay. Surely a piano that pleased Liberace was good enough for Mr. Bernstein? I looked around at the people meandering through the lobby at that late hour, and imagined LB entertaining them in his bathrobe as he studied Stravinsky's *Symphony in Three Movements*.

"It's very pretty, but surely a piano was delivered for Maestro Bernstein," I said.

"Oh yes," said the manager. "But the decorator placed it in a room down the hall."

"On the same floor?"

"Yes, here's the key," the manager said, handing me the key for what was prob-ably intended to be my room, but I'd settled into one of the bedrooms in LB's suite. Each of the suite's bedrooms had its own bath and sauna, and enough closets for a family of ten.

After enjoying a nightcap in the bordello suite, LB, Harry Kraut, and Ransom Wilson (flute soloist on this tour) helped me liberate the sequestered piano, an upright on casters. We shouldered it down the hall and into a little study at the bordello's rear, where the décor didn't matter. Where we put that piano was to haunt me a week later.

After three concerts in the city, a private jet spirited us to the old silver mining city of Guanajuato for an arts festival, then in its tenth season. In a diversion en route to the airport, LB received the Order of the Aztec Eagle. Harry Kraut insisted it was only one notch below the honor reserved for royalty. Back in the car after a solemn but brief ceremony, LB unpinned the chunky medallion from his chest and handed it to me, now keeper of the jewels. Fortunately, someone had handed me the hardware's presentation box, easily stashed in a carry-on bag.

The intimate opera house stage in Guanajuato couldn't accommodate all the forces for Stravinsky's *Petrouchka.* The IPO musicians spilled into the wings, the piano consigned to offstage obscurity. Ruth Mense asked for a floor lamp so she could at least see her music. Standing at stage left, I watched Ruthie deliver a perfect performance, even though she said afterward that she couldn't hear the orchestra at all. During the concert's second half, I stepped into the plaza where the whole town sat enraptured by a gigantic, profusely sweating Maestro on a jumbo screen.

After the first concert, the Guanajuato festival hosted a dressy affair for its patrons (wealthy, white Mexican aristocracy), who thereby reaped their reward: dinner with the Maestro. In seconds, LB determined whether these donors had actually listened to the concert (*what concert?*) and then he instigated a musical game.

LB sang the first line of "Mack the Knife" from Brecht-Weill's *Threepenny Opera,* replacing the lyrics with a well-known name, say, "Stephen Sondheim." He turned to the socialite at his left, who had to sing the next line; fortunately, the notes are identical. Inevitably, the person singing the fourth line got the notes wrong, so LB stopped to explain the structure of the song—how to listen was reason number one for this game—and pointed at the next bejeweled socialite to start from the beginning.

The song's rhyme scheme stopped the game again and elicited another lecture from the Maestro, but by then general hilarity had settled over the table, the effect of copious wine and the late hour, compounded by musical cluelessness.

The deeper point of this game emerged when a socialite, frantically trying to fit a name to the tune, blurted out a psycho-sexual Freudian slip. Full stop. "You know you said that," LB said over the high-pitched laughter, "because she," pointing to another patron, "said something that touched on your deepest fears," thus morphing a harmless after-dinner game into the boggiest of shrink sessions. People loved LB for airing their repressions and felt flattered to be in the spotlight beaming from the Chief Therapist of the Universe. From afar, the screams of laughter could have been mistaken for torture.

After the patrons had slipped away in their limos, LB said, "Let's hear some local music. Where can we go?" In minutes we were in a smoky dive where a guitarist was peacefully entertaining a full house. LB claimed he knew over 400

Mexican songs, picked up during his busy honeymoon in Cuernavaca, so he challenged the guitarist to a singing duel. In LB's voice, like a rusty handsaw gnawing through a hambone, many of those songs sounded alike, so I figured we wouldn't have to listen to every single one of LB's vaunted 400.

Sitting at one side, still in my concert tux, I nursed the beer in front of me. No one in the bar knew what to make of this white-haired Maestro, his eyes closed, head thrown back, his hands slapping the table. A soul spirited into a memory zone where no one else could go. The guitarist, stunned by this howling troubadour from outer space, stopped playing and stared mutely at LB.

At the end of each *canción*, everybody clapped and cheered and got another round of beers, but LB launched immediately into another howl. This was no longer a contest, but that didn't mean it would ever end; LB had three hundred and ninety-seven songs to go. I peeked at my watch: 3 A.M. Pretending to take a pee break, I stepped outside, away from the cigarette smoke and noise, into a cool and starry night. I was just drunk enough to try walking back to the hotel.

My sense of direction was always infallible, but after several blocks in total darkness, I worried about meeting up with a pack of wild dogs, or worse. A limo pulled up, a window rolled down, and LB leaned out. "What are you doing?" he asked.

"Walking to the hotel."

"Please don't do that," he said quietly. In the limo, Harry Kraut seemed genuinely concerned that I'd been abducted by bandits. I never did that again, no matter where in the world we were or how late the hour.

At the press conference before leaving Guanajuato, LB drank from a glass of tap water. Within days, his gastric distress indicated intestinal parasites, but did he cancel anything? Not a chance. For the next three months, I sought out one doctor after another, but we never stayed in one place long enough for lab tests, so for two months LB's parasites flourished, undiagnosed.

Back at the bordello suite in Mexico City, unaware that LB already had parasites, I filled bags with ice cubes from bottled water and placed them in an insulated cooler, seconds before trundling the concert bags to the limo. For LB's post-concert scotch, I couldn't be too careful.

For the final concert at the university on the opposite side of the megalopolis, our driver warned us to depart two hours before concert time. The concert bag holding the scores and a small bottle of Ballantine's sat by the door, ready to go, when I went into the kitchen to get the ice cubes.

The drive to the university really did take two hours. Traffic grew more chaotic the closer we got to the auditorium, due in part to the presence of Mexico's First

Lady and her sizable entourage. Our driver tooled along sidewalks as people dashed aside like frightened rabbits, until we stopped inches from the stage door.

Usually at a concert, as soon as the music started, I prepared for the intermission. I hung up LB's change of shirt and vest and placed the score for the second half of the concert on a table so LB could study. But before I could open the concert bags, Avi Shoshani, the IPO's manager, burst into the green room. "You have to help me count this!" he cried, brandishing fistfuls of pesos—the IPO's compensation for all six of its concerts in Mexico. "We have to divide this up into these envelopes," which he produced from his jacket pocket. "Before the intermission."

We still had twenty minutes to go in Stravinsky's *Symphony in Three Movements* and then a half-hour in Prokofieff's *Second Violin Concerto*, but Avi had nearly a hundred envelopes to stuff. He sat on one side of the table, Harry Kraut and I took the opposite sofa, and we counted pesos like they were on fire. At the end of the Prokofieff, Avi swept up all the envelopes—and the few remaining pesos—while I hurried to the wings of the stage to give LB a towel, a bottle of water, and a hit of oxygen from a tank the American Embassy had lent us. LB was in a good mood. So were the musicians, as they filed offstage and looked around for Avi.

In the green room, LB stripped off his tie, vest, and shirt. I toweled him off between his whiffs of oxygen and held up a fresh shirt. Sooner than expected, Marilyn Steiner, the orchestra librarian, knocked on the door and asked for the score of Stravinsky's *Rite of Spring*. I unzipped the bag where I'd put the score, and then frantically opened all the bags. No score anywhere.

"The score's missing," I said.

A dreamy look crossed LB's face. "Oh," he said calmly. "I know I saw it at the hotel. I think I put it on the piano,"—the piano we'd maneuvered into the study at the back of the suite a week ago. "I'm sorry. I thought you knew I left it there."

I hadn't checked the piano, and I hadn't seen LB take the score out of the bag. I'd been preoccupied making ice cubes. Stupid of me.

"What do we do?" I asked as calmly as I could. "There are only five minutes left in this intermission, and the hotel is a two-hour drive." The orchestra was already onstage.

Avi looked at LB. "Can you conduct without a score?" He was serious.

LB looked stricken. "It's not possible. It's such a complicated piece," LB said.

"I have an extra score," Marilyn Steiner said. In fact, she had two extra scores. No one was better prepared than Marilyn.

"But it won't have my markings or the re-barring in the last movement," LB said, almost whining.

Harry wondered aloud, "How quickly can our driver get to the hotel?"

The rest of us stood in stunned silence. Harry was out the door before we knew it.

LB, Avi, Marilyn, and I waited. There was nothing to do but wait. Avi said, "We'll have to make an announcement," because the audience had retaken their seats. Something was made up about the First Lady's security patrol causing a delay, but by then we could hear the audience stamping in rhythm, like war drums too close for comfort.

Forty-five minutes after he left, Harry returned triumphantly bearing the score. LB kissed it and handed it to Marilyn, who hotfooted to the podium. LB kissed his cufflinks and strode onstage, to scattered applause. In the green room, I asked Harry what the drive across Mexico City was like, but he couldn't speak. I'd never seen him dazed, so I poured him a glass of scotch.

As the end of the *Rite* shook the auditorium, I splashed scotch over the remnants of the "safe ice." Wild applause turned into a steady roar. In the wings, LB gratefully sipped the scotch, took a hit from a cigarette, and mused, "I don't know what it was tonight, but I didn't have to turn a single page." He had conducted the entire *Rite* from memory. I wanted to punch him, but he'd already walked back onstage to take another bow.

In a rapturous review, a critic snidely commented on the IPO librarian's unprofessional conduct. He assumed she'd misplaced the score and caused the tedious delay. Somehow Marilyn forgave me. After that night, I checked—and double-checked—the bags before heading to a concert. Yet another detail for me to obsess over.

WHEN WE ARRIVED in Houston the next day, we each showed some strain. I took the night off and LB attended a donors' dinner for Houston Grand Opera; the premiere of LB's opera *A Quiet Place* loomed only twelve months ahead. Even after he'd rested all the next day, LB still seemed uncommonly weary.

Toward the end of Tchaikovsky's *Francesca da Rimini,* the last piece on that night's program, LB dug into the music even more frenetically than usual. He leaned so far forward on the podium that he slipped into the orchestra, landing on his rear. But he continued to wave his baton, while shouting in Hebrew, "Keep playing, keep playing."

Behind the closed door at the side of the stage, I heard a solid thump but had no idea what had happened. Had a musician knocked over a music stand? The orchestra continued to play, but as soon as the door opened at the applause, I could see that LB was in pain as he shuffled toward me. "I slipped on the podium carpet but climbed back up. I think I bruised my tailbone," he said. His breathing sounded labored.

I asked the stage hands to hustle LB to the green room where I removed his tie and loosened his shirt as he collapsed into a chair. Did he need a doctor? He shook his head. The musicians filed in to see if he was all right, a few patting LB's shoulder as they claimed they'd never played as exciting a performance of that Tchaikovsky, and how impressed they were that LB had shouted in Hebrew. After a long while, LB regained his breath, but he wasn't moving easily. "I'm very sore," he said. "Let's go back to the hotel."

In the hotel lobby, LB said farewell to flute soloist Ransom Wilson, pretending to give him a kiss. Instead, LB bit Ransom on his lower lip. The embouchure—the area around the mouth—is the foundation of a flute player's technique. Some perverse lover's quarrel? Ransom nearly gave LB a sock on the jaw in return.

LB enjoyed an indulgent night with a young conductor/pianist and his partner, so I ordered three breakfasts the next morning, bearing a full tray of coffees into the bedroom. The tour had worn me down, but I methodically started packing up the suite. As soon as everyone was awake, I left with the luggage but didn't notice the driver took me to the wrong airport. The Southwest Airlines clerk checked the luggage to Dallas anyway and suggested I take a taxi to the right airport for my flight.

Confused and rattled, I left my datebook on the check-in counter. In it I'd scrawled dozens of private phone numbers: Dean Webb in Indiana, Ethel Kennedy at Hickory Hill, among many others. When I called Southwest later, a clerk said he had the datebook in his hands, but I never saw it again. On our one day in Dallas, I walked to Neiman Marcus and picked up a datebook at five times the cost of my old one, but I still felt irritated with myself.

Despite my exhaustion, I would miss the IPO musicians after this tour. As LB showered before the Dallas concert, Ruth Mense knocked on the door: could she warm up on LB's piano for Stravinsky's *Symphony in Three Movements*? From the steaming bathroom, LB shouted, "Of course!" and then padded across the suite in his bathrobe to give her an enormous hug. Her diligent arpeggios turned into cacophony.

As planned, Zubin Mehta took over the rest of the IPO tour, and we flew back to New York. Over the next five days, I unpacked, paid my bills, saw my dentist, and packed again—for the next tour. Oh, and I slept. Now, off to Italy. At least it was a country where I already knew the language.

14 | A Touchy Situation

LB'S SOUVENIRS FROM THE Israel Philharmonic tour ran the gamut, from the distinguished Aztec Eagle to the lowliest of intestinal parasites and a sore rear end. Back in New York, he wanted me to have a souvenir, too. Thinking a year ahead to the Houston premiere of *A Quiet Place*, he said, "Go buy yourself a pair of cowboy boots and charge them to me." In a fancy shop a block from the Dakota, I picked out a tawny pair at an absurd price, a week's salary. Cowboy boots in New York? What an affectation. Did people actually wear these in Houston?

One evening, Jack Gottlieb, LB's first assistant in the 1950s and now his music editor, came by the Dakota with the first printing of LB's "Touches," a set of piano variations commissioned by the 1981 Van Cliburn piano competition. Though generally good-humored and engaging, Jack seemed on edge. I leafed through the score while we waited for LB to get off the phone. Something in the music puzzled me, so I took Jack into another room where we wouldn't be distracting. Good thing I did, because Jack burst into a paroxysm of shouting and self-flagellation, whacking at himself with his hands.

I'd found a mistake, but I hadn't intended to push Jack over the edge, which turned out to be easy to do. As he humbly handed "Touches" to LB, Jack pointed out the mistake and magnanimously credited me for finding it. The incident left me wondering how rigorous an editor Jack was. In later years, I learned that in the publication of serious music, nothing is ever perfect.

The American Academy of Arts and Letters held its annual assembly that week. The two new members to be inducted were Arthur Schlesinger Jr. and LB. I suppose the magnitude of the honor was what roused LB from bed so early that day. When I arrived at the Dakota, he was already dressing and was ready well in advance of Maggie Carson's arrival in the car hired to take them both uptown to the Academy.

As press agent for the Academy in the 1940s, Maggie had been taken to lunch by a successful insurance salesman and offbeat composer named Charles Ives, who seemed interested in the Academy's objectives. Despite his reputation for gruffness, Ives responded to Maggie's vivacity and intelligence. "He wasn't gruff at all," Maggie told me. "He asked a lot of questions. A smart and charming man." Eventually, Charles Ives donated the royalties from his musical works to the Academy, funding prizes for deserving composers. Maggie never even hinted that her lunch with Mr. Ives had anything to do with his philanthropy, but that was the sort of classy deal Maggie routinely finessed, always with white-gloved politesse.

If I'd known that the ceremony was open to the public, I would have witnessed the final Academy appearance by Aaron Copland and Leonard Bernstein together, and heard LB's well-received speech.

At an intimate dinner afterward, the host seated LB next to a relative young-ster named Aaron Stern, who galvanized LB with a harangue on the lack of "a love of learning" in the United States. "It was no accident," LB said later, "that I met a younger Aaron [Stern] in the presence of the older Aaron [Copland]." Education— and Aaron Stern—took a central role in LB's remaining years, as LB founded edu-cation-oriented music festivals in Los Angeles, Schleswig-Holstein in Germany, and Sapporo in Japan. In addition, LB assisted Aaron Stern in establishing the Academy of the Love of Learning in Santa Fe, New Mexico, with a mission for "transformational learning."

The next day, eventful as only a day in New York could be, LB listened to cast auditions for his opera-in-progress *A Quiet Place* and then had dinner at Stephen Sondheim's house. The following morning over breakfast, LB breathlessly described Sondheim's newly trim figure. "I always thought of him as a slug," he

LB and his two Aarons: Leonard Bernstein, Aaron Stern, and Aaron Copland. New York City, 1982.

said, a little too candidly. "But I could hardly keep my hands off his buns last night." Yes, the Maestro said "buns."

A while back, when a gym opened across the street from his brownstone, Mr. Sondheim worked out with a personal trainer. His noticeable results inspired LB to hire his own personal trainer a couple years later, but by then, for LB, muscle tone was an unrealistic goal.

With less than a day to pack for a four-week tour, I opted to spend the night on the fold-out sofa in my office. Around it, I arranged the luggage like the monoliths at Stonehenge. Upon closing my eyes, things I'd forgotten to pack popped into my head. When I thought of one or two things, I wrote them down, but when I thought of three things I got up and packed them then and there—whereupon my brain formed a new list. I sprang out of bed eight times that night.

For the stint in Milano, Italy, Ann Dedman came along as chef and housekeeper, a perk for me. I'd hardly seen Ann in the three months since we'd decamped from Indiana. LB's European press agent, Dorothee Koehler, met us at the Milano airport with a van and then served us a delightful lunch. I kept keeling over in exhaustion, jerking upright whenever Ann poked me. Throughout my first year as LB's assistant, jet lag afflicted me like a chronic disease.

In the forty-eight hours before LB's arrival in Milano, we organized the apartment that La Scala Opera had rented for LB in the trendy Montenapoleone district. The sunny penthouse faced south, with two bedrooms in the back, away from the street. The first two nights, I tried out the bed LB would sleep in, to make sure that the blinds blocked out the sunlight and that the bathroom could accommodate LB's boxy medicine bag. Above the bed, a headboard in supple snow-white leather featured an articulated wall lamp, perfect for late-night reading. Cheap paperbacks of 1950s pornography in laughably ribald English, "quivering" body parts on every page, filled a shelf next to the bed.

On a morning walk, Ann and I couldn't believe our luck to be plunked down amid such sophistication. Freshly washed paving stones glistened beneath the feet of a well-tailored clientele who picked over a riot of imported delicacies. I knocked the rust off the Italian I'd learned as a teenager in Naples as we set up household accounts at a few shops. That afternoon, we climbed to the cathedral's roof, knocked breathless not by the stairs but by a vision of the Alps seemingly only an arm's length away.

I took advantage of the favorable exchange rate and picked up a few scores in the Ricordi music shop, especially the works in LB's performance schedule. Given that meals on the road and laundry done in a hotel helped stretch my salary, I could start to form a personal music library.

The genial librarians at La Scala welcomed me to their lair under the roof of the opera house when I delivered LB's orchestra materials, which included the *Rite of Spring* parts re-barred by Nicolas Slonimsky. As I explained the red and green ink in the "Danse Sacrale," it dawned on me that the La Scala musicians might never have played this work, at least not in concert. Seeing the parts bowed and ready for performance—including Stravinsky's *Petrouchka* and *Symphony of Psalms*—greatly relieved the librarians because the first rehearsal was only two days away. Then they indulged my passion for musical history, and for an hour let me poke around their painstakingly organized shelves. Heaven.

SUFFERING GASTRIC DISTRESS when he landed, LB instructed me to call Wally Toscanini to get a doctor. Meanwhile, he dialed his Milanese friends, the actress Valentina Cortese, and Madina Ricordi, of the music publishing family.

Wally Toscanini, named by her father Arturo Toscanini after the opera *La Wally* and called Countess Castelbarco after her marriage, readily recommended a doctor for her dear friend Leonard Bernstein. After he examined LB, the doctor said it looked as if the Maestro had parasites, but they were at too early a stage to detect conclusively. LB had to suffer from those parasites through six more weeks.

Happy to be back at the world's premiere opera house, where twenty-nine years earlier he had appeared as its first American conductor, LB dived into the grueling rehearsal schedule, dispensing compliments to the well-prepared orchestra and chorus. At the first rehearsal break I brought LB water and a towel, and got a shiver stepping onto the stage where, over the course of fifty years, Giuseppe Verdi had taken his opening-night bows. LB had a more personal moment of history in mind as we walked off stage right. In the wings, he grabbed me and pointed to the floor. *Now what*, I wondered.

In a dramatically low voice, LB said, "This is where Mitropoulos died." He pulled an ancient drachma on its chain out of his shirt collar. In the offstage darkness, it glinted faintly. "This was snatched from the neck of Mitropoulos and couriered to me, as Mitropoulos's final wish," LB said, his hands locked onto my shoulders. I believed every word of this mighty intense revelation.

LB later told me how close he had been to the conductor Dimitri Mitropoulos. As a student, LB had visited his revered Maestro in Minneapolis. "He lived like a monk," LB said. "Mitropoulos slept on a narrow cot, and I slept on a mat on the floor. Nobody believed that we weren't sleeping together," not a surprising deduction given LB's celebrated libido. "But we never touched one another."

Mitropoulos remained inviolable both physically and spiritually. His only wall decoration was a plain wooden cross nailed to the wall over his bed.

In the 1950s, Mitropoulos and Bernstein had shared the post of music director of the New York Philharmonic, duties assumed entirely by LB upon Mitropoulos's death in 1960. Seeing the very spot of his mentor's passing triggered high-voltage emotion in LB.

The third day of rehearsals started in the early afternoon and went on until midnight, a day that demanded heroic stamina from someone with intestinal parasites. In the brief evening break, we scampered downstairs to the ground-floor restaurant to join Wally Toscanini, the Countess Castelbarco, petite and elegant and of a certain age, at a back table. "This is the same table," LB insisted, "where I feasted [in 1953] with Maria Callas on *linguini con tartufi bianchi*, a dish that stinks like unwashed feet." The Countess broke into the most beautiful laughter. Linguini with white truffles was Callas's favorite dish.

Under the monumental bust of her father, Arturo Toscanini, in Milano's La Scala opera house, Wally Toscanini receives a rather chaste kiss from Leonard Bernstein.

Intense rehearsals continued the next morning, followed that evening by two more hours with the chorus. As she had done in New York, Ann Dedman brought us sandwiches and fruit, and she always had something for us to eat once we got back to the apartment. On the first completely free day, Madina Ricordi invited us for dinner in her home.

In her cozy kitchen, Madina's eccentric mother joined us, as did three of her four sons. At sixteen, the fraternal twins Carlo and Giovanni were stunningly beautiful youths: Giovanni dark-haired and intense, Carlo more auburn and relaxed, as if emerging from a magical sleep. LB immediately grabbed Carlo's chin and exclaimed, "Look at that face! That classical face, right out of the Cinquecento!" His face did have the fine lines of a Botticelli portrait. Carlo seemed not at all embarrassed and gave LB a smile. With their impeccable manners and precise, intelligible Italian, the Ricordis won me over instantly.

As the publisher of Verdi and Puccini, the Ricordis held a pedigree unequalled in the field of serious music, and music permeated their lives. In the years ahead, Madina and her sons turned up in Rome, Vienna, Tel Aviv—even New York and Houston. Always vivacious, Madina became my favorite personal cheerleader, even though her energy could verge on hysteria. Years later, LB let drop the witty phrase his late wife, Felicia, had coined for this fascinating, sometimes too-intense family: "the long-playing Ricordis."

After the first performance of the all-Stravinsky program, the Ricordis waited patiently in the hall backstage while LB indulged in the La Scala tradition of using the sink as a *pissoir*. No sooner had Madina, Carlo, and Giovanni seated themselves than Wally Toscanini, Countess Castelbarco, entered, quiet and stately, all in black, wearing a small box hat shaped like a cardinal's *biretta*. Immediately Carlo and Giovanni rose and remained standing. "*Per cortesìa*," Carlo said, and motioned the Countess toward the sofa. I'd never heard that phrase. Carlo later explained that it was a more polite form of "please," to be employed as a matter of course when speaking to the Countess. I paid close attention during that conversation in the green room and learned a lot about formal forms of polite speech in Italian.

After everyone departed the green room, LB broke into a slow waltz, so quietly that I could barely get his woefully approximate pitches.

With a sly grin, LB said, "I have no idea why that popped into my head."

Oh? A roomful of Italians? An organ grinder's tune?

"Adolph Green made that up during a set change in a Revuers act," LB said, referring to the comedy sketches by Comden and Green, and Judy Holliday—and sometimes LB at the piano—that entertained New Yorkers at the Village

Lu - i - gi, the e - le-phant keep-er, He sure love that e-le-phant, you bet.

He feed her on pea-nuts and crack - er- jack, and that e-le-phant, she ne-ver for- get!

(with a twisty wave of the hand: "well, maybe")

Lu - i - gi, the e - le-phantkeep - er, He sure love that e-le-phant ve-ry much.

(new key)

So on that fate - ful day when she tram-pled him to death, we were all sur - prised!

Vanguard in 1939. "The crucial moment is at the end," LB said, "when it veers off into a completely new key." LB's singing might have been centered on a key. But in his voice like gravel sliding out of a dump truck, it was hard to tell. I never heard Adolph Green's authentic version, so LB's rendition was all I had to go on.

After dinner at the apartment, LB insisted on an espresso. Ann found an ancient espresso machine, terrifying in its medieval enormity. After I helped Ann heft it onto the counter, she poured water in the reservoir and plugged in the cord. She let LB flick the switch. All the lights went out. Groping around in the dim light reflected through the windows, we found a dozen candles, dialed the caretaker's phone number and left a message. LB said he'd go to bed without an espresso, so I led the way to his bedroom bearing a tray of flickering votive candles.

As we stood by his bed talking about the next day's schedule, LB suddenly put his hand on my crotch. A solid pat, not exactly a grab. It was a repulsive thing for him to do, breaking the bounds of decorum so casually. I was too revolted and surprised to speak. But without missing a beat, I calmly took his hand away, raised his arm to pivot him toward the bookshelf behind him, and plopped his wandering hand squarely on the trashy 1950s pornography. Then I spoke. "You'll have a good time reading these." Without saying goodnight, I left for the hotel where I was staying a few blocks away.

During my short walk, I wondered if I should tell Harry Kraut about LB's breach of acceptable behavior. I hadn't previously considered what I'd do if LB harassed me in this way. In fact, this was new territory for me and I had to convince myself it actually constituted harassment. I'd never had a working relationship as personal as this. Where were the boundaries? I had decided early on to keep a temperate distance from everyone I worked with, and that definitely included the Maestro. Maybe LB sensed what a naïf I was, that I wouldn't tell on him if he made a wrong move. It was a wrong move, wasn't it? It certainly wasn't what I wanted and his grab made me feel compromised. My thoughts turned to Dimitri Mitropoulos, but he had nothing on me. I was just as inviolable, although I didn't need to display a cross over my bed.

When I brought LB his coffee the next morning, a hurricane had swept the shelf of porn books. He must have ransacked them all night.

After about three months into the job, all LB's assistants got a crotch-pat test, but I didn't learn that until after LB's death when I mentioned my experience to the assistant after me, Craig Urquhart. LB did the same thing to him, too, but Craig seemed less puzzled than I had been. I never quite resolved the weirdness of being propositioned by my employer.

After the third all-Stravinsky performance at La Scala, LB took the Ricordis to Positano on the Amalfi coast for a week at Franco Zeffirelli's luxurious villa. Harry Kraut departed for Florence, and Ann packed up to stay with a friend elsewhere in Italy. For a week on my own in Milano, I moved from the hotel into the apartment, did my own cooking, took long walks, and visited museums. I was unready for free time in an unfamiliar city. The sudden solitude shifted to loneliness, though I steered myself from depression by checking in with myself. Could I have a conversation, get out of bed? *Good*. Not like the depression that permeated my adolescence, when I went for weeks without speaking. It took another year for me to learn about making plans for the rare spells of free time in my job with LB.

I had one major repair to look after. The wall lamp above the bed had swung loose one night, and its light bulb landed on the white leather headboard where it burned a big hole. The stench of charred cowhide woke LB, fortunately. I congratulated him for falling asleep and for waking up before the whole place caught on fire. The caretaker who fixed the blown fuse said he'd repair the headboard. I never saw a bill, but it wouldn't have been cheap.

For the final performance of the Stravinsky program, in the Venetian church where Stravinsky's funeral had taken place eleven years earlier, La Scala provided a van and driver for the short trip to Venice. I'd been to Venice twice before, but never with fifteen pieces of luggage borne by a flotilla of rocking gondolas. I handed out tips right and left and nothing fell into the canal. After calling the opera office to confirm LB's arrival the next day, I lunched on the hotel's rooftop terrace—*risotto con frutti di mare* and a couple glasses of wine. It was a gorgeous afternoon, a perfect example of life's sweetness, which I'd missed so much ever since my teenage years in Naples.

Leonard Bernstein, Carlo Gavazzeni, Madina Ricordi, Giovanni Gavazzeni, June 12, 1982.

I got up early the day of the concert for a meandering walk. Back at the hotel, LB was reading his mail, delivered from the Bernstein office in New York, and talking with Madina Ricordi and her sons, Carlo and Giovanni. Normally, LB put on a bathrobe after getting out of bed, and there were plenty to choose from in the luggage I'd packed, but that morning he went casual. Very casual. He had on only his beloved Shark jacket, which covered him down to his navel. Nothing else. No socks, no underwear—nothing!

To hear LB conduct the *Symphony of Psalms* in the same church where that music had accompanied Stravinsky's own funeral made for a mystical experience. As if pre-ordained for that space, each phrase's slow-moving harmonies and rich timbres blossomed, reverberated, then died away as the next phrase bloomed. Critics often mentioned the glacial pace of LB's conducting in his last years, but in the church of San Zanipolo, LB clearly had the acoustics in mind for this particular music, and he changed forever how I hear the *Symphony of Psalms*.

We were all unusually somber the next morning. While I took the luggage directly to the airport in a water taxi, LB detoured to the island cemetery of San Michele for a moment at Stravinsky's grave, of course accompanied by numerous photographers.

After we changed planes in Paris, I overindulged on my first Concorde flight. The flight's hostess kept pushing lobster and champagne and I couldn't say no. Next to me, an enormous businessman lit one cigar after another. The engine noise, cigar smoke, rich food, and too much alcohol brought on a blinding headache, but I had to grin and bear it. In New York, we changed planes for Washington, D.C., where the next project was already under way: a concert on Stravinsky's hundredth birthday, June 17, 1982.

15 | A Day for Distraction

AT THE WATERGATE HOTEL in Washington, D.C., the production crew for the Stravinsky centenary concert had already assembled, overseen by Humphrey Burton, who filmed most of LB's concerts and special events for the German company Unitel. After I set up a bar in LB's suite and called for the head waiter—every script conference is fueled by alcohol, caffeine, and fatty foods—Humphrey acted as chairman for the business of writing a script for LB and Michael Tilson Thomas, once they'd decided on the program's half-dozen Stravinsky works. A famous BBC television director who had worked for eleven years alongside Leonard Bernstein, Humphrey deftly managed the four-day creation and rehearsal of this Stravinsky commemoration.

Reinforcements arrived from New York, notably Harry Kraut's secretary, Mimsy Gill, to update the script for the teleprompter, and press agent Maggie Carson to field interviews. Maggie also corralled her friends Fred and Irma Lazarus, Cincinnati's principal patrons of the arts. Similarly stylish, the two *grandes dames,* Maggie and Irma, ensconced themselves on a shaded seat of the National Cathedral's north porch, and summoned me to greet them, a moment so regal I bowed to kiss their hands. I'd said barely two words to them when Mimsy burst through the door and hollered at me to get back inside.

I'd never participated in rehearsals for a live broadcast. Everyone buzzed with caffeine, but Humphrey Burton maintained a magisterial calm. He moved the rehearsal forward in fits and starts, because, among other difficulties, the Cathedral swallowed up all sound. Music that should have been pointed and rhythmic, hallmarks of Stravinsky's style, came across as woolly and diffuse. I took a seat in the middle of the church where the nave and transepts intersect, to make myself conspicuous if anyone needed me, even though I wasn't in charge of anything. LB said two pages were out of order in his score of the Octet. Was anyone going to fix that?

The rehearsal slowed considerably when LB turned to the teleprompter, began to read, and then stopped to complain about typos. It also took a while to find the right spot for the teleprompter: close enough for LB to read easily, but out of television camera sight lines. A cathedral is certainly a theatrical space, but it isn't ideal for a live broadcast.

I planned to go to bed early that night, because the schedule started early the next morning with a videotaped dress rehearsal and continued through the evening concert. It would be a long day. But the guy in charge of the teleprompter came to my room at the Watergate and stayed the night. Hooking up out of the blue had never happened to me before. I was flabbergasted that he took the initiative.

I saw that LB was already awake when I brought him coffee the next morning, but he'd pulled the sheet up around his head; he wasn't ready to face the day. I eased apart the draperies to let in a minimal amount of light.

I hadn't yet figured out the best ways to wrest LB from the clutches of Morpheus. A previous assistant had told me to soak a washcloth in warm water and drape it gently over LB's face. That definitely worked, eliciting coos of delight in LB's cracked voice. Later that year in Vienna, I'd drop LB's hand into a big bowl of whipped cream. At the Hotel Sacher, there were usually two bowls of whipped cream—*Schlagobers* to the Viennese—that accompanied the coffee every morning. With his eyes still closed, LB licked cream from each finger, humming appreciatively as he edged toward wakefulness.

To jump-start LB for the brutally early Sunday-morning concerts in Vienna—11 A.M. on the dot—I'd play something familiar on the piano, like the "Aragonaise" from Massenet's *Le Cid,* a Boston Pops chestnut. If I played badly enough—on purpose—LB would put on a bathrobe and push me off the piano bench, growling, "What are you doing? It goes like this." A surefire way of getting the Maestro out of bed.

But that morning at the Watergate Hotel was June 17, 1982, and LB had something on his mind other than Igor Stravinsky's centenary.

"Do you know what day this is?" he asked as soon as I had set down the coffee cup. The strain in LB's voice told me not to answer. He rolled over onto his back. "It's the day Felicia died." I sat in the space at the edge of the bed and he extended his hand from under the covers. As I held his hand, he said, "It's the one thing I never joke about—Felicia's death."

The heaviness of his hand was nothing compared to his conscience. He went on, his thoughts circling around the suffering he said he had caused. "I know I exacerbated her final illness," LB moaned. "She knew it. I knew it."

From the rawness of the sorrow in his voice, the events of four years ago might have happened that very morning. (Felicia actually died on June 16, 1978, but Harry Kraut emphasized that June 17 was the day to keep LB distracted, to prevent him from slipping into an unmanageable depression.) From my own many depressive periods, I knew how it felt to be at a complete loss. But helping someone else? No one had ever helped me climb out of one of those pits of depression, and I had no idea what to do. I could tell that LB needed to verbalize his emotions—but to whom? No one in his family was on hand that week in Washington. I drew the short straw.

Over the years, I pieced together the critical moments in what was truly a grim story, though LB never shared the whole sequence of his separation from Felicia, the diagnosis of her lung cancer, their reconciliation, and finally her death. Julia Vega told me one unnerving detail: when she gently shampooed Felicia's hair and drew her hand away, all of Felicia's hair came with it. Though she rarely talked about it, Julia's sorrow seemed every bit as intense as LB's.

Yet how could LB not know how he affected those around him? The weight of his guilt must have been unbearable—when he acknowledged it.

Why guilt? I never completely understood that aspect of his grief. In fact, it wasn't until I read Humphrey Burton's biography of LB in 1994 that I grasped Felicia's central role in LB's life: her wit, grace, and polish, her talent as a pianist and actress, and how valuable the sense of normalcy was for LB in the home that she established for him. No more the randomness of his bachelorhood, the pickups to keep away the Saturday night blues—what LB called "the loneliest night of the week."

He had told me once about lying in bed with Felicia when he was at work on *Candide*. Writing a song for the character of the Old Lady, LB admitted he was stuck.

"I don't have a rhyme for 'a long way from Rovno Gubernya,'" he said, referring to the legendary origins of the Old Lady's patriarch. "Instantly," LB reported, "Felicia said, '*Me muero, me sale una hernia.*'" [I'm dying, I'm growing a hernia.]

Perfect rhyme, perfect poetic meter, winning wit. They must have giggled all night.

THAT MORNING AT THE Watergate Hotel, it took him a long time to come back to the present, but I knew LB was coming around when he asked me how my night was. He knew all about the teleprompter guy staying in my room. Later that morning, Harry Kraut congratulated me on snagging the one guy several men were chasing, including Harry himself.

What?

Was there a contest going on that I wasn't aware of? How strange to be employed by two men who not only kept track of who slept in my room but then dished out positive reinforcement.

I wished that I'd had a therapy hotline to help me process LB's inconsolable grief and his immediate randy, earthy curiosity—topped off by my befuddlement after one night not spent alone. But my health insurance didn't cover therapy, and besides, LB insisted that *he* was the world's best shrink.

<hr />

WE WERE ON TIME at the Cathedral, and the whole day went without a hitch. LB stayed only an hour at the post-concert party for the orchestra and chorus, and then headed for an informal dinner hosted by Fred and Irma Lazarus. For once, he didn't dominate the conversation. Maybe his unburdening that morning woke him to how those around him could help him through his most miserable private moments, especially this particular anniversary in June.

I also noticed for the first time LB looking at his colleagues with deep gratitude. He rarely offered spoken thanks, but occasionally he wrote short notes. I hadn't been involved much in the Stravinsky centenary, but seven years later, after I'd edited the performance materials for the recording of *Candide* with the London Symphony Orchestra, LB graciously raised a toast to me.

During that dinner in Washington, Irma Lazarus asked me pointedly about LB's health, his stamina, whether he had any control over his smoking, and how he was faring emotionally. I wasn't about to share what LB had said that morning, but the fervent look in her eyes told me that she understood the meaning of June 17 as a critical date for LB.

The most stalwart of LB's admirers, Irma Lazarus understood the privilege her life gave her, so she led by example. A passion for the arts inspired her every step. Besides founding the Ohio Arts Council in 1965, she served on the boards of the Cincinnati orchestra, ballet, and opera. She was once told she should be chairman of the Cincinnati Symphony Orchestra's board, but in the 1960s, naming a woman to such a prominent position was beyond the imagination of even the most progressive arts organization.

The warmth in Irma Lazarus's voice gave me a new perspective on the people around LB. Those who were trying to help him found their concern eroded to helplessness as he destroyed himself with cigarettes, Dexedrine, sleeping pills, and a brutal schedule. In my five months as LB's assistant, I had met a roster of women who either reminded LB of his promising early years or devoted themselves to his current well-being: Ann Dedman, Kenda Webb, Ethel Kennedy, Adrienne Barth, Martha Gellhorn, Halina Rodzinski, Ruth Mense, Dorothee Koehler, Madina Ricordi, Wally Toscanini, Valentina Cortese, Margaret Carson—and the indispensable keystone, Julia Vega. Now I was talking with the first among many, Irma Lazarus. She had an unquenchable inner fire.

Eight years later, Irma sought me out at LB's funeral in his Dakota apartment. Gripping my hand tightly as we stood together, she pulsed with an electric current channeling all the emotions we both felt for LB.

Back in New York after Stravinsky's centenary, I had ten days before heading off on the next stint: six weeks with the Los Angeles Philharmonic in a brand-new venture, the Los Angeles Philharmonic Institute. On my one free day, I saw my hapless doctor who continued to ignore my urinary infection. But then, no doctor had detected LB's intestinal parasites yet, either. When would LB stay in one place long enough for a proper medical diagnosis?

In no time, I had twenty-three newly packed pieces of luggage ready for the flight to Los Angeles. Harry Kraut had already settled into a motel in Brentwood. Ann Dedman, staying with friends in Venice, California, would move into the house at 1488 Moraga Drive the day I arrived, and the day after that, LB would fly to Los Angeles with Lee, the kid from Washington. Harry had hired him as a second assistant to LB for the summer.

Ann and I knew the schedule never had an end, but somehow we made everything fall into place.

16 | Far from Tanglewood

HOW SERIOUS WAS LB'S GRIPE that Jamie, his oldest offspring, "abandoned" him by moving to Los Angeles? "She's the only one of my kids who can't have dinner with me, because she's all the way across the country," he said, sounding genuinely hurt. Should I remind LB that he himself was in New York only one week out of five? Who was abandoning whom?

And now, because of what he'd experienced there the previous summer, LB abandoned Tanglewood. Harry Kraut spouted a half-credible tale about a former assistant who'd shipped *Fancy Free* performance materials to Tanglewood by surface mail from Israel.

I interrupted: "What, by boat?"

Harry continued without answering. "Nobody told Lenny those weren't his parts on the stands."

Wait, whose were they?

"They were full of mistakes. Lenny thought the musicians played wrong notes on purpose. He threw his baton at them and walked out."

I doubted that LB's assistant was responsible for shipping, and I knew no orchestra librarian would ship via surface mail from Israel. What was this story about? How much was LB to blame? The Shark Jacket Incident happened that same summer of 1981, when Tanglewood ushers ejected LB and his disruptive entourage from a concert. That was when LB's beloved Shark jacket was taken away, a rather puerile form of punishment, it seemed to me. Since then, LB and Tanglewood had pushed one another away, like the wrong ends of two magnets.

On the other side of North America, the manager of the Los Angeles Philharmonic (LAP), Ernest Fleischmann, quickly set up a "Tanglewood of the West" for the summer of 1982, while Jamie Bernstein scouted out houses for her father. She settled on one built on spec at the end of a ravine, a short commute from the Hollywood Bowl. With several bedrooms, indoor and outdoor Jacuzzis, a pool, and a tennis court, the house came fully furnished, including an oversize video screen in the living room and a sound system with outdoor speakers—which I forgot to turn off when LB played a video of Brahms *Lieder*. The neighbor's phone call was polite. The piano on loan from the Los Angeles Philharmonic fit in a sizable family room, and the piano from Baldwin lodged in a paneled study directly under LB's bathroom.

At the guardhouse for this one-street canyon, I handed over a list of names and the license plate numbers for our dozen rental cars. Ann Dedman, LB's chef and itinerant household manager, quickly hired an all-round helper. Harry Kraut and his partner, Peter, invited thirty "candidates" to a cocktail party. One of them, named Steve, became Harry's summer assistant. Steve's hair, of course, had a tinge of red in it. His show business experience made him unflappable, and he knew Los Angeles inside out.

Martin, son of the LAP's manager, took over as LB's driver with his own open-air Jeep. Martin turned out to be a Mental Jotto pro. In a normal round with a five-letter word, Martin stumped LB on his first try. "Gyros." LB said he'd never had a Greek deli sandwich, but admitted the word was a good one. (No one ever stumped LB.)

Lee completed the roster of assistants. After Lee had stood on the sidelines in Washington, D.C., Harry hired him for the summer, supposedly to help me; with two assistants, each could take an occasional day off. The real reason for this staff addition was that Lee's turmoil with his father had hooked LB. Imagine how flattering for a conflicted young man to have the world's presiding genius snoop into your angst.

Wait—that's how Harry hired my deputy?

OUR SIX-WEEK RESIDENCY began with a bang: a Fourth of July cookout at our canyon house, for the Los Angeles Philharmonic Institute and Orchestra (LAPIO) students and staff, over two hundred people. As the party percolated on its own steam, Harry Kraut's partner, Peter, suggested we venture into West Hollywood for a dip into local culture. We figured the party would take some time to wind down, and we had nothing on the next day's schedule. Ann said, "Sure, see you later."

So rarely away from the loquacious Maestro, I struggled making conversation with Peter. I said I looked forward to watching the conducting students that summer, hearing the works of American composers, and getting to know Los Angeles a little. The summer might bring a respite from the grueling schedule of the last six months. Clearly, I was delusional.

It didn't take us long to give up on the strip of unpalatable bars in West Hollywood and head back to the house. What had happened to the party? All the windows in the house were dark, and no cars were parked out front.

We found Ann in the kitchen, a butcher knife in each hand as she mimed a sacrificial evisceration. With an edge in her voice, she said Lee had gotten drunk and passed out shortly after Peter and I drove off. I apologized for leaving her to deal with such a mess and promised it would never happen again. "But wait, there's more," she said. "Somebody called the police and said drugs were involved." Good golly. Was this going to get in the papers? Mississippi Mud, in spades.

Ann said, "I stopped the police at the door and told them there weren't any drugs, but we had a guy who needed medical attention. The police agreed not to search the house." Ann gulped air as she held herself together. "An ambulance took Lee to the hospital at UCLA. He'll be released around 4 A.M."

"What about LB?" I asked.

"He went to bed," Ann said, with a little sardonic laugh.

I dropped Peter at his motel, then returned to talk to Ann before lying down for an hour. Driving to the hospital, I took a leisurely route, enjoying the stillness and cool night air just before sunrise. Lee couldn't stand, so Ann and I each took an arm and half-carried him to the car. Ann surprised me with her solicitousness, even offering to hold a barf bag, while I wondered to myself what LB saw in this guy.

For a couple days, Lee remained very groggy, but then, he never showed much energy anyway. If anything, he became more remote, and his overtly preppy reserve made communication even more stilted. I tried to be personable and pondered getting LB involved, but I doubted that would have helped.

Diagnosing LB's intestinal distress was more pressing. A reputable doctor gave me some stool sample cups, and the next day I drove back to his office with the plastic container bouncing on the passenger seat. I glanced over at LB's compact turds. They looked every bit like little truffles, and I thought, *What on earth are these worth*? I'd never imagined ferrying Leonard Bernstein's stool samples around Los Angeles, but I could picture a market for all sorts of celebrity relics. After all, fans had once collected Beethoven's hair.

The doctor quickly confirmed LB's parasites and put him on medication that knocked everything out of his system, including all his energy. Rehearsals and teaching sessions commenced that week, so LB resorted to his usual behavior, wolfing down Dexedrine to get through his commitments. What could I do about it? I got him out of bed, no matter his condition. Doing so took all the patience and resolve I had, which made for one very trying summer.

Betty Comden and Adolph Green came to Los Angeles for a trial run of their new musical, *A Doll's Life*, a peppy sequel to Ibsen's dour play, *A Doll's House*. LB caught a performance, and Comden and Green came to the house for a drink. Though I'd met Adolph in New York, our friendship began in LA when he asked me to dance.

Me? Dance? Adolph's arms told me I was Ginger Rogers, as he twirled me around to some mad Hungarian rhapsody that only he could hear. Stopping for a second, he asked, "Let's see you do a bell kick." I was no dancer, but I was even less an athlete. Adolph clicked off three vertical leaps—*one, two, three!*—as though he'd stepped out of his *On the Town* sailor garb yesterday, not forty years ago. This man was sixty-eight years old! Behind him, Betty Comden couldn't stifle her laughter, a sight I'll always treasure.

On a quieter evening, Richard Nelson brought the page proofs of *Findings*, LB's forthcoming book. I looked on as LB flipped through the oversize pages. To my untrained eyes, the proofs seemed polished and professional, but I kept my mouth shut. I was mindful of Jack Gottlieb's tantrum when I'd perused the first printing of LB's piano work "Touches" and had found a mistake.

As he departed, Richard took me aside.

"The proofs look great," I said.

With a crazed look, Richard barked, "Why didn't you say something?" and stalked out.

It took me years to understand about presentations to the Maestro. If LB was unusually silent, an observation from someone in the retinue could elicit a comment from him or even get a discussion going. Richard had expected me to contribute, but I'd held back, and LB had said nothing. There was still so much for me to learn.

Another evening, Jamie played her most recent songs from a polished demo recording that her friend David Pack had produced. A mysterious hiss in the a cappella "Angel de la Guarda" turned out to be several pairs of palms rubbed together in a pulse more subliminal than the finest sand blocks. Captivated by Jamie's musical imagination and David Pack's attention to detail, LB nearly forgave Jamie that evening for abandoning New York. He said later he was really proud of her.

Then we all jumped in the outdoor Jacuzzi, big enough to hold seven. So here I was, stark naked, with my employer—and two of his kids. Ann Dedman caught my eye. "Charlie, did you ever think it would be like this?" she said. The abashed look on my face made everyone burst with laughter.

———

REHEARSALS AT THE Hollywood Bowl start early, well before the sun edges over the Hollywood hills, when the heat is merciless despite the canvas awning drawn across the Bowl's proscenium. Maybe it was Dexedrine, maybe it was the anticipation of his first ride in Martin's open-air Jeep with a roll bar, but LB got dressed and ready to go sooner than any of us had expected. That first morning, I had to hustle for a change. I stuffed a bag with scores, batons, pencils, cigarettes, inhalers, Aquafilters, and powdered Gatorade, and threw *guayaberas*, T-shirts, towels, and handkerchiefs into a garment bag, and quickly hefted everything into the trunk of a sky-blue Mercedes convertible on loan from the LAP.

LB had never heard of a roll bar, but he eagerly climbed in beside Martin and stretched up his arms to hold on during the exhilarating dash to the Hollywood Bowl, cigarette dangling and Maestro hair flying. I followed with Lee in the sedate Mercedes. We were on time for everything that summer, thanks to Martin and his roll-barred Jeep.

After a similar morning rehearsal the next day, we hosted a party even larger than the previous one, to honor MTT's Hollywood Bowl opening concert and to celebrate Alexander Bernstein's birthday. Before Alex's arrival from New York, Ann had hinted that his favorite meal was a Big Mac. Harry's assistant, Steve, knew of a bakery for cakes in all shapes and sizes, so we ordered a birthday cake replica of a Big Mac, three feet in diameter. The bakery didn't take checks or make deliveries, so I cashed $600 and we carefully loaded the Big Mac replica into Steve's hatchback for a cautious drive back to the house.

After Steve and I carried the precious Big Mac into the dining room, a couple dozen people crowded around while LB made a speech. He began with the cost of this birthday cake. He had forced me to tell him, but how could a few hundred dollars be a big deal? Something was up. After saying a few words, LB smashed his right hand smack into the center of the Big Mac and worked his arm down to the bottom layer. He flattened most of the cake into a mushy mess and then slowly sucked the goop off his fingers. Nobody breathed. Alexander tried unsuccessfully to appear amused. I didn't know what to think. Was this how LB built up his guilt, first acting out, then attempting to atone for his behavior?

Ann sliced up the remainder of the cake, but no one wanted any after what LB had done to it.

The party turned more upbeat when the crowd arrived from the Hollywood Bowl concert. My Deutsche Grammophon pals, Jobst and Joachim, and their partners stayed late and joined me in the Jacuzzi. *This is almost like having a social life*, I thought.

Auditions for the conducting fellows took place at UCLA the next afternoon, a nine-hour session that lasted until nearly midnight. The selected fellows each faced LB and waved a baton through the opening of Beethoven's Symphony No. 7 in A, op. 92, while two pianists played from an orchestral score. The conducting technique on display ranged widely. LB groused later that one poor soul never figured out where his baton should go on the downbeat of the second bar. I had a book to keep me occupied.

The next morning, we were back at the Bowl for another rehearsal, followed by a three-hour class for the conducting students, and another two-and-a-half-hour rehearsal with the LAP—a ten-hour working day. In my pants pocket, I carried LB's parasite medication along with a small supply of "halfsies," Dexedrine tablets broken in half. I kept track of the hits LB took and made sure he increased his water intake.

The Hollywood Bowl concerts sold out, one program entirely LB's own works, the other an all-American feast with Gershwin's *Rhapsody in Blue* as the grand finale. Yet the *Los Angeles Times* music critic, Martin Bernheimer, griped that Bernstein didn't take the Bowl concerts seriously. Why not conduct Mahler?

"Bernheimer is never happy," LB said after digesting the review. "If I programmed Mahler, he'd say I ignored American composers. What can I do? He's got to show he knows more than anyone."

After the second week of concerts, I was looking forward to a free day while Lee took over. Lee had caught on to the post-concert routine: while LB signs autographs, ditch the sweat-soaked concert clothes into the Mercedes trunk—they get hung up to dry back at the house so they won't mildew before going to the cleaners the next morning. Meanwhile, keep LB's cup of Ballantine's scotch about half-full (fill it discreetly behind a closed door). Replace the autograph pens when they dry out, and cheerfully hand an LB publicity photo to anyone who asks for one. Lee needed only a few reminders to pay attention.

The morning after the second concert, Lee wasn't at the house, and the Mercedes was gone—with the wet concert clothes still in the trunk, though the trunk might be empty if the car had been stolen. I'd carried LB's conducting scores myself, so those sat safely on the piano. I called Harry Kraut. Had Lee said where he was spending the night? Harry didn't know whether Lee had any friends in Los Angeles. Call the police? Mississippi Mud? "No," Harry said, "Not yet." We carried on with the schedule and I filled in on what was supposed to be my free day.

When Lee eventually returned, a decision had been made for him. He'd leave for his parents' home in Chicago the day before we flew to San Francisco, and we'd slog through the remaining weeks in Los Angeles with one less person on the staff. So much for hiring someone to help me out.

———

THAT DAY'S CONDUCTOR try-out sessions determined the assignment of musical works for the Los Angeles Philharmonic Institute Orchestra (LAPIO) concerts, but I'd never seen such timid podium technique. I'd had a semester of conducting at Carnegie-Mellon, working with singers and the student orchestra, but I didn't have the take-charge temperament of a conductor and I'd never followed up. The first two LAPIO candidates had even less temperament than I. Enough of this; I took my book outside. It was a beautiful day, if only I'd had it to myself.

That evening, all the conducting fellows came to the house for a cookout. Still annoyed at not getting a free day, I lit the charcoal and grudgingly slopped ground beef from one hand to the other, in a half-hearted attempt at making hamburgers. At least I didn't have to entertain the conducting fellows, who all seemed dazed after their auditions.

LB wouldn't appear until dinner was ready. The silence on the patio turned prolonged and awkward, twelve guys trying not to stare at one another. I figured they each were thinking: *Who was going to have a career, and who wasn't?* Into this dismal scene entered Danny Kaye. LB had invited him over without telling me. As a comedian and musical nut, Danny Kaye had long been a hero to me, and now he sidled up to me as if to share a secret. I kept flinging the raw hamburger. Bits of it flew out of my hands and spattered the patio.

Not asking permission, he picked up a handful of ground beef and in seconds expertly massaged it into an edible unit with a recognizable shape. "What you're doing could be called 'mangling,'" he said with precision. That voice of his cut the air with the focus of a seasoned actor. "Those will fall apart in seconds, whereas," he said, scooping up another blob of beef, "if you allow the beef to shape itself into patties, they may be called 'hamburgers.'"

I had no idea what he was talking about. Should I laugh? Look serious? Transfixed with the subdued deadpan of his voice, I let him continue with the ground beef as a prop to his monologue. I didn't know that Danny Kaye was a celebrated chef. In no time, he formed a batch of shapely hamburgers. Then he turned to the conducting fellows, and lifted me off the entertainment hook. For once, LB had called up exactly the right person to help me out.

After dinner, LB enticed the conducting fellows into watching videotapes of *Tristan und Isolde,* his live-concert performances recorded one act at a time over the course of two seasons. I pulled down the video screen and cut off the outdoor speakers. Ann made big bowls of popcorn and everyone settled onto chairs and pillows. I cued the first tape and escaped into the kitchen to talk to Ann.

Even with the doors closed, after fifteen minutes we heard the "Vorspiel" come to an end. A sheepish Danny Kaye peeked around the kitchen door. "I *loathe* Wagner," he said, extending "loathe" into a cadenza. "How happy I am to find you both sitting here." He took a barstool and launched into an interrogation of Ann's food sourcing in Los Angeles. Because the hamburgers had been a success, thanks to him, I was happy to sit there and listen.

Two days later, LB, Harry Kraut, and I were off to San Francisco with the LAP. The change of scene gave us a jolt of adrenaline and it felt like we were playing hooky, scooting away from "the Tanglewood of the West." Deutsche Grammophon (DGG) recorded both concerts in San Francisco, along with early-morning retake sessions for the *Rhapsody in Blue*'s solo piano passages.

Rather than sit in the green room where Harry managed an ad hoc office, I slouched in the back of Davies Hall while LB attempted the first solo passage, a series of triplets ending with a loud, "Shit!" when he hit a clinker at the high end of the phrase—nearly every time.

In the intermission before the second performance of *Rhapsody in Blue*, LB commented on how stiff his hands felt. Among the people standing around in the green room, one young man claimed he knew the perfect massage to relax hand muscles and get the blood flowing, so LB held out his hands for a brief but intense hand massage. After the performance, LB came off the stage very upset. "My hands stopped working altogether," he said. "Whole phrases. That massage made my hands dysfunctional." We never saw that guy again. I suspected he simply wanted to hold LB's hand.

That encounter reminded LB of a fan, many years back, who'd offered a remedy for LB's profuse sweating on the podium. This loony fan theorized, "Doesn't deodorant keep perspiration in check? Roll some deodorant on your forehead, and it'll stop the sweat from going into your eyes." LB grabbed his Right Guard roll-on and rubbed it across his forehead a few times. Back onstage under the lights, LB's sweat carried the deodorant's alcohol and other chemicals into his eyes, blinding him during the performance. As LB told me this bizarre tale, he re-enacted wiping frantically at his forehead with the non-absorbent silk square from his breast pocket, while valiantly trying to conduct. "What an insane idea," he said. "What was I thinking?"

WE WERE BACK IN LOS ANGELES for the final two weeks of the LAPIO. The days began early again with sessions at UCLA, only a few minutes away. LB figured he could roll from his bed directly onto the stage in Royce Hall, an idea that made my mornings even more challenging. Now he swallowed a "halfsie" of Dexedrine with his first cup of coffee.

Harry Kraut's secretary, Mimsy, arrived as video director of the LAPIO rehearsals. Her job was to document the conducting fellows' podium time as the Maestro stood an arm's length away, in the same camera frame. Mimsy plunged into her assignment despite having no experience and immediately got grief from the phalanx of Hollywood-hardened cameramen. "Where do you get off, lady?" one macho operator growled into her headphones. After a crying jag, she rallied and stuck with it, thus giving credence to Harry's "sink or swim" on-the-job training method—an echo of my unenlightening experience in Indiana. Mimsy produced several dozen expertly directed tapes, and I schlepped them all back to New York. Those boxes of tapes brought my luggage count to sixty-four, a new record.

Over the stage in UCLA's Royce Hall, studio lights hung everywhere. They not only ramped up the intensity of the rehearsals, they also made it difficult for LB to see anything. For the Mozart Concerto for Three Pianos, K. 242, LB wore two pairs of glasses, his half-frame keyboard readers over folding-frame sunglasses, which he loved because they fit in the pocket of his *guayabera*. But what did the musicians see? Not LB's eyes, but a reflected panorama of the keyboard and a glowing nebula of Maestro hair.

Leonard Bernstein conducting and playing Mozart's Triple Concerto in Royce Hall, UCLA. July 1982.

On a rare free afternoon, LB turned on the Jacuzzi in his bathroom upstairs for a soak, but as soon as he flicked the whirlpool switch, I heard Ann yelling, "Turn it off!" Water cascaded through the ceiling in the study below, directly onto the

Baldwin grand piano. I ran into LB's bathroom and turned off the Jacuzzi while Ann stuffed the piano's soundboard with thick towels. LB took a shower instead.

I thought back to the espresso machine in Milano. What was it with LB and an electric current?

The outdoor Jacuzzi by the pool quit and a swarm of bees occupied the study with the waterlogged Baldwin piano. Chunks of stone around the kitchen's microwave oven fell off. The perils of a house built on spec. Did the crumbling wall make the microwave dangerous? Whenever LB nuked his vanilla ice cream, Ann and I stood twenty feet away. Silently, we counted the days until we'd be out of that house.

Two weeks before LB's birthday, at the final Hollywood Bowl rehearsal, the LAPIO surprised him by striking up the *Overture to "Candide"* as he walked onto the stage. LB stopped in his tracks, delighted. He crossed his arms over his chest, as if to prevent himself from conducting. He nodded now and then at the musicians, to keep the momentum going. Maybe their tempo was a hair too fast. The musicians got as far as the second theme, turned tentative, rallied, faltered a second time, and the run-through fell apart a quarter of the way through.

LB couldn't have been more tickled and turned their near miss into a teaching session. Looking at some of the wind players, he asked, "What didn't you do, were you not watching her?" pointing to the concertmaster. "And over there," reaching toward the brass players, "how do you stay with these guys over here?" sweeping an arm at the percussion on the other side of the stage. Without a pause, LB stepped onto the podium, gave the downbeat, and had them play the *Overture* again, but with his hands down at his sides, coyly leading with his eyes and nose— except for one gesture to stop them from speeding up.

These musicians had become an orchestra.

I've heard many performances of the *Overture* since, and the New York Philharmonic now regularly plays it conductor-less, but when I think of this music, I see LB on that beautiful morning in Los Angeles, beaming with delight at the young musicians in front of him.

17 | *"People Like Me for What I Do, Not for Who I Am"*

SIX MONTHS INTO THE JOB, I expected an all-night event at the end of every residency. No surprise that the raucous party for the kids in the Los Angeles Philharmonic Institute Orchestra went on for hours after the last Hollywood Bowl concert. For those young musicians, it was a once-in-a-lifetime party with Bernstein. As for LB, he'd planned to stay up all night anyway.

Somebody suggested a final jam session, so everybody ran to get their instruments for a run-through of Beethoven's Symphony No. 5—without the music, the kids making up whatever part they wanted to play. From afar, it sounded like a Looney Tunes soundtrack, but Beethoven should always be played with such gusto.

Ann Dedman and I had one day to pack up the house on Moraga Drive. I set aside a small bag for LB to take to Tesuque, New Mexico, for a ten-day stay with Stephen Wadsworth. LB hadn't met with his opera collaborator since February, so this August visit would be a dive into the depths of the opera. My datebook lists: *cigarettes, Aquafilters, bath supplies, opera, mss [manuscript] paper, letters, stationery, desk supplies, books (1 bag), scotch.* In 1982, airlines didn't care about bottles in luggage, and an unopened fifth of Ballantine's gave Stephen Wadsworth one thing less to track down on LB's arrival.

LB packed his own clothes for the trip. He could be surprisingly helpful, in a pinch, though he really wanted to have one last free-ranging conversation. We talked about the young LAPIO conductors, about the recording sessions a month ago in San Francisco, and about his daughter Jamie's life in Los Angeles. Everything was going in the right direction. Even his intestinal parasites had trotted out the rear door. LB seemed solidly healthy, at last. What a remarkable summer, all that music, and those talented kids.

I didn't allow enough time to get to the airport the next morning after packing a van with twenty-four pieces of luggage and forty crates of videotapes. Leaving my car at the curb of the airport terminal added a hundred dollars to the rental fee, but I had luggage on my mind as the van pulled up behind me. A dozen skycaps stapled sixty-four luggage stubs to my ticket, when suddenly the ticket itself, fluttering atop a suitcase on the conveyor belt, bobbed through the leathery straps into the terminal.

The skycaps apologized: they couldn't stop the conveyor belt. But how do I get on my flight without a ticket? A stern flight attendant appeared out of nowhere and accosted me with the one question that, if answered correctly, will unbolt even the portals of Hell: *What is your mother's maiden name?* What nonsense! I cut her off and stalked toward the gate for my flight. Somehow I had the nerve to bark that a ticket better be waiting for me at the gate. And it was! Had I become the commanding assistant of a Maestro, at last?

The next day I flew to Maine for my first break since January. I'd stayed many times with my Bostonian friends the Wadsworths (no relation to Stephen, LB's opera librettist) in their comfortably rustic home on the island of Great Cranberry, off the coast of Acadia National Park. How wonderful to be back in a familiar place among close friends. But how did I get there? My memory couldn't piece together anything.

I was bursting with energy, out of bed before dawn, yakking my head off. As I made coffee one morning, Jeanie Wadsworth grabbed my shoulders, summoned all her Boston Brahmin authority, and forced me to sit down. "Stop pacing!" she commanded. She'd never seen me so scatterbrained, so unfocused.

The Wadsworths sentenced me to hard labor, which always does the trick. I weeded their garden, picked blueberries, and played the piano during cocktail hour. I relaxed. It took some doing, but after four days I remembered how to be myself again. To see how things were going with the Maestro, I called Stephen Wadsworth's number in Tesuque.

"Lenny hasn't gotten out of bed for several days," Stephen said, his voice clipped and sharp. "I'm putting him on a plane to New York later today."

A rush of adrenaline jolted my nervous system. I threw my things into a bag, took the ferry to the mainland, and caught the next flight to New York. This vacation was over. I hoped to have one full day before LB's return. It didn't occur to me to ask why I hadn't been alerted to this change in plans.

My brain buzzed with anticipation concerning the schedule ahead. In four days we were to fly to Salzburg, via Paris and Munich, for a splashy Bernstein 64th birthday bash with an all-star cast of entertainers. Dorothee Koehler, LB's European press agent, was already in Salzburg, lining up her press contacts. Lauren Bacall, the emcee for this event, had already boarded her flight from New York. In fact, an army of singers and celebrities, each a close friend of the Maestro, was descending on Salzburg like troops massing before battle.

There was just one problem. The beloved Maestro wasn't going to show up. When LB returned to his apartment in the Dakota, he went to his room and wouldn't come out. He wasn't sleeping, he wasn't eating, he wouldn't answer the phone, he wasn't seeing anybody, and he refused to get out of bed.

THE DOWNSIDE TO Dexedrine, popularly known as "speed," is that when you stop taking it, you crash—the colloquial term is apt. That giddy feeling of dancing on a high-wire suddenly stops and you're crumpled on the dirt floor of the circus tent, unable to move, unable to find a reason to move. LB's summer diet of "half-sies" ganged up on him, precipitated a psychic crisis exacerbated by fatigue, and hurled him into a chasm of self-doubt, a predicament entirely drug-induced and not easily sloughed off.

Or *was* it entirely drug-related?

"Drink lots of water," sounds trivial to someone in this condition. "Pull up your socks," is downright callous. Climbing out of that bottomless pit takes a lot more than a few simple steps, as I knew from my own depressed adolescence.

WITHIN APARTMENT 23 at the Dakota, LB's bedroom had a hushed intimacy. Its deep russet wallpaper blended with the substantial architectural details: the elaborate window surround, the heavy doors, the mantel over the fireplace, all in a saturated brown oak. Even on the brightest day, the room stayed dusky, somnolent. The massive shutters inside the window were rarely opened, and thick draperies muffled the sound of the city. You'd never know about the madcap traffic outside, careening up and down Central Park West. Two or three table lamps cast pools of dim yellow light.

From the hall in the back of the apartment, a door led to a shorter, narrower hall with LB's clothes closets on one side, like a compressed dressing room. At its far end, an inner door led to LB's bedroom. If I turned the light on in this dressing-room hallway, it shone through the transom above the bedroom door and cast a tawny oblong into LB's room—a subtle signal. That oblong provided just enough light to see where I was going.

I pushed open the bedroom door and asked LB if he was awake.

"Yes," he said.

I set coffee and orange juice on the table by his bed.

"How are you feeling," I said, not making it a question. A long pause gathered weight. He reached for the lamp on the bedside table and turned it on to its lowest level.

"People like me for what I do, not for who I am," he said, with a weariness far deeper than melancholy. I settled on the edge of the bed and let his pause go on for a while, let it gather more weight.

I thought of all the glib things I shouldn't say: *Well, who* are *you and what* is *it that you do*, but that year I'd learned when not to be glib. My benchmark was the morning of June 17, when LB ruminated mournfully on the death of Felicia. He had his own pace. I waited.

Music, anagrams, phone calls—LB's brain never emptied. But this specific dichotomy—what he *did* and who he *was*—must always have been in the back of his mind, and it surged forward when everything else dropped to the side. I hadn't heard LB express this depth of doubt before. It sounded as though he hadn't had this conversation with anyone in a long time. Dexedrine fueled a manic energy that pushed doubt away, but without the drug, he was spent, unable to see his way through physical depletion, and unable to bear his staggering emotional burdens.

Finally, he began speaking. He reviewed the events of the summer: the master classes, the Hollywood Bowl concerts, the performances and recordings in San Francisco.

"Those are all about *doing*, not about *being*," he said. More was to come: concerts in Vienna, recordings to fill out a Brahms cycle. To his exhausted mind, the activity of the past seemed without much purpose, and the projects in the future looked endless. This wasn't merely a philosophical remark. LB was taking stock, as well as he was able to in this frame of mind. What was the point of all this ceaseless activity? I didn't have the nerve to ask that out loud.

I let him talk. Occasionally, I latched onto a noun he brought up and asked him to elaborate, one aching concept at a time. My patience would never run out as long as he continued speaking. After an hour, he begged to be left in bed for the rest of the day. He told me he'd cancelled the Salzburg party but had every intention of honoring the next commitment. Later, Harry Kraut said he'd feared that LB might cancel everything through the rest of the year.

I sensed that LB had already turned a corner, though he wasn't going to say so. He knew I was there, and that I'd be there the next day and the day after that. In February, LB had turned solicitous when I drove off the road in Indiana, broke my nose, and had to cancel my first travel assignment with him. Now it was my turn to show empathy. What kind of bond this was, I couldn't figure out—not like any employer-employee association I'd ever heard of.

How could I understand the way he perceived his life, the path that had been laid out for him? Not merely a musician, but a political activist, educator, a force of nature for the entire planet? His life was complicated, his history was intricately entwined with everything around him, his achievements beyond my comprehension. Yet, the role of his assistant, lowly and subservient, was determined, in a way, by LB's sense of himself. That week as LB lay in his bed in the dark, I felt a strengthening of devotion in myself, surprisingly heartfelt and resolute.

That August, it was my turn to be solicitous and keep the world at bay, while LB huddled in his darkened room, pondering where his focus had gone, trying to revive his psyche. I'm not sure he ever put the whole puzzle together. He was too immersed in the vortex of Dexedrine abuse, sleep deprivation, and depression. But he understood that I'd be there, along with Julia Vega and his family, whenever he put his feet on the floor, stepped to his bedroom door, and opened it.

CH -
Where is sketch for song about "I should never have gone to that party . . ."
(yellow sheet on bedroom piano in Brentwood)

During those hushed days in New York, this Post-it with the quote "I should never have gone to that party . . ." appeared on my desk. The handwriting is small and steady, as if LB were determined to regain control: of his hand, his thoughts, his life. There are no flourishes with the pencil, and the text is centered like an artist's drawing.

I never found the page he was asking for. Maybe it was lost in Tesuque. At least he did not have to go to that "other party" in Salzburg.

18 | Name the Nine Muses!

DESPITE THAT DEBILITATING DEPRESSION on his birthday in August, LB vowed to fulfill his autumn commitments with the Vienna Philharmonic. I quickly packed sixteen pieces of luggage for a relatively cheap overnight flight to Vienna, two days before LB and Harry Kraut would take the far more expensive Concorde.

I'd visited Vienna only once, never dreaming I'd stay at the century-old Hotel Sacher, an establishment that eternally promoted itself as the refined epitome of the long-gone Austro-Hungarian Empire. As I followed the luggage into the hotel, the liveried staff shouted "*Grüss Gott!*"—a quaint greeting somewhat like "God bless" in Tennessee. The forced gaiety and chirpy Viennese accent grated on me like singing animals in a Disney movie. Their arch mannerisms made me think the Viennese must be the most delusional people in Europe.

That afternoon, I accompanied the porters who hefted the music trunk to the Musikverein. I had to wait until the next day to see the fabled *goldener Saal*, the room in which Vienna redeems itself of its many sins. Regarded since its opening in 1870 as the ideal performance space for serious music, the Musikverein is more steeped in history than any other concert hall. Brahms and Bruckner conducted on that stage, and except for replaced light bulbs, little has changed since Gustav Mahler's last rehearsal there in 1901.

The Vienna Philharmonic is a self-governing ensemble, and its day-to-day affairs are handled by a general secretary—in 1982, the lively Brigitta Grabner. I warmed to her immediately, especially when she referred to the musicians as "my boys." We sorted through the music and she introduced me to the stage manager, Herr Kraus. Why would they need a librarian? Dependable Herr Kraus always put the music onstage himself.

Back at the hotel, I domesticated Suite 314 with sharpened pencils, books, and family photos in their silver frames. Moneto, the white plush monkey, and his new partner Kenda, a petite piebald seal, tried out LB's bed pillows. Between the two bedrooms, a sitting room in red and pink, splashed with gold, resembled a box at the opera, symptomatic of the "red and gold disease" that infects most opera fanatics. A big black Bösendorfer grand piano offset some of the frou-frou, and although it was as cumbrous as a limousine, it left enough space for a dining table, a sizeable desk, a bar, a sofa, and expensively upholstered chairs. Characters from Greek myths busied themselves in antique oil paintings. A balcony overlooked the elegant Albertinaplatz and the rooftops of the Hofburg, the imperial palace, beyond.

LB's bedroom, away from the street, was quiet and dimly lit. I took the other bedroom in the suite, at the front of the hotel, with the traffic noise. Every morning, I had the option of watching the ballet corps take their class in the opera house across the street, though all I could see were their bouncing heads.

LB and Harry arrived at midnight, but they had determined to stay up late anyway because the next day's rehearsal wasn't until 3 P.M. I handed LB the gifts dropped off by his Viennese admirers, and he read the cards aloud and explained who these friends were. Though tired, he seemed happy.

Amongst the flowers, chocolates, and books sat a large cookie tin. LB gasped as he tore off the lid. Inside, pale stars nestled on tissue paper. I put one in my mouth and an otherworldly suspension of sugar and whipped cream evaporated on my tongue. The card's signature looked like pendulous loops, not letters. LB pointed out the dots on each swoop: nipples on a massive "W," the insignia of Renate Wunderer, *eine Wiener Verlags- und Kulturdame* (a woman of great cultural value to Vienna in music and in publishing). LB said, "Wait until you meet her and behold the heft of her bosom." He loved hugging those breasts to his chest while wailing at the top of his lungs, "Renate Wunderer," to the tune of "*Santa Lucia.*"

At the Musikverein the next afternoon, shouts of *Grüss Gott* accompanied LB up the stairs as he detoured to the side rooms where the Deutsche Grammophon (DGG) and Unitel (video) recording crews had installed their gear. Seeing the two gay DGG technicians, Jobst Eberhardt and Joachim Niss, perked me up; maybe I'd have a social life on the road. As before, Hans Weber headed the DGG crew, Humphrey Burton would direct the video for Unitel, and John McClure would manage the video's soundtrack. I'd already met everyone except John McClure, though I knew his name from LB's Columbia recordings with the New York Philharmonic. Collegial admiration permeated those offstage rooms.

Heading down an aisle of the legendary concert hall, the *goldener Saal*, LB stopped, grabbed my arm, and pointed to the huge canvases on the ceiling.

"Who are they and what are their names?" he said.

I looked up at several women dressed as ancient Greek goddesses. "There are nine, so they are probably the Muses," I said slowly, stalling for time. "Thalia, Terpsichore, uh, Calliope." I scratched my head. "Um, Erato," I said, looking for clues up above but not finding any. "Euterpe?" That was more than half.

LB said, "Good," and walked on to the stage.

That was close, nearly another "fetch me my Chambers" moment. First thing

I did on returning to the hotel was to open a reference book and memorize the entire batting order.

At the end of that first rehearsal, the concertmaster, Herr Professor Doktor (HPD) Gerhart Hetzel, approached the podium with questions. Standing behind him, a student and budding photographer, Thomas Seiler, clicked his shutter right after I draped a towel over LB's shoulders.

Left to right: the shoulder of Dr. Gerhart Hetzel, Leonard Bernstein, Charlie Harmon. Onstage in the Musikverein, Vienna, Austria. September 1, 1982.

In this photograph, as I hold my affected pose, I'm paying close attention to HPD Hetzel's question, trying to decipher his Austrian accent, and am mindful that I might have to fix something in the orchestra parts. LB is listening not only to HPD Hetzel's question, but also to the Brahms symphony replaying in his head.

Without much effort, I too can replay in my head the sound from that day even now, along with LB's exhausted voice from the week before: *People like me for what I do, not for who I am.* Here he is *doing*—conducting—rather than *being*—father, educator, composer, but in rehearsal he assumed the role of conductor-as-composer, a dual capacity that LB explored all his life. In an all-encompassing performance, LB inhabited the mind of the composer—*being*—by making the music come alive—*doing*. The look on his face says that he has given in completely, resolved despite his exhaustion to create this music from the inside out.

That week, LB's two daughters, Jamie and Nina, settled into rooms on the same floor of the Hotel Sacher as LB's suite, lifting LB's spirits enormously. When he knew his daughters would have breakfast with him, he got out of bed without any prodding.

Jamie and Nina explored Vienna every morning. In the Brueghel room at the art museum, the painting of a peasant wedding reminded Jamie of a poem she'd learned in high school, "The Dance," by William Carlos Williams. I fetched *The Oxford Book of American Verse* so she could read it aloud, which elicited a cheer from LB—*being* a happy father.

Every few minutes, the Sacher waiters replenished the pots of coffee, bowls of *Schlagobers*—whipped cream—and platters of pastries. Not healthful but irresistible.

The night before the dress rehearsal, a sophisticated, youthful couple, Fritz and Sigrid Willheim, hosted a party at their apartment nearby. A close friend of LB's, Fritz advised LB as his European legal counsel. Sigrid, a teacher and sponsor of education reform, shared LB's educational ideals. Jamie and Nina added luster to this get-together, where I met more of LB's Viennese friends, foremost among them the witty Susann Baumgärtel and studious Peter Weiser, later the translator of LB's book *Findings* into German.

With the Vienna Philharmonic, LB asked for very few rehearsals. One reading of Mozart's *Overture to "Don Giovanni"* and the piece was ready to go. The ease of rehearsals was offset by the peculiar schedule for the concerts: Saturday afternoon at 3:30 followed by a Sunday performance at the ungodly hour of 11 A.M. In between on Saturday night, LB caught Plácido Domingo's performance in *Otello* at the State Opera. LB anticipated each dramatic moment in highly audible stage whispers. Just before Margaret Price, as Desdemona, hit her high A-sharp at the end of the "Willow Song," LB emitted a walrus-like grunt, but no one told LB not to sing along. Later he mused, "I wish I could record *Otello*." He'd need a sound-proof box from which to conduct, but it was only a dream. It never came true.

In his new capacity as general manager of the State Opera, Lorin Maazel visited LB at the Sacher late one night. Returning to the hotel after an evening out with the DGG crew, I saw a grim-faced Maazel walking out the door. Moments later in the suite, LB said disparagingly, "Lorin wants to put his feet up on a desk and smoke big cigars. That's his idea of managing an opera house."

Nevertheless, after the Sunday concert, Maestro Maazel joined us for lunch at an outdoor terrace in the Wienerwald, the famous Vienna Woods. Jamie and Nina strove to maintain the stilted conversation with Maestro Maazel, but their efforts ended abruptly when LB walked away to have a cigarette. I followed him to another part of the patio, where he took a seat and began singing, in his usual growl, a rhythmic setting of his favorite lyrics, by John Lennon:

I'm a moldy moldy man
I'm moldy thru and thru
I'm a moldy moldy man
You would not think it true.
I'm moldy til my eyeballs
I'm moldy til my toe
I will not dance I shyballs
I'm such a humble Joe.

LB lightly slapped his hands on a table top in a five-beat pattern, and when Jamie and Nina sat down, he nodded at them to enter in turn, in canon. Think of trying to sing "Row, Row, Row Your Boat," but in a complicated rhythm, to a tune you've never heard before. Singing a canon while listening as it was improvised proved too challenging for me, but Jamie and Nina managed to do so effortlessly.

LB improvised three versions, each in closer rhythmic imitation than the one before. Then we all took a stroll in the Vienna woods, the full extent of exercise that month.

———

MY SECOND TOUR with an orchestra—the first had been that spring with the Israel Philharmonic— covered only two cities in five days, virtually a walk around the block. Jamie and Nina came along to the first stop, Munich, where LB always occupied Suite 680 in the luxurious Vierjahreseiten (The Four Seasons). The suite came with a key for the door to the hotel's indoor swimming pool, so LB or his guests could go for a dip at any hour.

Jamie's friends from Los Angeles, David and Gale Pack, surprised us at the hotel. They wanted to help celebrate Jamie's thirtieth birthday the next day. LB's outlook improved even more, now that he was surrounded by family and friends.

Harry surprised me with a ticket for the concert in Munich. I had a hard time sitting still, but the performance of the Brahms Double Concerto grabbed me; the Vienna Philharmonic had this music in their DNA. LB's pace clarified the entire arc of this work, which I'd heard only once before as a student in Pittsburgh. Afterwards LB asked me, "Did the piece hold together?" though he knew the answer. It seemed ideal to me.

Nothing held together at Kai's Bistro, a loud, campy nightclub where LB felt compelled to make an appearance so that newspapers could feature him the next day. As patrons threw handfuls of glitter at one another, I drank a lot of sweet German champagne, to take the edge off the thudding disco noise. Afterward, LB invited many of the Vienna Philharmonic's string players to have a swim at the hotel, all of us stark naked. I innocently agreed to Gale Pack's challenge of racing the pool's length, unaware she'd starred on her high school swim team. She beat me by a mile, but then she had less booze in her system than I did. LB accurately described my swimming as "laughable."

The next morning LB said goodbye to Jamie and Nina, who were off to Paris as we flew to Berlin. I'd never had a travel day with a concert that same evening— truly an endurance test: pack up in one hotel, schlep to the airport, unpack at the next hotel, prepare for a concert, get through the concert, stand and smile at a reception. LB slept all the next day while I explored unfamiliar West Berlin to find a *regalito* for Julia.

Again a surprise: only minutes before LB walked onstage in Berlin, Harry handed me a ticket for a seat in the hall. As I rushed out into the concert hall, I wondered how I'd get backstage afterward in time to pack things up so we wouldn't be late for the most important reception of the VPO tour. I'd written "Austrian Consulate" in my datebook, but I didn't know where that was. I hadn't seen any invitation.

By the time I made my way into the green room and helped LB into a fresh shirt, everyone had departed for the reception except Dorothee Koehler. She said, "I'll see you there," and left. I guessed our driver knew where to go. But the building he took us to looked deserted, and no one answered the buzzer. Where was this reception? LB didn't have a clue either. Maybe there'd be a message at the hotel.

Nope, no message. I accompanied LB to his suite. We ordered some food and waited for Harry, who stormed in very late. Beyond enraged. As always when something went wrong, Harry contrived a self-exculpating scenario.

"I put the invitation on your desk," he said, glaring at me.

What desk? I wondered mutely.

"At the Sacher," he insisted.

That was three hotels ago. I'd submerged the Sacher's dainty escritoire under the orchestra parts for the Brahms Serenade No. 2. Had an invitation crept into the part of the first oboe? Not that I'd noticed, nor had I seen Harry in my room, nor had he ever given me a verbal reminder. I'd written the reception in my date-book because it was on the calendar. Everybody in the entourage got a copy of

LB's calendar, but it didn't include locations. I looked at Harry but I didn't have the nerve to ask: what exactly was this accusation about?

After that evening in Berlin, Harry never handed me another concert ticket, except when I asked on behalf of friends. For the next three years, I listened to LB's performances over tinny speakers in the green room.

Depressed the next day, I hid out in the hotel. When LB trotted off to a party, I said I wasn't up for that, stayed in, and packed for our next-day flight back to Vienna. In fact, at this stage of Maestro assistant-ship, the physical activity of packing up had become a reliable stabilizer. It made me feel purposeful, and it almost offset my low spirits.

When I carried a cup of coffee into LB's bedroom the next morning, a young man in LB's bed sat up and extended his hand. "Hi, I'm Robert," he said brightly, as he took the coffee cup to wave beneath LB's nose. I was about to call for a larger pot of coffee, but Robert put on a bathrobe and took care of that himself. Then he opened the draperies and cajoled LB into consciousness.

"I was so happy to see Lenny again at that party last night," Robert said. I wasn't used to hearing the Maestro referred to as "Lenny" by someone my own age, but Robert seemed altogether affable, someone you'd want at a party. I was to learn that, as an actor and a model, he always made himself presentable, even dashing. He could talk to anyone, as he was now talking to me.

Over breakfast, LB giddily re-enacted bits of the previous night's louche party, more amusingly than if I'd endured it in person. Despite my shaken equilibrium about the missed consulate reception, LB and Robert managed to cheer me up. But for the rest of the tour, I remained watchful for a repeat of Harry Kraut's machinations.

The one comfort in LB's interminable travels was an occasional homecoming. It calmed me to be back at the Hotel Sacher that evening, and familiar faces lifted my spirits. Susann Baumgärtel told some new jokes. Fritz and Sigrid Willheim brought me a book of German poetry. LB ordered *Tafelspitz* to satisfy his rhapsodic craving for the Austrian edition of New England boiled dinner: a beef rump boiled with root vegetables and served with horseradish, applesauce, and tubs of sour cream. It reminded me of the one thing my mother could not overcook: boiled corned beef. Later, LB divulged his own mother's culinary cluelessness, which far outclassed my mother's mere antipathy. *Tafelspitz* must have reminded LB of his childhood, too.

The final performances, in the Konzerthaus a few blocks from the Musikverein, concluded this chunk of the Brahms recordings: the Serenade No. 2 in A, op. 16, and the Concerto for Violin, op. 77, with Gidon Kremer as soloist. Getting dressed, soaking in the bathtub, or padding around in his bathrobe, all that week LB sang the oboe's big tune in the last movement of the Brahms Serenade, with Edwin Denby's lyrics in Aaron Copland's *The Second Hurricane*.

Two octaves lower, but astonishingly at pitch. An endearing way to share a tune that wouldn't leave his head.

LB often made a point of observing Rosh Hashanah at Hitler's table—well, he claimed it was Hitler's table—in the restaurant Zum Stadtkrug. He liked to invite members of the press so he could expound on why it mattered to be a Jewish conductor in Vienna, a city that, in LB's opinion, would never face up to its anti-Semitic past. But in 1982, LB's devoutness guided him to temple instead, alongside the Israeli ambassador. In a different kind of celebration, the recording crew took me out for dinner, but not at Zum Stadtkrug.

Before returning to New York, LB wanted to visit the pianist Justus Frantz, who had injured his back when he slipped on a wet bathroom floor while on a concert tour. After cancelling the remainder of his tour, Justus returned to Germany on a stretcher but then decided he'd recover just as well at his house in the Canary Islands.

On automatic pilot after nine straight months on the road, I summoned all my concentration and walked to the airline offices a couple blocks from the Hotel Sacher. The concierge could have done this for me, but the flights to the Canary Islands had to be paid separately from the hotel bill. Thank goodness for the Amberson credit cards. Meanwhile, LB called Justus Frantz, who promised that no matter what hour we arrived at Gran Canaria, somebody would meet us with a car. I arranged with John McClure for him to take most of LB's luggage to New York, having proffered the bonus of a limo to his apartment only a few blocks from the Dakota. The travel plans fell into place quickly, though the details took up a lot of space in my datebook.

Before immersing himself in the celebrated Norton Lectures that he delivered at Harvard in 1973, LB had taken a break on Gran Canaria, where he met a striking "big blond" German aristocrat, Justus Frantz. Well-connected, blessed with charm and a formidable pianistic technique, Justus soon shone as a bright star in Bernstein's personal firmament. They'd stayed in touch ever since.

When LB and I landed at Gran Canaria around midnight, Justus met us himself—he'd recovered enough to sit up and drive—along with Robert Dawson, who had arrived a day earlier from Berlin. Buffeted by the tropical air, we rode in Justus's Volkswagen convertible up the precipitous byways to his hilltop villa. After a couple hours of talk, Justus showed me to a bedroom on the ground floor, where I conked out.

My bladder woke me up, but where was the bathroom? More generally, what country was I in? The bedroom's sliding glass door looked onto a tropical landscape. I stepped outside and peed into some convenient foliage as the sun peeked over a rugged far-off ridge. For a moment, I savored the stillness, the idyllic warmth of the clean air. Such a long way from Vienna. No one else was up, so I opted to sleep one more hour.

The next thing I knew, three wide-eyed faces peered at me around the bedroom door: LB, Justus, and Robert. I had slept through the night and the following day and well into the next evening. They thought I'd slipped into a coma. The entire week on Gran Canaria, I slept over ten hours every night, even after a lengthy afternoon nap. LB claimed that all he needed was one night of deep sleep, and he was ready to tackle his usual schedule. I didn't doubt it, but not so for me. I needed weeks to recover. Especially after the past nine months.

Three other guests plus Justus's mother lodged that week at La Casa de los Musicos. One night we all squeezed into a car for dinner in Maspolomas, down a steep twisty road to the ocean. LB drove, the first time I'd seen him handle a gear shift. At a steep climb after one hairpin turn, the car lurched backwards toward a sheer drop. We six paralyzed passengers shrieked as one, while LB griped, "Why is everyone screaming?" A week later in New York, I described LB's daredevil road mannerisms to Julia Vega, and she said simply, "He go with God." That winter I learned that when LB drove, Julia simply refused to get into the car.

Another evening we played some piano four-hand music, two people at one piano. Justus had the Bach orchestral suites in a nineteenth-century arrangement, a thick and almost unplayable edition. LB, ever the muse of meddling, divided up the counterpoint, taking over some of the lines on Justus's pages and vice versa. He turned a complicated arrangement into a complete impossibility. That was my introduction to LB's famous way with four-hand arrangements. Although in the years ahead when I played Mozart duets with LB, he allowed that Mozart knew what he was doing and did not reassign the notes.

On the flights to New York, first heading northeast to Madrid before the long flight west across the Atlantic, the Iberia Airline planes rattled so much I expected all the rivets to pop loose. LB chided me for being overly fatalistic, but I didn't know that his destiny did not include dying in a plane crash. I hadn't yet heard Julia say, "He go with God."

Queer Al,
police goddess!
(8)

First, ignore the punctuation.
Queer = make an anagram.
Al police = the letters to be rearranged.
Goddess = the definition.
(8) = the number of letters in the solution
("al police" is eight letters).

The solution is Calliope, muse of epic poetry.

The Rebbe's quiz after my first visit to the Musikverein.

19 | What Takes Nine Months to Gestate?

RIGHT AFTER WE RETURNED to New York, City Opera's rehearsals of *Candide* got under way. Those free days on Gran Canaria certainly helped—I'd never had to change focus so quickly before. As I sat next to LB in the theater at Lincoln Center, I wrote down his copious comments. Ten seconds into the *Overture*, LB said, "No screaming." The cast ran onstage, tossed props around, and hollered as if liberated from an insane asylum. Why bother playing the *Overture* if nobody could hear it?

In a glum frame of mind after the rehearsals, LB's outlook worsened as he read a terse letter from Lillian Hellman. "Permanently and irrevocably," she withdrew the book she'd contributed to the original 1956 production of *Candide*. LB re-read the note aloud, including her final line about "standing in a closet facing death" every day. He asked, "What am I supposed to do? How do I respond to this?" Wasn't it obvious? No one could make Ms. Hellman happy.

The opening night, we got to the theater at the last minute. I scooted to my seat between Ann Dedman and Alexander Bernstein in the front row, while LB picked his way through the middle of the theater, stepping over the feet of dozens of seated New Yorkers. Please, couldn't he be seated off to the side, so he could step out for a cigarette or a pee break? Anywhere but the middle of a row. As LB reached his seat, the audience recognized him and broke into applause. LB said later he couldn't have been more irritated.

The curtain went up, the trumpets played their fanfare, and the cast bolted onstage and screamed through all six minutes of the *Overture*. But Harold Prince's inventive production was a success. Broadcast live one night, it revived interest in *Candide* from many opera companies.

LB's schedule was intentionally travel-free—almost—for the next nine months. He needed an unbroken stretch to move forward on the opera, allowing first a two-week buffer (which turned into six weeks) to transform himself from a conductor into a composer. He said it always took a while to get the music of "those other composers" out of his head—the Brahms and Stravinsky he'd conducted in 1982. After seven hectic months of airports and hotels, I looked forward to the sedate version of the assistant job, maybe an entire winter holed up in Connecticut.

In Connecticut one morning—before LB's return—Julia Vega became alarmed when the caretaker didn't answer the phone. She walked up the driveway to the caretaker's cottage and found him on the floor, dead from a heart attack. Julia often managed to be the first witness on the scene; she'd dashed heedlessly to the Dakota driveway seconds after John Lennon's assassination.

Languishing without a caretaker, the Connecticut house needed work, plus there were no office supplies, no typewriter. And how could LB write an opera without music manuscript paper? As LB drove up the Merritt Parkway, tossing out five-letter words for rounds of Mental Jotto, I scribbled in my datebook: get the furnace cleaned, fix the garage door, install storm windows ("storm," that's a good Jotto word), maintain the two cars—they got us back and forth from the city—pick up train schedules, and find a photocopy service in Connecticut. A replay of the stint in Indiana, except here in New England I didn't have Dean Webb to lean on.

One October afternoon, executives from the Phillips record label drove to Connecticut for a formal presentation of LB's recording of Wagner's *Tristan und Isolde.* LB put on his in-the-country outfit: shorts, sandals, and his favorite *schmatta*, a ratty windbreaker. Not bothering to shower, he lubricated his armpits with Ultra Ban while crowing, "Let's fox 'em!" I don't know whom he thought he was foxing. Any dog could have tracked him from the musty scent in his general vicinity.

Photographer and family friend Henry Grossman asked me, "Is Lenny going to get dressed?" He didn't look like the conductor of a major opera. In the driveway, LB accepted the boxed set of LPs and went back to his studio. I asked the Phillips chiefs if they'd like to come inside the house, but they retreated into their car for the drive back to the city.

During dinner, LB put the third act of *Tristan* on the record player—not exactly light-hearted background music. Hildegard Behrens had been ill during the final recording sessions. LB said she took big gulping breaths in Isolde's final solo, the "Liebestod," during the performance, but the spliced-in retakes made her control sound faultless over the Bavarian Radio Symphony Orchestra's sustained intensity. LB seemed pleased.

After a pause of several seconds, loud applause reverberated from the speakers in the living room, clapping that sounded like it might go on for quite a while. LB threw his fork. "What? I never allow applause on my recordings," he said. I turned off the record player. "Call Harry," LB said and stalked off to his studio in a funk. The first pressing of *Tristan und Isolde*, five thousand copies, had to be destroyed.

MEANWHILE, LB'S SLEEP went down the tubes. Awake all night, he might doze a couple hours after sunrise, but he never mastered the discipline of preparing to go to bed. A few scotches before dinner, a chocolate bar later on, after-midnight phone calls with his sister Shirley about the crossword puzzle in *The Guardian*—all the while raising his pulse with four packs of cigarettes a day. And in the months without any conducting, he got no exercise.

What about a sleep disorder clinic? Harry Kraut settled on the Sleep-Wake Disorders Center at Montefiore Hospital in the Bronx. LB filled out a lengthy survey of his sleeping habits, alcohol intake, medications, and exercise, his first assessment of his overall anti-sleep habits in a long time. (He'd had to keep a log during an attempt to stop smoking, but that was years before.)

Dr. Thorpy—a name that thrilled LB as it seemed impossible to anagram—cleared a weekend slot at the clinic, and I called to get the protocol: what clothes LB should take, whether there would be a personal phone line. We decided not to have a piano delivered—a piano? What were we thinking?

On a Friday afternoon in November, I drove LB to the Bronx and left him in a chilly, overly bright room with a single bed smack in the middle, like a slab awaiting a sacrifice. Room 101 in Orwell's *1984* came to mind. Creepy one-way windows encircled this Spartan chamber, to allow observations from every angle while LB slept—or didn't. That weekend, LB's household staff got two days completely free. We paid for it later on.

When I picked LB up at Montefiore late on Sunday, he bubbled with energy and sleep statistics, gleaned from the electrode-fed data that the observation crew had analyzed. Still, it was literally a coldly clinical study. LB said, "I woke up because I'd kicked the covers off and got chilly. I realized I was lying there flat on my back, completely naked, and fully erect. What must they think?"

"Those guys are professionals," I said, not taking my eyes off the Merritt Parkway. "No one else will ever know. Besides, they've probably seen that and more, many times over." A thought hit me between the eyes. "And it proves you were asleep," I said. "Congratulations."

The clinic determined that LB's ideal cycle was seventeen hours awake, seven hours asleep. Nothing unusual about that. Dr. Thorpy set up a rigorous schedule to attune LB to this cycle, starting that night. LB had to stay up until 4 A.M.—hardly a challenge—and get up exactly seven hours later, at 11 A.M., whether he thought he'd slept or not. More challenging: total abstinence from medical helpers during his waking hours. No "halfsies." And keep a log: how did LB feel through his seventeen hours awake? I notated and underlined this schedule for five days in my datebook, and then the schedule shifted one hour later each day.

Back in the city, LB's social calendar filled up: a poetry reading by Seamus Heaney followed by dinner at author and editor Jean Stein's apartment; a party hosted by Irma Lazarus at the Algonquin; a book signing of *Findings* at the

Doubleday store on Fifth Avenue, where one very tall woman in a massive fur coat crashed to the head of the line. It was Joan Sutherland, who thrust a forearm under each of LB's armpits, power-lifted him to his feet, and gave him a bone-crushing hug. The line of autograph seekers clapped and cheered.

Later that same afternoon, LB screened for final approval his Vienna Philharmonic films of the Brahms Symphony No. 4 in E Minor, op. 98, and *Academic Festival Overture*, op. 80, and Mozart's Symphony No. 39 in E flat, K. 543. I carried the scores around all day, though LB didn't need them in the screening room. He shouted over the music—at bar 18, I noticed from the score on my lap—"I wish I could be Mozart at that moment!" when Cs and D flats crash together, the harshest dissonance in Western music.

All in all, a fairly ordinary day. According to the sleep-wake schedule, LB had to be in bed with the lights out at 7 A.M. When I woke him seven hours later, I asked, "Are you sticking to the schedule?" and he said, "Yes," with genuine enthusiasm. Good. This son of Harvard was giving it the old college try.

Then the sleep-wake schedule got rocky. LB's waking hours shifted later each day by three hours: in bed at 10 A.M. on Sunday and 1 P.M. on Monday, with the goal of a normal schedule by Thursday, Thanksgiving Day. Meanwhile, the rest of us stuck to ordinary daylight hours. After all, Ann Dedman had to get groceries when the stores were open. Julia never grumbled and made LB breakfast at whatever hour he asked. A bowl of oatmeal at 9 P.M.? *Sí, Señor.*

On Thanksgiving Day, LB woke at two in the morning and was in bed by ten that night, even though the full house of family and friends stayed up late. Standing on the sidelines that weekend, I at least got to meet LB's mother, Jennie, who arrived from Boston in a chauffeured car. I loved her gregarious curiosity and inexhaustible kindness. After she returned to Boston, Jennie phoned me weekly. "Can you get Lenny to stop smoking?" she'd ask every week, though neither of us had a clue how to end his addiction. When LB asked what I talked about with his mother, I said, "Your smoking, and how to get you to stop." He never looked more sober than when he heard that.

Did I really have to spend a holiday with the Bernsteins? Probably not, but I'd forgotten to ask for time off. Besides, I hadn't made any plans of my own. From the Dakota, I'd hauled the typewriter that the Amberson office had leased for me, and I figured writing thank-you letters would occupy me all weekend.

LB's brother Burtie arrived and immediately organized a touch football game, dubbed the "Nose Bowl" in honor of the Mount Rushmore-sized schnoz that he and LB sported on their faces. (Though he wasn't there that day, Aaron Copland possessed the biggest nose. In one letter to LB, Copland even signed himself,

"Old Judge Nose.") Everyone except Julia was expected to participate in this football game.

How could I explain the sheer terror I felt at having to participate in an organized outdoor game, of any sort? I had no skills with a ball of any size or shape. My stomach clenched whenever I saw a football being tossed around. It made me physically nauseous. All the high schools I'd attended had compulsory physical education, which consisted solely of competitive sports. On the days when I had P.E., I'd vomited first thing in the morning.

I should have understood that the Nose Bowl was simply a bit of friendly outdoor running around. Instead, I'd retreated to a little room used for storage off LB's studio, where I'd set the typewriter on a tiny desk. As I tried to write a thank-you in German to DGG's Jobst Eberhardt, a loud cheer from the lawn outside rattled me. LB opened the door a couple inches, saw me huddled over the typewriter, and said, "Look at how scared you are!" I looked at him in a panic and went back to typing. I was never more grateful than when he closed the door and left me alone for the rest of the afternoon.

As it turned out, that cheer I heard was for the Nose Bowl's most accomplished and graceful athlete, Betty Comden, when she made the winning touchdown.

⁓

THE PHOTOS THAT Henry Grossman had taken of the *Tristan und Isolde* presentation landed on LB's desk, awaiting his say whether they could be used for publicity. LB set one photo aside as particularly useless, and when I saw it, I blurted, "But it makes you look so vulnerable." What did I know about publicity?

And what did he know about my nickname? Somehow it morphed into "Chasito." But he was right about one thing: vulnerability.

During his days in the city, LB scheduled visits from Helen Coates. Having been his first serious piano teacher fifty years previously, Helen knew LB better than anyone except his mother. After LB's Philharmonic debut in 1943, Helen gave up her teaching career to be LB's secretary and business manager, but by 1982 she had surrendered almost all her responsibilities except invitations and fan mail.

LB received about a dozen invitations every week—the gravy on a celebrity's plate. On some of them, LB wrote "A/C" as shorthand for "accept and cancel." He understood that his name on a guest list created a buzz, so he'd lend his name but not always his presence. Then it was up to Helen to call slightly before the event with the Maestro's regrets: the "cancel" half of "A/C." As for fan mail, an envelope vaguely addressed to "Leonard Bernstein, New York" might go first to the Philharmonic but eventually would find its way to Helen's desk.

For Chasito who really understands vulnerability.
Affectionately, LB

She also maintained the repository of awards, photographs, manuscripts, and recordings in the small apartment on the second floor of the Osborne, an historic building diagonally opposite Carnegie Hall. Returning from overseas, I'd drop in at her apartment on the Osborne's ninth floor and deliver bundles of newspaper reviews and mail for her to file. In her schoolmarmish way, she was all business and never permitted me to take a seat or stay long.

To her credit, Helen never threw anything out—except the invitation to the composer David Diamond's 70th birthday concert (no A/C scrawled on that one). Mr. Diamond had personalized the card to LB with an endearing note, and Helen angrily ripped it to shreds. Later, she told me she had organized a fund for David Diamond's psychotherapy during his early years of depression. "He never thanked anybody," she said. "I spent a lot of time contacting people, going to the bank, keeping that account in good order." Besides, in her opinion, "The therapy didn't do the slightest bit of good."

Helen habitually produced a clucking noise when she made an emphatic point. Ripping up that invitation from David Diamond brought on a cadenza of cacophonous clucking.

LB and Harry Kraut each shared with me a sorry detail of Helen's professional behavior. For two decades, she had been invited to a monthly business lunch by the secretaries to the directors of New York City's major musical entities: the Metropolitan Opera, New York Philharmonic, New York City Opera, City Ballet, and Carnegie Hall. In the days before faxes and e-mail, their off-the-record chats served a purpose.

Helen never attended. Of course, she never said why.

Sometimes LB's friends and colleagues asked me why LB stuck with a secretary so out of the loop and subject to irrational fits. The more trusting colleagues added an aside about Harry Kraut's duplicity and penchant for sowing chaos. To reach LB, an outsider had to thread a path between these two captious creatures. Why?

As a true musician, Helen must have been an inspired teacher and foreseen the career LB would achieve. LB never forgot that. Harry, though he could read music, admitted he had no musical memory. His management of LB's life seemed blatantly self-serving as he manipulated LB's prestige into a bartering chip in contract negotiations. But LB knew they handled his career in ways he could never manage on his own. Say, opening a hundred pieces of mail every day or fine-tuning a recording contract. The forbidding quality of the Helen-Harry barrier? That came with the territory.

Leonard Bernstein and Helen Coates in LB's old studio in the Osborne, Apartment 2 DD, 205 West 57 Street, New York City.

In December 1982, two dozen Christmas cards arrived every day, and the kitchen doorbell rang constantly as presents got trundled off the service elevator—a huge crate of Jaffa oranges from Zubin Mehta in Israel and chocolates from fans in Germany. I doggedly logged all the names and addresses for Helen's files.

LB picked one of his 1982 recordings to give to his closest friends, and Deutsche Grammophon delivered over a hundred copies to Helen's apartment. In her nearly indecipherable scrawl, she addressed several dozen manila envelopes. "Charles," Helen said on the phone in her most officious tone, "you will deliver these next week." I knew not to suggest a delivery service. Besides, what else did I have to do?

A few addresses I couldn't decipher at all, but the rest I organized into Manhattan neighborhoods, and for two days I drove the Buick station wagon around the city while a helper dashed into lobbies and handed LPs to doormen, somewhat like a city kid's idea of Santa Claus in a *New Yorker* satire, minus the reindeer in front of the car.

The indecipherable addresses I took home, where I puzzled over Helen's runic loops until they triggered a hunch. The next day, I nailed the solution in the massive Rolodexes on my desk. By early January, I'd delivered all the LPs.

IN LATE DECEMBER, composer-conductor, protégé, and friend Michael Tilson Thomas celebrated his 38th birthday with a quiet party at his apartment on East 10th Street, where I happily connected with many people I'd met in my first year as LB's assistant. After a few hours, I reminded LB that he'd been invited to another party that night, hosted by his opera librettist Stephen Wadsworth on the same street just two blocks west. The town car waited at the curb, but LB said, "It's such a fine night, let's walk." He asked Stephen Sondheim to join us as I led the way to 19 West 10th Street.

Mr. Sondheim extended his hand and introduced himself. "I'm Stephen Sondheim," he said affably. I was flattered, but LB got as flustered as comic actor Edward Everett Horton in his fussiest role—with a tinge of Margaret Dumont's grandiosity from the goofiest Marx Brothers sketch. "Oh, I'm sorry, I thought you'd met," LB blustered. "No, really," LB continued, wallowing in his measured capacity for not introducing people to one another. At least he didn't treat me as a joke, as in the Dakota courtyard when he introduced me to Lauren Bacall as, "My new assistant, Charles Manson." (Thanks, Maestro.)

At Stephen Wadsworth's apartment, a boisterous party turned to dead silence as I ushered Leonard Bernstein and Stephen Sondheim into a cozy gathering of aspiring singers. Stephen Wadsworth took over with introductions, after chiding me in a quick aside, "How could you do this? Wrecking my party by bringing

Lenny and Sondheim?" Gee, I thought I was doing him a favor. Stephen still regarded me as the low-level assistant in Indiana, the fetcher of font balls for his typewriter.

Not much interested in what happened next, I walked home, after I made sure the town car waited in front of the right address.

The week before Christmas, the Bernsteins hadn't decided whether to stay in the city or go to Connecticut, but there had to be a tree in the Dakota living room. "Call the florist on Columbus Avenue," Ann Dedman suggested. Only one tree remained that could live up to the seventeen-foot ceiling. That tree plus the delivery charge equaled my weekly salary and disrupted my paltry cash flow for quite a while.

Julia helped me move furniture and we retrieved boxes of ornaments from a remote closet. After a family day of tree-decorating, the biggest indoor tree I'd ever seen looked glorious.

The next day, the Bernsteins decamped for Connecticut. I called Julia.

"What happens now?" I asked.

She replied in her typically explicit way, "The decorations go in the boxes, and you cut the tree into little, little sticks. You find garbage bags in the laundry room, and when you fill the bags, you take them to the basement."

The living room had to be cleared because LB's daughter Nina had planned a New Year's party for a few friends, which turned into over three hundred Harvard undergrads crashing her guest list. I found Julia's tiny garden shears, suitable for a potted avocado plant, and went to work on the nearly seventeen-foot tree.

The dismantling took all day and the clippers gave me blisters. Who could help me? Everybody I knew had holiday plans. As usual, I did what was expected of me, wasting an entire day. At least I got reimbursed for the tree, later.

———

WASN'T LB WRITING AN OPERA?

———

AFTER RETURNING TO THE STATES, he hadn't written a note. Directly after Christmas, Stephen Wadsworth got himself to Connecticut, determined to make some headway. I hung around answering the phone and drove back and forth to the city every other day, picking up mail.

After a few days of intense effort, LB and Stephen wanted a break and asked me to get seats for the new Dustin Hoffman film *Tootsie*. Remembering what I learned from Adolph Green, I called the theater in Westport, where the manager said, "Oh yeah, we get this kind of request from Paul Newman all the time." I'd forgotten that Mr. Newman lived close by. When the manager showed us to our seats in the middle of a packed theater, I discreetly put a twenty-dollar bill in his hand.

The lively audience drowned out most of the dialogue with continuous waves of laughter, so Stephen suggested afterwards we go to a nearby diner and reconstruct what we'd missed. I sat across from LB and Stephen in a booth, anticipating a discussion of the movie, but I couldn't get a word in. Those two cracked jokes nonstop that only they could understand in a pretty good imitation of a newly smitten couple.

At a certain stage of collaboration, the project-at-hand infuses all the references in every conversation. LB and Stephen had arrived at that stage. Additionally, for an immersion in the suburban milieu of *A Quiet Place*, there could be no place more apt than tony Westport, Connecticut. Earlier that day, I'd overheard Stephen lampooning what he claimed an elite WASP considers a satisfying light meal, and I couldn't get it out of my head: a turkey sandwich on white toast with extra mayonnaise and a glass of milk. Even now, that's what I most enjoy the day after Thanksgiving.

As I placed my order with the waitress, the randy self-referential dialogue from the two guys opposite me came to an abrupt stop. I had just let them know that I was in on one of their jokes. In fact, I was occupying their planet, or at the least, we were sharing a booth in a diner. Stephen sputtered, "Did you overhear us . . . ?" and I nodded, "Yes." Their stunned silence made it difficult for me to keep a straight face, but I relished the whiteness of what I was eating, especially the extra mayonnaise and the milk. I felt no obligation to join in their conversation.

Even if I didn't have my own life any longer, I could carve out an occasional quiet place in the three-ring circus around Leonard Bernstein. I'd need those quiet places for myself because there were many months to go before the opera came into the world.

20 | The Two (Other) Women in Leonard Bernstein's Life

IN EARLY 1983, despite some loose ends in the schedule, the opera-to-be-written edged into LB's calendar in a casual pattern of two or three days in Connecticut followed by an overnight in the city.

On one of those overnight stays, LB saw his son, Alexander, in a play at the HB theater in Greenwich Village. At the time, Alexander was dating another HB actor, Cecilia Peck, daughter of actor Gregory Peck and his wife, Veronique Passani, so Alex invited Cecilia to Connecticut for dinner. At the round table in the living room we enjoyed an amicable dinner, but afterwards there was plenty of drama: a cut-throat intellectual slaughter masquerading as a game of anagrams.

LB decided we'd play a "half-game," won by the first player to form five words. He opened the antique tin box of anagram tiles, and we rapidly turned the hefty black squares face down on the table top. A game of anagrams at the Bernsteins started off orderly, but at the revelation of the fifth letter—the minimum word length—mayhem ruled: it was everyone's turn, all the time.

You see a word, you shout the word, you grab the tiles and position them in front of you. You lose that word when someone else adds a letter from the tiles in the center of the table to anagram your word. You think "harmonica" is safely in your possession? If an "S" turns up, anybody could shout "anachronism" and take your word. ("Harmonicas" isn't allowable because it doesn't change the word's root.) You didn't see that anagram? Stephen Sondheim saw it and played it—and the Bernsteins talked about it for decades. Anagrams with the Bernsteins were dazzling, nonstop, and emasculating.

I was doing pretty well that evening, as was Cecilia Peck. We each had four words, only one more needed for a win. LB had only three words. I don't remember Alexander's side of the table, but he was more interested in Cecilia than in anagrams.

LB ostentatiously cleared his throat. "Charlie, you haven't said anything lately about the issues you have with your father," he said in an uncompromising tone, as though I'd gone AWOL for three hundred therapy sessions. My concentration went down the drain and LB won the game, though he congratulated Cecilia for doing so well.

Back in the city, LB underwent a lengthy root canal procedure, taking Perco-cet for the pain, swallowed with a shot of Ballantine's scotch.

"It's like floating six feet above the ground," he said.

"You'll be six feet underground if you keep up that combo," I said, trying to sound severe.

LB sang:

Marche funèbre

Where will we be in a hun - dred years from now?

On cue, I sang the next line of Chopin's funeral march, "Pushing up the daisies, pushing up the daisies."

What is mortality? A jest.

At the end of January, Hans Weber, chief of the Deutsche Grammophon (DGG) crew, brought a trunk of tapes from Germany for an approval session. (CDs were rumored to exist in Europe, but hadn't yet made it to the USA.) Normally those sessions happened on the road, but with no travel for a while, LB had to slot a lis-tening day in Connecticut: seven works by Brahms, and all the American works recorded the previous summer, a baker's dozen.

LB got through half the tapes in one afternoon. It was a lot of listening. At the dinner break, LB launched into a tirade on how much of his time was taken up in recording projects just to pay the bills. Alexander Bernstein picked up on the busi-ness aspect and observed that LB was the employee of a family-run corporation—not what LB wanted to hear. Angry and hurt, he threw a dinner roll at Alexander and stalked back to his studio, where the listening sessions continued through the night.

One interruption lightened the mood. In the Brahms Symphony No. 4, LB and Hans Weber distinctly heard an insistent triangle at the wrong moment. Annoyed, Herr Weber exclaimed, "I spliced this myself!" and stopped the tape. The ringing continued; it was the telephone on LB's desk, sounding exactly like a triangle. LB's sister, Shirley, had a question about that week's crossword puzzle in *The Guardian*, a perfectly legitimate phone call for LB at that late hour. LB said he'd call her back, because there were still a few works to go in the listening session. That phone-as-triangle still gets a laugh in the DGG offices.

Meanwhile, Houston Grand Opera hired Peter Mark Schifter to direct the new opera, though his credentials in television soaps didn't impress Stephen Wadsworth. I continued to make photocopies for two pianists and an ever-expanding roster of singers, and Stephen scheduled workshops. My biggest headaches were keeping enough cash on hand to pay everybody (ATMs existed, but not yet for my bank branch near the Dakota) and keeping family and friends posted so they could drop in and listen.

But a bigger headache loomed. During her brief vacation in the Caribbean, Ann Dedman ate an improperly prepared fish, probably a pufferfish. Back in New York a week later, she had a very rough time. She couldn't really grip anything with her hands. I caught her mopping the kitchen floor by side-swiping her legs with paper towels fastened under her feet. With the schedule ramping up to the opera premiere, Ann had no time to recuperate, though she wanted to stay busy and not feel sorry for herself.

Then Harry Kraut obliterated Ann's last shred of morale. He knew that Port Arthur, Texas, not far from Houston, was Ann's hometown. She planned to entertain in a big Texan way during our month at Houston Grand Opera. But Harry decided we'd stay in a hotel, not a house. "Tell Ann her services won't be needed," Harry instructed me bluntly.

I'd never done Harry's dirty work before. Ann's eyes filled with tears as I broke the news to her. We both had looked forward to recapping our weeks in Milano and Los Angeles. Harry's excluding her from Houston denigrated her professional skills. It made me feel disloyal, too, as if I had to choose sides. Of course Harry's side always won: he signed the checks.

Soon afterward, Ann said she would continue as LB's chef through the August stint in Tanglewood, but those two weeks would be her last. LB never knew what emotions she had to suppress. Harry finagled a similar telling off with me two years later, when he flushed me away as so much effluvia, a true "toilet paper job" moment. I had no one to console me then; I should have called Ann. Those moments of humiliation stick with you forever.

Snow fell heavily the afternoon of February 11, but the surprise party for Schuyler Chapin's 60th birthday went on as planned at the Century Club in Midtown Manhattan. LB couldn't miss it. Definitely not an "A/C" event. Schuyler had once been LB's record producer at Columbia and his business manager before Harry Kraut. Schuyler had held several positions central to the arts in New York: vice president of Lincoln Center, general manager of the Metropolitan Opera, dean of the Columbia University School of Arts. At LB's death, Schuyler was one of three executors of the Bernstein estate. At the same time, he was named cultural affairs commissioner of New York City by Mayor Rudolph Giuliani. Schuyler's kindness and decorum endeared him to everyone he met and added luster to his many accomplishments.

The temperature dropped that evening and snow accumulated quickly. I went home early, not long after LB left for the party in the hired car. Mid-morning the next day, I was surprised to find LB up and very lively.

"Go to the Olcott next door and pay the bill for a couple who checked in last night," he said. Who would stay at the shabby, bug-infested Olcott, the most decrepit building on West 72nd Street?

"When I left Schuyler's party, I found my driver weeping in the lobby of the Century Club," LB said, somewhat breathlessly. "He kept the engine running to stay warm in the car and it ran out of gas. Poor guy, he didn't know what to do. I gave him some cash so he could go home and I walked to Sixth Avenue to hail a taxi, but the streets hadn't been plowed and there was no traffic, so I waved at the first car I saw."

My hair stood on end. Hitch-hiking alone in a blizzard? The middle of the night? Had he been robbed? Where was this story going?

"What time was this?" I asked, more than merely curious.

"Around one or two," LB said. "I got in the back seat and told the couple where I wanted to go, but they had no idea where they were. They were looking for a hotel to spend the night. They said something like 'Hotel Baffy,' but they were unintelligible."

The more LB told me about this couple, the queasier I got. They sounded pretty savvy at getting lost in blizzards.

"When we got to 72nd Street, I got them a room at the Olcott," LB said. "The bill has to be paid by noon. They're probably ready now to drive back to Boston."

"You know, Maestro," I said, inserting the honorific for emphasis, "the Century Club has a staff and a phone. Someone there would have called a taxi. You're very lucky you weren't robbed and dumped in the Bronx."

The Olcott's manager said the vagabond couple liked their room and wanted to stay a few days. It must have been many rungs higher than the Hotel Baffy. I paid for one night, and said it was up to the hotel to get them out of there. At the Dakota office, I alerted Miss Winnie at the desk: do not allow these people upstairs. Sure enough, the couple showed up a little later, begging to see their new friend in Apartment 23, a message I didn't pass to LB. I was afraid he'd run into them if he went out, but LB didn't leave the apartment that day. He certainly trusted in a benign universe. Julia's phrase, "He go with God," echoed in my head all day.

Mid-February, LB and Stephen Wadsworth completed another scene of the opera, which I distributed for another workshop. LB itched to go to Connecticut, so we drove up late and headed back to the city the next afternoon so LB could see his son, Alexander, in another play at the HB Theatre on Bank Street.

February 23 was sunny but cold and very still, a manifestation of the "quiet, the heavenly quiet" praised by the singers in *Trouble in Tahiti*, LB's opera about an unquiet suburban family (and the source for *A Quiet Place*). The same musical phrase about the blissful quiet gets recapped in the final act of *A Quiet Place*, sung not by the cast onstage but by an offstage chorus. When LB reached that scene, he handed me his manuscript and asked me to fill in the chorus staves. "You know what I want here," he said, "Or look at the passage in *TNT*"—his nickname for *Trouble in Tahiti*. This was new: trusting me to write in the notes myself.

I've always enjoyed being a nerd. My "fun" bookshelf that year included *Fowler's Modern English Usage* and the scores of Handel oratorios, chock full of choruses. At transcendent moments, Handel writes the tenor line up near the alto and leaves the bass out altogether, an ethereal effect. That unsupported sound aptly caught the rapture of the phrase in *A Quiet Place*, I thought.

A QUIET PLACE
ACT III

LB asked later why I had left out the basses (the staff labeled "B."). *Because it's an ethereal moment.* Satisfied with my Handelian rationalization, he let those bars stand as I wrote them.

That February afternoon, a deep chill heightened the quiet in Connecticut. I brought the Mercedes to the side door of the house and loaded the trunk as LB got behind the wheel. Gigi Cantera, the maid, got in the passenger side, and I asked LB if there was anything else.

"I forgot my gloves," he said.

Reaching up to the shelf in the foyer closet, I put my hands right on LB's nubby rawhide gloves, as big as potholders. As I closed the closet door, I heard footsteps upstairs, the slapping sound of hard-soled sandals on the bare floor in Nina's room, the bedroom over the kitchen.

There were always too many people and things to keep track of, and at that moment I couldn't add everything up. Wasn't the house empty? LB and Gigi were in the car, the two dogs and the parakeet were in the station wagon, Julia was in New York with Ann Dedman. Who was upstairs?

As I opened the door to the back stairs, I said, "Who's there?" as two legs in a grey skirt, just at the knees, walked from Nina's room onto the carpeted hallway at the top of the stairs. The change in the flooring altered the sound of the footsteps, from *rat-a-tat-tat* to a muffled drumbeat. Svelte, shapely legs, a well-tailored skirt: it was Felicia inspecting the house.

She walked purposefully towards the front bedrooms. A calm reverence came over me. Something was being confided to me, even more trusting than LB asking me to score two bars for the chorus in his opera. Seeing Felicia was like being in a room already occupied by a couple who were very much in love, but unaware anyone was there with them.

I quietly shut the door to the stairs and went out to the driveway. Only a minute had passed since I'd left LB there. I said, "I'll see you in the city," as I handed his gloves through his open window. After he drove off, I sat in the station wagon a minute, peering up at the windows of Shirley's room, which had once been Felicia's. I didn't expect to see anything. I thought about all the times I'd seen departed people, dogs, a few cats—never spooky, but inexplicable, and always a surprise. *Hearing* Felicia before seeing her—that was a first.

I couldn't wait to speak to Julia, so I was grateful to find her sitting at the kitchen table when I entered the Dakota apartment. Even before I placed Gaucho's birdcage on the countertop, I said, "Guess what I saw," and without missing a beat, Julia said, "And what was she wearing?"

I said, "A grey dress and summer sandals," and Julia, slightly ahead of her cue, remarked, "I see that many times." The grey outfit? Yes, but she also meant the vision of Felicia inspecting the house. Julia, as imperturbable as bedrock, made me understand it was no big deal to see Felicia. Still, I needed a crutch. "May I make two pisco sours?" I asked. She chuckled. "Of course." When Julia was amused, her "of course" made an upward leap of an entire octave.

Julia and I talked for quite a while because LB arrived very late. As I helped him get dressed to go to Alexander's play, he said, "I ran the car into a construction barrier on the Cross-County, and the front of the car gouged into the tire. I found a gas station where some guys unbent the metal a little. You'll have to take it in to be fixed."

"But you're okay?" I said.

"Gigi's a little flustered, but she tried not to show it. The guys at the gas station kept calling me Maestroy. 'Yeah, we'll fix it for you, Maestroy.' I had to put the bill on my credit card," LB said.

Another thing for me to look after.

The governor of New York had presented Zubin Mehta with the license plate MAESTRO, but an observant aide in the governor's office noticed a name printed above Maestro Mehta's on every Philharmonic program: the Laureate Conductor, Leonard Bernstein. The governor hurriedly ordered a MAESTRO1 license plate for LB. Most people read the number "one" as the letter "I."

LB was so busy telling me what happened, I forgot to say anything about seeing Felicia. After he left for the evening, I made another pisco sour, for Gigi.

On a beautiful spring day many weeks later, traffic slowed to a complete stop on the Merritt Parkway. LB could legitimately take his eyes off the road, so he looked at me and asked, out of the blue, "What did you feel when you saw her?"

I knew he would ask someday, but I was taken by surprise and had to think for a moment. I said, "I was being shown a great love—her love for the house and also her love for her family."

After a pause, LB said, "I'd give anything to see her." He gripped the steering wheel more tightly. "Just once."

Julia had confided in Nina what I'd said about seeing Felicia that February afternoon, and Nina had told her father. But it disturbed me that LB had had an accident that same afternoon I saw Felicia. I couldn't shake an ominous hunch that those two events were somehow connected.

At the end of February, I brought Julia a blooming azalea for her birthday, her one hundred and twenty-sixth, she claimed. My bond with Julia deepened with each year and azaleas became a birthday tradition. Julia knew just what to do with them. All told, we planted twelve in a shady area of the Connecticut garden.

For several weeks, I drove from Connecticut into the city almost every day, distributing scenes from *A Quiet Place* to an ever-expanding cast. When LB's friends who'd attended a workshop called, I wrote down their comments, such as from the composer Lukas Foss: "LB invented a new vernacular American opera, a recitativo style as important as Wagner's 'through-composed style.'" Exactly what LB and Stephen were trying to do.

How far could this vernacular go? LB and Stephen argued for a week about the word *fuck*. Houston, Texas, for all its sophistication and wealth, is securely buckled in America's Bible Belt, and when the character Dede says to her brother, "It's *not* fuckin' Christmas," there would be shock waves.

Stephen Wadsworth and Leonard Bernstein in 1982.

After LB and Stephen had spent the day delving into the misaligned family at the center of *A Quiet Place*, I'd drive Stephen to the train station for his return to the city and go straight back to the house to take the five o'clock ice bucket to LB's studio. Sometimes LB wanted to talk about the soul-searching that he and Stephen put themselves through that day. *A Quiet Place* explores the emotions of a compact family bound up in loss, as well as delusional ambition, sexual identity, and the mechanics of avoidance. To reach the emotions of an audience, the authors must scrape their own emotional membranes to the bone and forge what was personal into a universal drama.

This exploration of LB's loss of Felicia, Stephen's loss of a beloved sister in a car crash, and the ensuing psychological repair lit LB's creative fire, possibly pushing LB further than any previous collaboration. In a way, LB and Stephen morphed into a self-help group of two. They opened up to one another ever more honestly, and worked through a winter of introspection toward a springtime resolution, their combined vision flowering in an opera. In *Trouble in Tahiti*, the character Dinah dreams of a garden. In the last act of *A Quiet Place*, Dinah's family seeks comfort in the garden that she'd made real.

———

LB INVITED TWENTY PEOPLE for Passover in 1983. The day before, after cancelling the opera workshop on the afternoon of the Seder, he said, "Call for a car to take you to the airport to meet my mother." Jennie Bernstein's flight landed at Newark at 10 A.M., so I had the limo pick me up at home. My landlord noticed that I'd gone up in the world.

As the first person off the plane, Jennie was all business. "Where's the wheel-chair? Let's get my luggage. Is there a car?" A few minutes later, seated in the back of the limo, she wanted to talk.

"Charlie, what is it you want to do?" she asked.

I already had a job that took up all my time. I even enjoyed most of my cart-load of responsibilities. I hadn't thought about wanting to do anything else in the near future, but I remembered a fantasy from my student years.

"I'd like to write music for the theater," I said. I hadn't thought about this since I graduated from college ten years ago.

She digested this for a few seconds. "How are you going to do that?" she asked.

"I don't have a plan," I said, "but there are few basic steps I could take."

"Are you taking those steps?" she asked without a pause.

"Well, no," I said, feeling pretty deflated.

Placing her hand firmly on mine, she said with the clarity of a sweetly sono-rous shofar from a mountaintop, "You'll never know till you try."

I glanced at the industrial landscape of New Jersey, where all hope seemed to have been abandoned generations ago. I thought of the incongruity of us two in a luxury limo—a Russian immigrant grandmother next to a feckless, over-educated, and lazy gay man—talking about ambition. What was mine, compared to hers? She'd never finished school, working instead in the grim mills of Law-rence, Massachusetts. Yet her optimism, her ambition for something better, never left her. I looked at her face, her extraordinarily bright eyes. In her sagacious curi-osity, there was an inextinguishable hope, encased in kindness.

Jennie's adoration of LB beamed on him like sunshine his entire life. Such nurture, such steadfast encouragement. What a difference one supportive person's love makes in the life of another. While Jennie and I talked through the rest of the car trip into Manhattan, I wondered how to ask LB about his mother's crucial bit of counsel: *You'll never know till you try.* How often had he heard her say that?

After everyone had gathered in the apartment that evening, LB surprised his mother with a song he'd written for her 85th birthday. As the star of this family, LB enlisted his three offspring and his two siblings, assigning them each a verse. I'd typed up his final draft and distributed copies as family members arrived in advance of a brief rehearsal in LB's studio. Shirley seemed apprehensive. It wasn't easy for her to perform for her mother, especially as a sidekick to her stage-hogging older brother, LB. As everyone gathered in the living room, Phyllis Newman cried out, "Oh! Look at the moon!" The fully ripened Passover moon lodged itself smack in the middle of the window behind the piano. In a mock-scolding voice, LB said, "What a Phyllis thing to say!" and everyone laughed. That brushed away the nerves and the performance began with LB singing first.

Grandma Song
LB: Jennie dear, you're eighty-five.
Year by year, you grow more live.
Classy, sassy,
That's my Jennie
Righter, brighter
Than any penny.
Love from . . . Lenny.

A few days later, I recorded another performance in the living room, similarly bluesy music but on a radically different subject. Harvard's male vocal ensemble, the Krokodiloes, showed up at the cocktail hour to perform "Screwed on Wrong," an a cappella number LB had written for the Kroks in 1980. The chromatic harmonies and punchy off-beats proved so difficult that several years went by before the group felt secure enough to perform it. Maybe the annual turnover in this group of Harvard undergrads extended their learning curve, but the Kroks of 1983 felt ready to sing this number for the composer.

I recorded the entire hour as these talented lads sang the number once and then absorbed LB's expert, if colorful, coaching. He gestured expansively with his outstretched arms, asking them to imagine that the rhythm, "like all jazz, is in one," meaning one big beat to each bar. "It's like fucking," LB said.

The Kroks whooped with laughter and gallantly sang the number three more times, each rendition more secure in pitch yet more free in rhythm (within that one big beat per bar). As an encore, they threw in "Sophisticated Lady," and then LB had to depart for a four-hour opera workshop.

It didn't occur to me to turn on the tape recorder for a follow-up conversation with LB's mother, Jennie, but her voice remains strong and clear in my ear: "You'll never know till you try."

21 | A Quiet Place in a Noisy, Noisy World

BY LATE MARCH 1983—less than three months before the premiere of his opera *A Quiet Place*—LB realized he needed somebody else to tackle the orchestration, the actual writing of every note that the orchestra would play. He called the one colleague who could manage it brilliantly: Sid Ramin, credited with seemingly a hundred Broadway orchestrations, including the credit shared with Irwin Kostal for *West Side Story*.

LB and Sid had met as teenagers in Massachusetts and remained friends ever after. Sid said he was in awe of LB from the start. They both remembered the day a typewriter appeared at a friend's house. Everybody pecked shyly at the machine until LB waltzed in, took one look at the layout of the keys, and began typing like a pro.

Sid spoke with a precision that perfectly illustrated why LB was so fond of him. Simply put, Sid never put a note wrong, though he claimed his only lessons in orchestration came from LB and working alongside Irwin Kostal, whom he called to help him out with *A Quiet Place*. In the next few weeks, I learned more watching Sid and Irv at work than in all my previous years of musical study. I regard Sid as a true mentor, and with his wife, Gloria, among my most trusted friends.

As with the orchestration of *West Side Story* twenty-six years previously, LB reviewed each page of his manuscript of *A Quiet Place* with Sid and Irv: here's where the percussion takes over, these chords should be brassy, but keep the rhythm clear. A few days later, Sid and Irv returned with a sheaf of oversize orchestral pages for LB to evaluate. The score progressed swiftly. Not only were Sid and Irv the best in the business, they knew the sonic vocabulary of LB's mind. When LB completed the instrumental interludes at the last moment in Houston and orchestrated those passages himself, the integrity of the sound remained seamless.

In the middle of this upbeat spell, an advance copy of the May issue of *Harper's* magazine arrived by special delivery. LB subscribed to *Harper's* and *The Atlantic Monthly* specifically for the notoriously cryptic puzzles. Why this extra copy?

Featured on the cover, an essay promised to reveal "The Tragedy of Leonard Bernstein" as divined by Leon Botstein, president of Bard College and an aspiring conductor (he eventually became music director of the American Symphony Orchestra). The *Harper's* essay set an impossibly high expectation for the new opera, as Botstein griped that LB never focused his skills to achieve the Great American Work, of which he was so clearly capable. Unfortunately, Botstein's critique came across as a personal grudge. Was he miffed at not being invited to the workshops for *A Quiet Place*? LB thought it was less than that, musing, "Hmm, wants to be a conductor and his initials are L. B."

LB decided the thing to do was to write a note to *Harper's*, to thank the publisher for the extra copy of the May issue because the puzzle—the real reason why LB subscribed—was an especially good one that month. Now he could share that puzzle with a friend. Yours sincerely, Leonard Bernstein.

Essay? What essay?

The upbeat mood continued through a two-night excursion to Winston-Salem, North Carolina, for the dedication of the renovated theater at the North Carolina School of the Arts (NCSA) as the Roger L. Stevens Center for the Performing Arts. With Harry Kraut away on a global junket of his own, only Maggie Carson accompanied LB and me. Maggie cagily noted how simple these short trips could be when Harry wasn't around to muck things up.

After a day of rehearsals, LB led off the gala evening honoring Roger Stevens by conducting the NCSA students in the *Overture to "Candide."* I stood in the wings with a tumbler of water and LB's cigarette, and was stunned to find myself between the actor Gregory Peck and the former First Lady, Lady Bird Johnson. They were the hosts of this gala. When I told Julia Vega later that I had met those two extraordinarily noble people, she sighed like a heartsick teenager, "Mr. Gregory Peck, he is such a *hann*-son man!"

As we left the theater for the gala dinner, Isaac Stern asked if I was going to the hotel first, and handed me his violin. I must have looked stunned, because he chuckled and said he'd pick it up later, if that was all right. His gesture lifted me to a level where "the toilet paper job" had no meaning. Thank you, Mr. Stern.

The NCSA students besieged LB with questions, but where could we all go for a drink? Nowhere in that dry county of North Carolina, not even the hotel bar, and I hadn't brought a bottle of Ballantine's. It hadn't occurred to me to research the local liquor laws before packing. One enterprising student volunteered to drive to the next county and bring back some scotch. Hired! I handed him a wad of cash. Two dozen students followed LB to his hotel suite and arranged themselves on the floor in front of him. These sessions could be numbingly dull if LB got stuck on himself or on radical politics. Now, I'd give my right arm to hear him rant. But the kids at NCSA were exceptional: balanced, generous, and eager to listen to one another. For once, LB didn't dominate but carried on a spirited symposium. These kids possessed well-rounded minds.

With a genuine, mutual affection in the air, LB kept the discussion going until four in the morning. Then he drew it to a close with a rendition of "P.S. I Love You," a 1930s song by Gordon Jenkins and Johnny Mercer. As usual, LB skipped the first verse.

Dear, I thought I'd drop a line.
The weather's cool. The folks are fine.
I'm in bed each night at nine.
P.S. I love you.

Yesterday we had some rain,
but all in all I can't complain.
Was it dusty on the train?
P.S. I love you.

In her room down the hall, Maggie Carson must have tossed and turned. She'd begged me for months to record LB singing her favorite song. I decided not to wake her.

BACK IN NEW YORK, the circus came to town! The Saturday show was a benefit for the Gay Men's Health Crisis (GMHC), an organization that offered assistance to anyone diagnosed with AIDS, which had rapidly become an epidemic. In New York and California, AIDS decimated the population in the arts. GMHC tried to address the gaps in health care, public awareness, and fund-raising, but AIDS carried the stigma of a "gay disease." There was almost no public discussion and not much serious medical research. LB understood that fund-raising was critical, but very few celebrities participated in AIDS-related publicity at that time. It was a big deal when LB conducted the circus band to open the benefit as Shirley Verrett sang the "Star-Spangled Banner."

I handled ticket requests from LB's circle of friends; Betty Comden and Lauren Bacall were the first to ask. Well before her son's death from AIDS complications, Betty Comden volunteered tirelessly for AIDS relief organizations around the city. She and Lauren Bacall knew they'd be recognized by the star-struck benefit patrons that night, the largest gathering of gay men and women that year.

After the performance, the animal-tamers Siegfried and Roy escorted us alongside the cages of their ferocious show-biz beasts. Strapping athletes strutted around, flashing their sequins. Not the usual post-concert backstage scene. The circus performers said they'd never played to such a responsive audience, but of course, it was a crowd supremely appreciative of spangles and tights.

DURING MY NIGHTS AT LB's house in Connecticut, I slept in a bedroom off LB's studio, accessible through a modest utilitarian bathroom or by a door that opened to the driveway. With both bathroom doors closed, I couldn't hear LB at his piano in the studio, and I usually stayed up late reading in bed, the only hours I had for myself.

When LB composed, he sat at his desk or the piano, or stood at a slanted working surface, a long desk where he could write on several pages laid next to one another. (This furniture is now at the Jacobs School of Music at Indiana University, where LB's studio is being recreated for public display.) Sometimes LB stretched out on the sofa with his eyes closed and replayed music in his head. Julia remembered warning Nina, the youngest sibling, "Do not disturb your daddy on the sofa, he is not a-sleeping, he is working," but Nina insisted, "Daddy's taking a nap. That is not the same as working."

One corner of LB's Connecticut studio in 1990. The stand-up desk is at center, with a recently added drafting board and swivel stool. The four-legged stool at right was a gift from the Vienna Philharmonic, but its squeaks kept LB from using it during rehearsals. Inked under its seat are the letters "GM"—Gustav Mahler.

Composing music is largely an abstract mental procedure for anyone who has learned how to manipulate purely musical thoughts. LB supplemented that thinking with hours at the piano, playing chords and harmonies while reading from his sketches—to anyone else, mere random patches of sound. LB's most intense musical thinking hatched during those hours, and sometimes the notes came together in unanticipated ways, the "note that costs" always the goal.

One night in the bedroom off LB's studio, I was sitting up completely absorbed in a good book, a single table lamp on, oblivious to the late hour or anything else going on in the world. Around 3 A.M., I heard a timid knock on the door from the bathroom. LB shyly cracked open the door.

"I saw your light on, so I thought you were awake," he said. He sounded so hesitant. Was there a problem in the studio? A burned-out light bulb, firewood all gone?

"I need two more hands to play the piece I just finished," he said, still sounding apologetic. "Could you help me?"

I put on a bathrobe and padded into the studio. Several pages lay splayed across the piano's music rack. Neatly copied notes ran in sequence from one page to the next. LB sat down at the treble part of the keyboard and I drew up a chair at the bass. As we looked at the music, he explained which lines I should play in a complicated imitative passage scrawled across several staves—his usual short score notation.

He gave a downbeat, occasionally conducting with his left hand when I lost the underlying beat, and we played what eventually became the "Prelude to Act III" in the finished opera. I'd never done this before with a composer, play through a piece only minutes old. What a serious—and extraordinary—assignment, the deepest I'd ever ventured into LB's creative domain. Stepping across an invisible threshold into his musical thinking, I calmly surrendered to the Zen-like focus of another psyche.

I recognized all the musical motifs, but the new combinations took me by surprise. I stumbled through the concise development passage, so we played the entire "Prelude" again.

This time, I asked a few questions. Would the sparky "Little White House" phrase sound clearly? There was an awful lot of counterpoint crammed into a few bars.

"Yes, that's my concern," LB said. "Whether the imitation is clear."

"I think the climax is too brief," I said, indicating the passage where I stumbled.

"Trust me," LB said. "The proportions are fine."

"I don't remember what comes after this," I said. In the middle of the night, my memory of the opera hadn't switched on.

"Dede's aria," LB said, croaking, "Morning! Good Morning," in a voice like the balky ignition of an old car.

One sequence puzzled me, so I steeled my nerve and asked, "Is this what you really want?"

He took my question seriously and explained the underlying harmonic progression, out of which he'd constructed his melodic instrumental lines. LB's harmonic language always had a richness to it, though in his short score he wrote only the necessary notes, nothing extra. Imagine the lushest jazz chords as simple as a hymn in four-part harmony.

What an inspired illumination, that last response of his. Could I explain that passage now as he did then? Not likely.

We played through the "Prelude" one more time, talking only a little over our playing, and then played it once more, carefully and securely, without saying anything. The music was right. He hadn't changed a note. LB said he was satisfied. It held together, it had the right balance of harmonic drama and counterpoint, and its shape was right for that moment in the opera.

I didn't know how crucial this moment would be.

By 1983, I'd had a remarkable education. I'd talked with LB after he'd conducted his own works. I'd seen him alter his early works, say, by adding staccato dots to woodwind passages when the accompanying strings played pizzicato, or making sure he'd written dynamics both before and after a crescendo. Incomparably articulate, LB easily explained every detail of his musical thoughts, although at first his choices might not appear straightforward. The range of options from his original musical thoughts stayed with him even after years of performances. "Why did I write it this way?" he sometimes asked in the middle of a rehearsal.

To play through the "Prelude to Act III" that night may have helped narrow his thinking, to focus on one musical path. To answer my questions was, maybe, like defending a thesis, clarifying an argument. He certainly showed me how the notes go together, though I'd always written music in a similar way. First, imagine the music in your head, then play it again and again—mentally, or on your preferred instrument—until it's exactly what you want. Then write it down.

That night, oblivious to the rest of the wide world's noise, I immersed myself in one hour of intense musical study with a master, in a room off a quiet country road.

ONE GORGEOUS SPRING DAY in Connecticut, Stephen Wadsworth looked up from the script in front of him and saw a woman in the garden. She wore a straw hat, but he couldn't see her face. Later he asked Jamie and Nina about the mystery gardener, and they showed him their mother's straw hat, still in the front coat closet. That was the hat. So Felicia appeared to Stephen, too. Jamie, Alexander, and Nina later gave their mother's straw hat to Stephen as an affectionate opening-night present.

With only one more workshop, a five-hour session partly covered by a crew from CBS news, the pressure was on. All my attention focused on the opera premiere a month away. Friends of LB's requested hotel rooms in Houston and asked to be put on a list for tickets.

One week before Memorial Day, a van picked up me and the usual fifteen pieces of luggage at the Dakota, drove a few blocks south to get Harry Kraut and his two bags, and took us to La Guardia. LB traveled the next day with Maggie Carson and Jack Gottlieb. In Houston, Harry and I immediately headed to the rehearsal hall to take the conductor John DeMain out for dinner. John had a thorough grip on the rehearsals, but he looked tired and disarmingly pale and thin.

What did I know about the stamina required to premiere an opera? After a month in Houston, we all looked pale and tired.

The piano in LB's Connecticut studio. At rear, Grammys and Emmys fill the top shelves.

22 | Houston "Grand" Opera

THE PAGES IN MY DATEBOOK at the end of May 1983 filled up quickly with the names for contacts at Houston Grand Opera and room numbers at the Four Seasons hotel for LB's retinue. My first day in Houston, I found a dentist for LB, a masseur, a replacement electric shaver, and for me, the local YMCA, where I actually got some fitful exercise. Amid so much peripheral information in my datebook, I drew boxes around the rehearsal sessions to make them stand out from the scribbled chaos.

The trail-blazing first female mayor of Houston, Kathryn Whitmire, welcomed LB to her city, plopping a ten-gallon Stetson on LB's head to certify that the Maestro had arrived in Texas. LB never wore a hat, but I'd stealthily estimated LB's hat size by getting him to try on a hat of my own. Mayor Whitmire's Stetson fit perfectly.

The opera company's donors sponsored a fancy lunch after the welcome ceremony, in the First City National Bank dining room. I'd written "skywriters" under "$150K" in my datebook—probably the bank's donation to the production of *A Quiet Place*. LB marveled later about Houston Grand Opera's fund-raising. During dinner at Lynn Wyatt's house, LB thought he was making table talk, speaking about his and Stephen Wadsworth's attempt to put the American vernacular onto the operatic stage. But the women on either side of him retrieved checkbooks from their purses and—he said this happened simultaneously—each wrote a check to Houston Grand Opera for $50,000.

When he told me this later, he asked, "Who keeps that much cash in a checking account?"

"This is Texas," I said.

The first orchestra rehearsal started at ten the next morning with *Trouble in Tahiti*, now the first half of an operatic evening called *A Quiet Place*—after an intermission, the new opera would be performed as a separate work. With two breaks that day, rehearsals lasted through the next twelve hours.

Musicians call a disastrous rehearsal a "train wreck." When an angry percussionist pushed over the buffet-size marimba, it sure sounded like boxcars flying off the rails. Wooden slats clattered to the floor and brought the rehearsal to a stop. Why was this percussionist so crazed? Parts had been copied and delivered according to the Houston Grand Opera's schedule. At dinner that evening, LB led a discussion on whether Houston Grand Opera's orchestra had the capability to learn this music over the next three weeks. Based on what we'd heard that day, Jack Gottlieb and Harry Kraut expressed their doubts. LB said the rehearsals had to go forward, no matter what.

Against LB's wishes, Harry Kraut wedged a concert with the Houston Symphony into the two blank days after the opera's premiere. "Why do I have to do this?" LB moaned, genuinely aggrieved at the extra work. When I delivered LB's performance materials for the *Overture to "Candide"* and the *Symphonic Suite from "On the Waterfront"* to Jones Hall, I snuck a look at the stage where LB had slipped off the podium, only a year earlier. That was the end of a road trip and now I was back in the same place at the beginning of a long stint on the road. Nothing much had changed in my role as LB's assistant, though maybe I was a little less exhausted now than at the end of that IPO tour. If exhaustion was quantifiable.

Irma Lazarus's sister in Houston, Elsa Kaim, called to invite LB out for dinner at a tiny Mexican eatery near the dockyards. Elsa equaled Irma in intellect, vivacious charm, and support of the arts. When the strikingly tall, white-haired sisters pulled up to the hotel in Elsa's convertible, LB whooped with delight. Naturally, he insisted on taking the wheel. Nothing pleased LB more than tooling around in a convertible, the wind in his hair and traffic whooshing around him. It may be that LB had an easier time seeing where he was going in an open car, given the wide visual angles and abundant light.

Over dinner, we put away several pitchers of margaritas and an enormous amount of food, although I went easy on the margaritas in case I had to drive. Of course, LB begged to drive the convertible back to the hotel, with Elsa as co-pilot. A few near-misses reminded me of Julia's adage, "He go with God." In no time my shirt was soaked through with perspiration, not just from the south Texas heat and humidity.

One morning, I called LB's secretary, Helen Coates, to report on how we—and the opera—were doing, and I gave her the number for the private phone line in LB's suite. A couple days later, that private phone rang as we headed out the door.

"If you answer it, we'll be late for the rehearsal," I said to LB.

"It might be somebody important," LB said.

"I bet it's Helen," I said. "You can call her later."

His face fell into a grimace when he heard Helen's schoolmarm voice over the phone, and I couldn't resist grinning. He leaned forward and punched me, hard, on the arm. That really hurt and it wiped the grin off my face. I didn't understand the love-hate relationship LB had with his secretary until many years later, but his unfriendly punch told me a lot about his irreconcilable emotions regarding Helen.

At that rehearsal, Stephen Wadsworth took LB aside. Stage director Peter Schifter had said something like, "Let's see how it goes," at the first rehearsal and let the singers meander around on their own. Stephen wondered if anyone was in charge; Houston Grand Opera's staff seemed unnervingly hands-off about this production. LB demurred from interfering, but the groundwork had been laid: Stephen would direct the next production of *A Quiet Place*, at La Scala, one year from now.

Thanks to conductor John DeMain, the opera came together musically in those piano-vocal rehearsals. Afterwards, LB sat at the piano and reviewed the spacing of certain harmonies. As valuable as those leisurely musings were, he was always due elsewhere. One evening, that doyenne of upper-crust fund-raisers, Lynn Wyatt, stalked across the set towards LB. No one introduced me to her, but I didn't mind staying out of her way. Like cleats on soft turf, her spiked heels would have aerated anyone in her path. LB's musical meditation was delaying the *soirée intime* at her chateau in River Oaks.

LB and Charlie Harmon, at a rehearsal that should
have ended already.

The opera company hadn't yet cast anyone as Dinah in *Trouble in Tahiti,* so for four days LB sat through auditions, and I wrote down all his comments, except for one clearly audible stage whisper.

"Dinah is not a floozy," LB said after a disheveled soprano flounced through her audition like a streetwalker from *Threepenny Opera.* All the Dinah recruits were tall, brittle, teeth-baring women, right off the Texas beauty-pageant runways, but Dinah is a smart, suburban 1950s housewife. Clearly, no one at the Houston Grand Opera had read the script.

The Houston newspaper reported that Diane Kesling had an upcoming performance on her recital tour. In New York, she'd participated in the opera workshops, and LB liked her personality, her rich voice, and her faultless diction, so she was invited to audition. She turned emotional as she told LB that her boyfriend had been murdered in Mexico and that a bureaucratic snafu prevented the return of his body to the United States. In despair, she admitted she couldn't sing her best—but in her audition, she clearly *was* Dinah. Later, she confided to LB that immersing herself in that role probably saved her life.

That night, I joined Stephen Wadsworth for dinner with the cast and strengthened a bond with these dedicated singers. As with the rehearsal of every libretto—or any play—quotes from the text peppered the conversation. "Good for you" and

Leonard Bernstein, Tim Nolen, Sheri Greenawald (visibly engaged), Peter Harrower, and Ted Uppman.

"Do I have to have the same conversation with everybody?" became useful punch lines. Clearly, Stephen had a knack for the vernacular. Then we all hit a bar with a dance floor where I learned the basic two-step, the Cotton-Eye Joe. Those boots LB had given me after the IPO tour at last served their purpose. They made dancing as easy as falling off a log.

Finally, the rehearsals moved onto the stage in Jones Hall. An expensive conveyor belt across the lip of the stage paraded shiny appliances while the trio in *Trouble in Tahiti* crooned about the advantages of suburban life: an abundantly stocked refrigerator, a dishwasher full of sparkling dishes. "Too distracting," said LB. At the first rehearsal, the stagehands couldn't off-load all those appliances quickly enough, and the rehearsal ground to a complete halt. The stagehands held a powwow and the appliances stayed in the production.

Later in *A Quiet Place*, Dinah's friends gather in her kitchen, where they sit on bar stools and commiserate after her funeral. Rather than exit through the kitchen door, the cast moved offstage—still on their bar stools—via the downstage conveyor belt. No one thought to do a test run. Atop a wildly wobbling stool, alto Caroline James jiggled like a mound of Jello, beamed her brightest smile, and waved "bye!" as the conveyor belt jerked her into the wings. The crew's guffaws drowned out the orchestra. Another complete halt. The conveyor belt got cut from that scene.

Another rehearsal came to a standstill when Sheri Greenawald as Dede, Dinah's daughter, attempted a quick costume change. She was to exit briefly and return in Dinah's dress. But behind the set, Sheri had to manage her dress zippers on her own. She re-entered on cue, but her bodice was still unzipped, "her tits flying," as the snide producing director put it. Sheri was justifiably furious. The crew duly designated a helper backstage, but what a senseless waste of rehearsal time. More evidence that no one in the production company had looked at the script.

A Bernstein entourage assembled in Houston. Madina Ricordi and her sons, Carlo and Giovanni, arrived from Italy. Madina had smuggled an enormous, illegal *bresaola*—a hunk of cured beef and one of LB's favorite foods—in her brassiere. My energy had begun to flag, but Madina cheered me up considerably. While we waited for LB to get dressed one morning, I translated a raft of Helen Keller jokes into Italian. *What drove Helen Keller crazy? Reading a stucco wall. Why did Helen Keller play the piano with only one hand? She sang with the other.* Yes, I'd gone batty, but Madina had never heard these jokes before. I loved her throaty laugh.

Dorothee Koehler arrived from Germany to line up the foreign press. The composer David Diamond showed up not only to hear the new opera, but also to feast at a fashionable Italian restaurant run by a former partner of his. From New York, Ned Davies arrived to assume his duties as Harry's assistant, taking off my hands the requests for rehearsal passes, as many as eighteen every day.

LB's three offspring met up in Los Angeles and drove across the desert. Jamie, Alexander, and Nina shared a suite on the same hotel floor as LB so they could drop in for morning coffee. Julia had prompted me to stock their favorite foods, such as two jars of peanut butter, one refrigerated and one at room temperature. Julia also carefully packed elegant gowns from Felicia's collection, important for social events in Texas, where gowns were de rigueur for passage through the front door of Lynn Wyatt's mansion. Jamie and Nina looked smashing in their mother's couture; alongside Alexander in a tux, they made a very sophisticated trio. With his family around him, LB was back in his element, *being* rather than merely *doing*.

Press agent Maggie Carson set up interviews with music critics in LB's suite. I paid scant attention while attending to other things—the phone, mail, answering the door, letting hotel maids tidy up the bedroom. One double interview started off impressively. A conservative male critic and a liberal female critic had both done their research and easily grasped LB's nuanced comments. But their reviews after the premiere came as a surprise: the liberal critic was slightly hostile and confused, whereas the conservative critic fully supported LB's intent and what *A Quiet Place* represented as an American opera.

"I expected each of them to write the opposite kind of review," LB said. "How could I have been more convincing, what could I have said to make them understand more clearly?"

What was the stumbling block? The opera itself.

Few critics were kind, though Andrew Porter in the *New Yorker* and Leighton Kerner in *The Village Voice* wrote appreciative reviews.

A rubber duck bath toy became one of my *AQP* obsessions. In the "double duet" in Act II, Sam and his daughter Dede find the duck in a box of odds and ends. Dede recognizes it as her brother Junior's bath toy, and Sam asks if he can see it. He squeezes the duck—perhaps a metaphor for his negligent handling of Junior's upbringing. The duck squeaks, Sam and Dede chuckle. It's a tiny moment, but it says something about the family's nearly-forgotten bonds, and about Dede and Junior as kids. LB wanted the duck's squeak to stand out, and he notated it as a solo sound, in the clear.

I had a hunch that the squeaking duck would be overlooked, so before leaving New York, I'd bought a large rubber duck with a resonant squeak. In Houston, I presented the duck to the props crew, but I should have bought several rubber ducks because the one in Houston never took wing. A year later, the duck at La

A QUIET PLACE
ACT II

Scala was a mute, and LB noticed. I asked the La Scala orchestra percussion to play a "squeak" at the right moment, but it didn't always happen.

In my datebook I wrote the time and location for the premiere on June 17, but no other notes.

At the fancy dinner for the donors three hours later, LB made a rambling speech. He referred to Houston as a "cow town," offending everyone in the room. Texan geography wasn't LB's strong suit, but he knew that the stockyards of Fort Worth lay somewhere to the north. "Cow town" stood for Houston Grand Opera's production standards, in LB's assessment. A recalcitrant orchestra, virtually no forethought in the stage direction, and a breezily cavalier administration gave the impression that the company wasn't much involved.

The Sunday after the premiere was Father's Day, so as a present for LB, I made French toast in his suite. I followed Julia's guidelines because her French toast was famously the best in New York. LB said my effort rivaled Julia's, a compliment I wish I'd had him write down. Then we headed to the hall for *AQP*'s matinee, where I sat at LB's left to write down everything he said.

The rows in front of us had sold out, but half the seats behind us were empty. The matinee crowd seemed elderly, the men tall, lanky Texans, the women comfortably upholstered, with enormous, immaculately maintained hair. Everybody looked dressed for church, every Sunday's primary obligation.

Imagine attending your conservative Baptist temple where you get your fill of your favorite hymns and then you have a nice brunch. Satisfied in stomach and soul, you head to the opera house. In the second act's very first scene, you hear the word "asshole."

Those people had sat placidly through *Trouble in Tahiti* and returned to their seats after the intermission. *A Quiet Place* was well under way when the entire row in front of us stood up, as if at a signal. It was in the middle of a scene. Couldn't they have waited another couple minutes? Were they offended by a four-letter word? Was it the lackluster staging? Had they expected hummable tunes, say, "Maria" or "Glitter and Be Gay"?

The phrase "completely unengaged" crossed my mind.

As they lumbered out, slowly and ponderously, like cattle in no hurry to cross a road, one towering Texan paused in front of us and bellowed, "Lurleen, where'd you pork the core?" (*Park* the *car*, but I think his wife was already out of earshot.)

LB put his face in his hands, so as not to watch this retreating parade, maybe also to weep unseen. Forget about the American vernacular. This audience had no interest in his work. I resisted the urge to say something consoling or grab his hand.

Unhappiness descended after that depressing weekend. Stephen Wadsworth and LB met for five uninterrupted hours. They laid the groundwork for structural changes in the opera and decided that scenes from *Trouble in Tahiti* should be incorporated as flashbacks within the larger work titled *A Quiet Place*. (John Mauceri claims the idea was his. Could be.) Houston's haphazard staging had to be ditched completely. Stephen insisted that he himself should direct the production at La Scala next year, followed immediately by performances at the Kennedy Center.

We could all have benefitted from a two-day break, but the following day in Jones Hall, LB rehearsed the Houston Symphony in the *Overture to "Candide"* and the *Symphonic Suite from "On the Waterfront."* In the car to the rehearsal, LB complained about being forced into this display as a conductor, which shoved extraneous music into his head when it was already overflowing with the new opera's sounds. LB was even less enthusiastic after a rehearsal at the outdoor venue for the concert. Houston swelters in late June, an unbearable climate for outdoor concerts.

Two days before we were due to leave Houston, LB's sister arrived. Shirley caught two performances of *A Quiet Place*, attended an elegant dinner at an Amnesty International fundraiser, and then after only forty-eight hours in Houston, packed her suitcase, ready to fly back to La Guardia with us. In the airport's first-class lounge, we sat together and stared out the windows into a soupy miasma, the city totally invisible in its toxic oil-boom smog.

Shirley put out her cigarette and delivered the most incisive line I ever heard her say. "Let's never come here again," she said flatly, a reaction not only to the pea-green atmosphere outside the window but also to the whole Texan landscape: the haphazard Houston Grand Opera, Bible-thumping Baptists, power-crazed women with big hair and bigger checkbooks. Quite a list. I silently added the despondency around the opera's premiere. Let's never repeat this, please. The despair we felt after *A Quiet Place* should not be revisited.

LB accepted Franco Zeffirelli's offer of his villa in Positano; the Ricordis were already en route. I almost tagged along but barely managed returning to New York before I collapsed and slept for two solid weeks.

23 | The Restorative Greens of Tanglewood

NOT MUCH COULD HELP ME pull myself back together after that debilitating month in Houston. As I squinted at what lay ahead in 1983, cluelessness fell on me like the lead blanket of depression: how to find the energy, the presence of mind?

I didn't even have my own life, defined as I now was as "Leonard Bernstein's assistant." Introducing myself, I was once asked, "So, you give him blow jobs?" Even as a joke, that shocked me. It could be just as hazardous not to open up. People assumed I hid sordid secrets if I didn't mention the Bernstein connection right off. After I resigned two years later, I first heard the term "star-fucker." What on earth? You mean me?

Even though I'd had two weeks of sleep, my nerves were on edge. I found a shiatsu masseur for some soothing but fleeting relief. I should have searched for a shrink, but since I'd never experienced this level of exhaustion—physical and emotional—I didn't know how badly I needed one. Doggedly, I threw myself back into the grinding schedule.

We were about to lose Ann Dedman. She'd found a less stressful position, so I scheduled chef auditions—and then the gas line to Apartment 23 at the Dakota broke, followed by a Con Ed strike. Only that utility company could repair the gas line. Stepping into a kitchen reduced to a pathetic toaster oven and a hot plate, some chef candidates didn't bother wasting their time with an interview.

To ease the strain, Harry Kraut invited LB for dinner at his house in Nyack, just north of the city, together with Aaron Copland—a chaste get-together of elderly gay men and their younger assistants. None of us suspected that this could be the last meal Bernstein and Copland shared. Copland was warm and funny as ever, but his mind sometimes slipped, and when LB called him a few days later, Copland admitted, "You know, I can't remember what you look like."

LB hung up, devastated. "He doesn't remember me," LB said.

"No, not at all," I said. "He simply can't picture the way you look now." But LB may have been right, and he brooded for days on his mentor's mortality.

A week later, Ann and I drove to Tanglewood to scope out the house that the Boston Symphony (BSO) had rented for LB. I also had orchestra parts for the BSO's library. We arrived at Tanglewood's main gate during the lunch break, so I headed to the nearby cafeteria, but was stopped in my tracks by the most beautiful lawn I had ever seen, an expansive, verdant sea, shored by venerable pines. As the saying goes: *What God could do with Nature, if only He had the money.*

I asked a group where I could find the assistant librarian, Marty Burlingame.

"Who wants to know?" said the guy at my right, as wary as if I'd flashed an arrest warrant. It was Marty himself, who grudgingly walked me to the library. Although actually pleased to meet me, Marty kept up his gruff façade. Rehearsals started in two days and he'd had scant information from the Bernstein office.

What a library! Once again, I stepped into a major repository of serious music, in awe of everyone I met, the atmosphere blessedly calm—temporarily. After we'd become friends, Marty described Bernstein's meteoric appearances at Tanglewood. Summer hummed along in a well-planned way until Bernstein and his entourage swept like a hurricane through the Berkshires. The instant the Bernstein horde decamped, serenity prevailed again, and everyone at Tanglewood looked around, stunned (Marty said), and asked, "What was *that?*"

Ann and I met with Richard Ortner, our principal contact, who supplied us with parking passes, names and phone numbers for the vast Tanglewood staff, and a detailed schedule. Richard was certainly the right person for his job—later, he became New England's most transformative arts administrator. Graciously relaxed, he took the edge off my trepidation over how much I had to do in the next two days.

Richard drove us south through Stockbridge to a trim white house hidden from the road by dense trees, a perfect retreat: a rear wing for LB and, up steep New England stairs, separate bedrooms and baths for Ann and me. Best of all was the dining room, paneled to the ceiling with book-crammed shelves. Richard requested that this personal library of the house's owner remain precisely in place. He wasn't aware that LB had appropriated a Lewis Carroll first edition (duly returned) from a Scottish castle, but we all knew too well how LB couldn't resist messing with books.

Across the road, trees hid the only neighboring house. On a warm morning a week later, I got up early to float on a raft in the backyard pond and gather my thoughts. A cello played nearby. Yo-Yo Ma, in the house across the road, greeted the day with a Bach cello suite. *Magical.* Music wafting through the landscape is Tanglewood's circulatory system.

LB started his stay at Tanglewood by staying in bed until 7 P.M. He seemed fine once he got up, but I suspected a post-Dexedrine crash. In his datebook, I crossed out that evening's André Previn concert, and the next morning LB asked me to cross out the 10 A.M. rehearsal. Over the phone, I gave Richard Ortner a status report, but after a lethargic morning, LB pronounced himself ready for his first conducting class that afternoon, to be followed by a three-hour rehearsal with the student orchestra.

The conducting classes took place at the Koussevitzky house, Seranak—which I consistently misspelled until LB explained the acronym: Serge (SER) and Natalie (ANA) Koussevitzky (K). Driving there along roads he'd known for over forty years, LB had a story for every mile. Here's where Aaron Copland hit a cow! Copland's car survived, but not, alas, the cow. After reporting his bovicide to the police, Copland fell into prolonged remorse.

"Imagine, Aaron inconsolable," LB said. "He was always so perky. When he opened a newspaper, he'd turn to the obituaries and say in his cracker-barrel voice, 'Let's see who died!'"

West of Lenox, LB gestured toward a sloping field.

"That was the place for 'nookie' after dark," he said, "But it could get very muddy. You should have heard Roger Englander screaming when his car got stuck." Roger Englander produced the televised Young People's Concerts in the '50s and '60s, but I hadn't known that LB's association with him went back that far—thirty years ago.

"How did *you* know about the muddy field?" I asked LB, but he pretended not to hear my question.

LB piloted his Mercedes up Seranak's shady driveway and parked in the grassy oval in front of the house as if staking a claim. I pocketed the keys to move the car later. The panorama through Seranak's doorway clinched LB's geographical narration: the blue of the Stockbridge Bowl—a sizable pond—backed by the purple ripples of the Berkshires. Golly, the North American ideal, a wilderness sublime, despite the Massachusetts Turnpike slicing right through it.

In a ground-floor room, two grand pianos faced one another with enough space between them for one fledgling conductor. A full-length portrait of Dr. Koussevitzky, in the white suit he bequeathed to LB (who'd worn it for his wedding to Felicia), gazed on benignly. Students and curious onlookers filled rows of chairs. I stood in the back for a while, until absconding for the sunny lawn outside, where I stretched out beneath an open window so I could continue to listen.

LB sat in front, fiddling with an Aquafilter, and coached up to half a dozen budding conductors over a two-hour session. Simulating an orchestra, a pair of almost identical women played faultlessly from orchestral scores at the two pianos.

These supplicants—the conducting fellows—congregated at Seranak for a kind of laying on of hands. Orchestra conductors claim a lineage about as exalted as that of the Bishops of Rome—from Saint Peter to the present Pope—and nearly as mystical. Holy anointment might manifest itself in that room on that very day, with the passing of the Maestro's baton from one generation to the next. Or not. Two years later, LB cried out, "Where are the young conductors?" bemoaning a dearth of developing talent.

Afterwards, we headed to the theater-concert hall, where the student orchestra waited to rehearse Milhaud's *Le Bœuf sur le Toit*. I sat onstage behind the violins, next to Tanglewood's "Artist in Residence for Life," Maurice Abravanel. What an honor! Maestro Abravanel, cheerful and winningly wry in his eightieth year, had lived in music's beating heart straight through the 20th century. It seemed that everyone he worked with became a close friend—Kurt Weill, George Balanchine, Bruno Walter. I could see why. He was the most engaging man I'd ever met.

That afternoon, he spoke warmly about his friend Darius Milhaud, and I had plenty of questions as I'd fantasized about studying with Milhaud once upon a time. Maestro Abravanel dubbed *Le Bœuf sur le Toit* "the well-tempered tango" in a droll allusion to Bach's "Well-Tempered Klavier." Milhaud's music lurches through its key changes, whereas Bach's progresses in an orderly way. At the break, Abravanel chatted with LB about the student orchestra's exemplary musicianship. LB enthusiastically concurred.

That evening over a cozy meal at Seiji Ozawa's house, Maestro Ozawa promised that his shiatsu masseur would grapple with LB's need to regain some stamina for conducting. With that help, LB turned a corner, though his only exercise was waving his arms from a podium. And LB's sleep? The sleep-wake clinic might as well have never happened.

Sunday afternoon, LB dispatched me to fetch Christoph Eschenbach to the house after Eschenbach's BSO concert. Around this Maestro, mine was indeed a "toilet paper job." Spying the Mercedes with the top down, Eschenbach enthroned himself in the back seat, the better to savor gliding about in a car with MAESTRO1 plates, with the Maestro's lowly assistant as his chauffeur. Later he granted me the privilege of hefting his luggage through the Pittsfield airport. Eschenbach never spoke a word to me, though I half-expected a command to shine his shoes. His supercilious behavior contributed to a day of disaster a year later, an incident I still find difficult to forgive.

At the opposite end of the ego spectrum, Todd and Helen Perry invited LB, Ann Dedman, and me to their home for a family dinner. Todd Perry had recently retired as manager of the BSO; I didn't know until that evening that he and Helen had attended Philadelphia's Curtis Institute of Music together with LB in the

1940s. Like affectionate siblings, LB and the Perrys brimmed over with reminiscences, but Helen kept an eye on the clock, mindful of LB's 10 A.M. rehearsal the next morning. LB cherished his lifelong friendship with those two.

After sharing a concert the next night with three conducting fellows, LB put in an appearance at the student cookout, compelled as he was to maintain the reputation of these Tanglewood blowouts. To anyone who could hear him over the din, LB explained and demonstrated the recent history of American popular music, pounding away at the piano through pop songs of the 1940s, '50s, and '60s. He shifted gears (circa 1964) with The Kinks' "Girl, You Really Got Me" to an even more intense repertoire built on rock's "power chords." You know them when you hear them, though no one could hear anything at this raucous shindig.

After a year of these parties, I'd adapted. Conversation? Not at a kegger like this. As the designated driver, I nursed a diet soft drink in the quiet of the Mercedes and caught up on back issues of the *New Yorker*. LB's post-concert high could go on for hours. Around 4 A.M., struggling to keep my eyes open, I gingerly steered the Mercedes toward Great Barrington while LB continued his lively monologue. To keep myself awake, and to show I'd listened to the concert, I commented on a finely played solo or a brass player running out of breath. (LB encouraged the student musicians to prepare for the summer humidity and learn to work around it.) I even critiqued the conducting fellows, but I always kept those pre-dawn conversations down the empty Berkshire roads strictly between us.

An evening with the composing fellows was a lot more engaging. After dinner at Seranak, four of the composers played recordings of their most recent works, followed by an intimate discussion with LB. Later, LB and I discussed the Thirty Second Test: if a new piece failed to grab his attention within thirty seconds, he knew the piece wasn't going anywhere. That evening, all four works passed the test; all those composing fellows now have rewarding careers.

The next afternoon, LB took the podium in the Shed, Tanglewood's principal venue, for his momentous return to the BSO. He rehearsed his own Symphony No. 1, "Jeremiah" with Gail Dubinbaum in the work's last movement, the "Lamentation." Gail's voice bore a striking resemblance to Jennie Tourel's, whose power and pathos LB had always considered the ideal for this work. Happy that the day had gone so well, that evening LB played tapes of *A Quiet Place* for his dear friend, the composer Yehudi Wyner, and Tanglewood's director of contemporary music, Theo Antoniou—a collegial get-together possible only at Tanglewood.

I half-listened from the next room, and I had to admit that the music of *AQP* carried its weight; it had something to say. *AQP* definitely passed the Thirty Second Test.

Bursting with enthusiasm the next morning, LB growled bits of "Jeremiah" in his cement-mixer voice. We got to the Shed for the 10 A.M. BSO rehearsal with time to spare. The weight of those weeks of *A Quiet Place* in Houston had finally lifted.

As the orchestra ran through Beethoven's Symphony No. 3, the "Eroica," LB dispensed an affectionate aside at every brilliant flourish. "That's my Doriot," he said, over Doriot Dwyer's flute solo in the last movement. The first woman named to a principal position in a major American orchestra, Ms. Dwyer had blazed a trail for women in 1952. LB's fondness for her extended into an embrace of the entire orchestra that morning.

Afterward, principal librarian Victor Alpert sauntered into the green room, and in no time was re-visiting the summers he and LB had spent together as teen-agers in Sharon, Massachusetts. In 1936, Mr. Alpert had played Ralph Rackstraw in Gilbert and Sullivan's *HMS Pinafore* under the direction of Leonard Bernstein, age eighteen. Watching them re-enact that production as vividly as if it happened only the week before, I couldn't stop smiling, for once.

HMS Pinafore ran aground when Joan Peyser barged in. I'd forgotten her scheduled interview, ostensibly for revisions to LB's entry in *Grove's Dictionary of Music and Musicians*. I'd booked LB for a haircut followed by a photo session, so LB suggested Ms. Peyser tag along. Driving into Lenox, LB chattered with unin-hibited volubility about his love life, past and present. Thank goodness Peyser had no notepad—this stuff wasn't for *Grove's*—but she got a provocative earful.

I'd never heard LB so candid, rattling on about sharing a house one summer with David Oppenheim, Helen Coates as the exacting warden. I leaned forward and cleared my throat, in case I had to interrupt ("Mississippi Mud!").

Smart but mighty brassy, Peyser actually had another goal that day, feeling her way around LB in order to snare a publishing contract for a Bernstein biography. I got raked over the coals when her book revealed much of what LB had told her on that drive to Lenox, though her gullibility brought into question whether she was even remotely credible. Calling me about LB's quote that conducting Mahler was "orgasmic," she asked, "Are there stains in his pants after a Mahler perfor-mance?" What a daffy question—and a great laugh.

Summer storms occasionally interfere with the Tanglewood schedule, but there's also "Lenny weather" when, hours before a concert, a storm sweeps through, refreshes the grounds, and leaves the air washed and cool. Thunder drummed above the Berkshires the morning of the BSO concert—my first at Tanglewood— but the evening turned idyllic. An elegant crowd settled into sumptuous picnics on that perfect lawn, that Eden where reverence for music quells all noise from the imperfect world beyond.

After an especially stirring Beethoven performance, LB seemed preoccupied. Before greeting his fans in the green room, he said to me, "In the second movement [a funeral march] I saw somebody walking across the back of the stage. I wondered why anybody would be back there."

"Who was it?" I asked.

"Koussy," LB said, his face suddenly drawn, the lines going deep.

I stopped what I was doing. Dr. Koussevitzky, founder of Tanglewood, died in 1951.

"I'm certain of it. It was Koussy," LB said.

⁓

ACCORDING TO SOME SOURCES, an astrological convergence took place that night, a once-in-a-million-years alignment of stars and planets. At the Seranak post-concert party, a hardy group—led by LB—resolved to stay up and absorb this exceptional energy, predicted to peak at 4 A.M. I left the party to pack up the house, returning to Seranak as faint colors sneaked into the eastern sky, and found the "convergence" party still going strong.

The dynamic energy of the universe? It emanated from one man holding a cigarette and a glass of scotch.

24 | Bi-Coastal Blues

THE MONTH IN HOUSTON for *A Quiet Place* drained all the blood out of us, but two weeks at Tanglewood made us human again. If only we had stayed longer!

After packing up the Tanglewood house all night, Ann Dedman and I drank several pots of coffee before she drove us to the airport in Albany, New York. Ann had often been my only confidante over the past nineteen months. On her last day, I couldn't imagine life around LB without her. I said a brief goodbye, but LB turned genuinely affectionate. The past two weeks had been extraordinary, in large part thanks to Ann's meticulous daily management. After leaving us that day, she said she stopped the car and cried for a while, making me wonder what my own as yet inconceivable departure might be like.

With a change of planes in Chicago, the flights to Los Angeles seemed like short hops, allowing no nap time. Besides, among other pressing requests, LB insisted on a duel to see who could complete the *Financial Times* crossword puzzle first. (I almost won.) Awake for thirty-six hours straight, again, I relied on caffeine to get me through unpacking at the Beverly Hills Hotel as LB went into raptures about snagging one of the hotel's bungalows, finally. Thirty years earlier, LB had been lodged in the main part of the hotel when Gore Vidal called him, claiming that "two Marine Corps cadets" were performing all sorts of pornographic scenarios in his bungalow. LB should come see for himself. But LB was busy and never made it to Vidal's lair. He'd pined for a bungalow ever since. He said that in a bungalow, he could sneak somebody right off the street, say, a brace of Marines, bypassing the snoopy front desk. Oh no, what were we in for?

I said, "This could be a dangerous fantasy, Maestro. Besides, given Mr. Vidal's active imagination, those 'cadets' were probably skanky hustlers from Santa Monica Boulevard." I allowed they might have sported eye-popping "Marine Corps" biceps.

No, no, LB insisted, "Gore's story was true, in every detail."

As I finished unpacking, Michael Tilson Thomas (MTT) walked into the bungalow, eager to review the next day's conducting seminar, the start of the second season of the Los Angeles Philharmonic's Institute (LAPIO), the "Tanglewood of the West." As MTT and LB pondered which conducting fellow would tackle Mendelssohn's *Hebrides Overture,* I said, "I'll see you tomorrow. I'll close the front door as I go out." But LB said, "No, leave it open. We've ordered some food and we won't be interrupted if the door is open."

In my room in the main part of the hotel, I took a mild herbal sedative to keep me asleep after I got into bed. The phone couldn't be unplugged, but its long cable enabled me to sandwich it between pillows in a drawer. Somehow I knew that's how Marilyn Munroe always put her phone to bed when she was desperate. Then I sank into a profound sleep.

Hammering on the door woke me up, far too early—the conducting class didn't start until 2 in the afternoon. It was Harry Kraut, in a pink bathrobe that matched the raging color on his face, his chinstrap whiskers looking like a ring of fire.

"Where were you last night? Out carousing!" he screamed, in a fine impersonation of an operatic mad scene. "I called every gay bar in Los Angeles, trying to track you down! What do you have to say for yourself?"

I had nothing to say, but my jaws wouldn't have worked anyway, they had fallen open too far. I gestured to the rumpled bed behind me, the phone still stuffed in the drawer. This man did not know how I lived my solitary life. When did I ever stay out all night? *Never—except when the job required me to.* Or go to gay bars? *Once, very briefly, a year ago.* In fact, had I ever been known to "carouse"? I let Harry continue, but it took a while before he became coherent.

"Lenny and MTT were robbed at gunpoint last night," Harry sputtered. Apparently, the robbery had occurred only minutes after I'd left the bungalow door open—at LB's request. After the thugs left, MTT called the front desk. The police showed up, followed by a hotel crew who moved everything to a suite in the main building. "Why weren't you there to help?" Harry demanded.

"This is a shock," I said. Without a pause I added, "But how would I have been helpful, as a sleep-deprived zombie?" I thought of all the cash in my wallet. "Besides, if I'd been there, the robbers would have gotten a lot more cash." All they snared was fifty bucks from MTT. "And by the way, is LB all right?"

Harry grunted.

"Has everything been removed from the bungalow?" I asked. "The medicine bag, the white-noise machine, the framed photos, the orchestra scores, the books?" A dubious look clouded Harry's pink face.

I quickly got dressed, went to the lobby and asked if I could get into Bungalow 12. I still had the key. In fact, the hotel staff had been thorough and had left behind only a few pencils. Upstairs in the main part of the hotel, in a suite that was definitely not a bungalow, I found LB already dressed and in a foul mood. When I asked if he wanted any breakfast, he griped he'd already ordered it, and why hadn't I asked whether he was all right? Having a gun pointed at him had shaken him, and he was not in a forgiving frame of mind.

I heard later that on sitting down in the suite after all that hoopla, MTT exhaled and said jovially, "So, who conducts the *Hebrides Overture*?" making them both laugh.

We were twenty minutes late for the first conducting seminar, far out in the Valley. The vibes were not positive. We had two cars but only one parking permit, thus pitting me against a formidable parking matron. While she read me the riot act, I saw in my rearview mirror that Harry was laughing so hard, tears streamed down his face, now pink for another reason. Wimpy Charlie, getting confrontational! I wasn't amused.

LB rehearsed the LAPIO in two works: Copland's ballet *Billy the Kid*—"Perfect music for the morning," LB said (it was mid-afternoon)—and the second movement of Tchaikovsky's Symphony No. 4. LB challenged the oboist, a demure young girl, to play her entire twenty-bar solo in one breath, "as Mr. Gomberg did" in the New York Philharmonic. Inspired, she managed it faultlessly. Then the cellos entered messily, so LB stopped them: "You play like *that* after she just gave you that fantastic blow job?" Classic Bernstein: beyond the bounds of decorum, but making a memorable, if slightly off-color moment. It was a turning point; the rest of the day felt far more upbeat.

———

LB'S RENTAL CAR was a Ford Mustang convertible and a piece of junk. As I drove it that morning, the steering wheel fell into my lap. I made sure it was fastened securely before LB got behind the wheel on our way back to the hotel. As we climbed over the Santa Monica mountains, rain came down in muddy splats. Naturally, the car's top was down. LB fiddled with the dashboard, trying to figure out the top's mechanism, but he was in the passing lane for the trucks, all gunning their engines to get up that hill. I asked him to pull over to the road's shoulder because the top's mechanism worked only in neutral and park. I shouldn't have said that. He nonchalantly shifted into neutral, the car crawled to a stop in the middle lane of dense traffic, and a mammoth semi swerved to the side of us, missing us by inches. Horns blared all around us. The Mustang's top popped up, I hefted it forward and quickly fastened both front clamps. LB calmly shifted into drive. I couldn't find my voice until we got back to the hotel, when I asked him never to do that again. "Do what?" he said.

When Julia said, "He go with God," she was more right than she knew.

Jamie had booked a table at Michael's, a pricey restaurant in Santa Monica, and she'd invited a few friends. Twelve, in fact. We kept the restaurant open until very late. When the waiter handed LB the bill, he turned white, quite a feat given his perpetual tan. He asked me beseechingly, "What do we do?" This wasn't an act. The bill was fourteen hundred dollars, beyond the limit of his credit card (I never understood why that was so). LB hadn't paid for anything himself since the mid-1950s, so he had no idea what dinner in a high-end restaurant would cost, nor that $1400 came mighty close to my monthly salary. Still feeling light-headed after the near-death experience on the freeway, I said we'd have to wash the dishes. LB thought I was serious. He looked so stricken, I thought he might start to cry.

My Amberson American Express card took care of the bill, but in the morning, I called LB's accountant, Charlotte Harris, to verify all the charges in Los Angeles, and to reassure her that every one of those was a business expense, including the exorbitant tab at Michael's.

It rained the next day, so the top of the Mustang was closed the entire day, hooray.

When LB drove back to the hotel, he took a different side street, and pointed out a house where, years before, he'd had drinks with the actor Van Johnson. According to LB, "Van Johnson said something that few, if any, others have heard: 'Fuck me, Leonard.'"

I looked askance at LB. *Why was he telling me this? What did he mean with the qualifier, "few, if any, have heard"?* I wondered if that moment with one of Hollywood's leading actors had been an embarrassment for LB—or one of his cockiest conquests. Was LB testing me? Whether I would repeat something so outrageously lurid?

If only I had the gumption of Joan Peyser, to follow up with *So, did you*?

Harry devised tests all the time, and he told me about them. Harry would say something peculiar as though it were fact, and then wait to see how it got back to him, how it got distorted, and who repeated it. He relished this sort of conniving. It winnowed the people he shouldn't trust from those he could.

Once when LB asked how I was getting along with Harry, I decided to try Harry's tactic. I said to LB, "I don't appreciate Harry's turning things into an operetta if he doesn't get his own way. When his voice goes up an octave, I back off."

The next morning my phone rang, well before 8 A.M. It was Harry, his voice in the coloratura range. "I do *not* make everything into an operetta!" he yodeled. LB must have repeated that almost instantaneously. At least the quote was accurate.

———

BETWEEN TEACHING SESSIONS out in the Valley, we had lunch at a nearby falafel place with MTT, his partner/manager Joshua Robison, conducting fellow Michael Barrett, and Michael's partner, violist Leslie Tomkins. No sooner had we sat down than "Maria" from *West Side Story* came over the sound system. LB said casually, "That pays for lunch!" (As if he knew the price of falafel in a pita.) It was a sweet moment and we all laughed; we knew how blessed we were to be the beneficiaries of LB's royalties. But MTT brooded over it later. Around LB, securely embedded in the cultural mainstream, anyone could feel small in comparison.

My mother and sister drove to Los Angeles from Oregon that week, so I offered to take my mother to lunch at the Polo Lounge at the Beverly Hills Hotel (my sister wouldn't be up that early). I figured my mother would appreciate the guaranteed celebrity-spotting, but she stared down at her plate throughout lunch and never uttered a syllable. I wished LB could have seen that; it's what I grew up with. LB had once chided me, "I never hear you say how proud you are" in assisting him with seminars, concerts, and recordings. But I was brought up not to draw attention to myself. Whatever success I achieved, I was forbidden to gloat.

I finally achieved a sense of satisfaction—a far cry from pride—when I put the spell of my mother's lifelong depression behind me. Though it could still sweep over me like a drop in air pressure before a storm, there was never the right moment to explain this to LB, and he would have said I was making excuses. He was the Chief Psychoanalyst of the Universe, but where was he when you needed him?

Harry departed for Boston on the day of LB's Hollywood Bowl concert with the LA Philharmonic, a repeat of the BSO program at Tanglewood, minus the apparition of Dr. Koussevitzky during the Beethoven. Humphrey Burton managed the Bowl that summer and hosted a terrific post-concert party. Instead of dozing in the car, I played piano duets with Humphrey, thinking again about a four-hand arrangement of LB's "Divertimento," which I didn't get around to for another five years.

The next morning we took off for Lawrence, Massachusetts, to celebrate LB's 65th birthday in the city of his birth. Once again we were flying over the Grand Canyon, once again checking into a hotel, once again I set up a suite, though this time LB actually helped me unpack so he could get to bed. We were all cranky, and the day ahead would be a long one.

The sun hadn't come up when I woke with a start. I couldn't reconstruct the previous day, except that we had traveled, but from where? Where was I now? Looked like a hotel room. Should I call the operator and ask what city I was in? Under the phone, I found a phone book: "Boston." Whew. I thought only rock stars on tour and campaigning politicians got this dislocated. Bit by bit I remembered why I was there, but what an unsettling moment.

That day I stood on the sidelines as LB got a hero's welcome at Lawrence's city hall, where all the local left-wing politicians put in their sound bites. LB maintained an unearthly grin—almost a rictus—for the cameras and crowds. I wondered how long he could hold up. Next stop: the tenement where he lived as an infant, on newly-christened Bernstein Way, followed by a ride in an open antique car to a park where an outdoor stage was named for him. (After LB died, a theater group staged *West Side Story* in that park, cast with at-risk youth from Lawrence's decaying neighborhoods. LB would have been buoyed by the community involvement, despite the down-and-out reality.)

A picnic by the Merrimack River brought a moment of calm, with LB surrounded by his family. He went for a swim, despite jocular warnings that if he drowned, the rest of the day would be a shock wave of cancellations. Then we forged onward to a rehearsal of the Boston Youth Orchestra under Eiji Oue, followed by an outdoor concert by the Merrimack Valley Community Orchestra. I stood at the side of the stage, the limo at the ready whenever LB gave a signal, so I caught Shirley Bernstein's guffaw when the principal clarinetist got lost in

Nina, at right, warily eyeballs Jamie, who lifts a fork to LB, who thinks he recognizes the room service waiter . . . oh, of course, that's not a waiter, it's Alexander. He's looking for . . . (Felicia?). On the terrace of Suite 916, the Watergate Hotel, Washington, D.C.

selections from *On the Town*. Not entirely the musician's fault—the parts for *On the Town* were notoriously illegible.

LB took a bow onstage, then we were off to a VFW hall, where the women of Lawrence descended on LB like hens on cracked corn. The crowd quickly got out of control, shoving themselves at him, picking at his sleeves for a thread of celebrity. I'd never seen LB truly angry.

He yelled, really *yelled,* "Leave me alone!"

Harry materialized, cleaved the frenzied matrons apart, and asked for some air. I dragged Shirley to the door where the limo waited. LB followed. Instantly, we were headed back to Boston. Inside the car, Shirley smoked one cigarette after another as LB ranted. By the time the limo arrived at the hotel in Boston, the three of us had calmed down, despite a feeling of unresolved antagonism.

We had a peaceful drive to Connecticut the next day. I sat in the back seat of the Mercedes as LB drove and Shirley smoked. Jamie, Alex, and Nina followed right behind us in another convertible. Thank goodness we took backcountry roads. I swear LB never stopped at a traffic light or stop sign the whole way.

25 | "Why Do I Have to Work So Hard?"

SEVEN WEEKS IN ONE PLACE, a rare luxury—and it was autumn in New York! A friend called to offer his spare bedroom, basically a windowed closet, in his spiffy Greenwich Village apartment. My share of the monthly rent ate up a week's salary, but the short commute to the Dakota won me over and, for the first time, the condition of where I lived wouldn't embarrass me. I borrowed the station wagon and made the move in one trip.

The search continued for LB's chef. I lined up three professionals for audition dinners at the Dakota, with the kitchen still hobbled by a defunct gas line, and followed through with the guest lists LB drew up. The candidates sailed over the single-hotplate hurdle, and LB relished sizing up their personalities. But nobody was hired.

Helen Coates decreed that Bachrach, the photo studio famous for headshots of newly married couples, should photograph LB. She conferred about this with no one, and for once Harry admitted that battling Helen was pointless; if LB was agreeable, then go ahead. LB owed a great deal to his secretary, whose rule over his life began with his first serious piano lesson in 1932. Eleven years later, she was his secretary, manager, and housekeeper. Nearly a decade after that, LB wanted a change and had tried to fire Helen, but she tore that letter up in front of him.

The humorless session at Bachrach took only half an hour, but the result prompted LB to say, "I look like a banker." The portrait of a Bernstein-as-financier quashed any hint of personality. I suggested LB autograph it for an upcoming AIDS auction. Helen purred (without a single cluck) over the copy I gave her and proudly placed it on her piano. Shortly afterwards, the Bachrach window featured a dozen "bankers," all apparently spawned from one pod, LB indistinguishable among them.

For the Metropolitan Opera's Centennial Gala, the day before our departure on another tour, LB kicked off the evening gala with Beethoven's Leonore Overture No. 3. As I guided LB toward the elevator for the orchestra pit, the most famous divas in opera mobbed him with kisses. Then the elevator doors opened. Fronting a flock of sopranos, Diane Kesling and Gail Dubinbaum saw me and shouted, "Charlie!" I blushed to my toes. Reduced to chopped liver, LB asked glumly, "Friends of yours?" Afterwards, as we stepped out the stage door, a gauntlet of autograph hounds screamed. I heard "I got Nilsson!" as LB commented, *sotto voce*, "It's the retardos." But he signed every scrapbook thrust his way.

It astonished me that LB was up and dressed for a 9:30 A.M. flight the next morning. The lure of the Concorde? Aaron Stern hadn't been around in a while but he tagged along on this tour, prodding LB into motion and making my mornings a cinch.

For a stint with the orchestra of the Accademia Santa Cecilia in Rome, we stayed close by the Vatican. The first of four concerts was in the papal reception room, the jewel box Sala Regia. One pair of doors led to the Pope's apartments, another to the basilica of St. Peter's, but the most imposing doors gave on to the Sistine Chapel. After the first rehearsal, LB's personal Swiss Guard gestured nonchalantly towards the chapel and asked if we'd like to take a look. He turned on the lights, we spread our coats on the floor, and we lay like spokes with our heads at the hub of a wheel: LB, Aaron Stern, Franco Amurri (the screenwriter who'd visited LB in Indiana), the composer Alessio Vlad (now the director of Teatro dell'Opera in Rome), and me. Harry Kraut lounged in a cardinal's chair somewhere. We were in no hurry.

For Aaron's benefit, LB expounded on the lavish illustrations while Alessio, Franco, and I concentrated on the entablatures teeming with prophets, patriarchs, and ancient sibyls. Look, the Sibyl of Cumae! It was like espying portraits in the clouds of a summer sky. I thought I knew Michelangelo's magnum opus pretty well from previous visits, but I never imagined myself stretched out on the Sistine Chapel's floor for an entire transcendent hour.

The ceiling's restoration was under way, so on a visit a few years later, LB took a hydraulic lift to within an arm's reach of Jeremiah, his biblical godfather. Naturally, LB caressed the prophet's luxuriant beard, leaving an inconspicuous handprint on top of Michelangelo's own fingerprints.

Our Swiss Guard took us behind the altar into a little room furnished with a tiny porcelain stove. "*Questo forno fa il Papa*," he said matter-of-factly: *This oven makes the Pope*, as though a bejeweled and mitered pontiff burst out of that minuscule oven like the Pillsbury Doughboy. He meant the stove's *chimney* conveys the signal of a Pope's election—black smoke to white—to the outside world. Three days later, we were still breaking up with laughter.

LB finagled an audience with Pope John Paul II, and took Aaron Stern along, despite Harry's warning that the Vatican protocol limited a papal audience only to family members. Nobody seemed to mind, and LB took over the session as he lectured the Pope on contemporary social norms. Later, LB badgered his Swiss Guard cohort about life in their barracks. They gave him a heart-stopping account of nude sunbathing on the roof of the Sistine Chapel, which LB excitedly recounted for me that evening. I was skeptical, remembering Gore Vidal's "Marine Corps" cadets in a Beverly Hills bungalow. Naked Swiss Guards seemed like a tale tailored for LB's secret cravings.

Aaron had friends in Gerona, Spain, who were unearthing evidence of Catalonia's ancient Jewish presence, so Aaron and LB flew to Barcelona while I headed to Munich for the next batch of concerts with the Bavarian Radio Symphony Orchestra (BRFO in German). What a treat: two days of museums, long walks in autumn fog, and a catch-up lunch with Dorothee Koehler, all without a single Maestro-oriented concern.

With my concentration restored, the intensity of LB's rehearsals of Bartók's *Music for Strings, Percussion and Celesta* burrowed deeply into my brain—until Harry dispatched me to mollify the die-hard Bernstein fans at the stage door of the Herkulessaal. Among them, a nonagenarian autograph dealer, a hard-bitten Frau dressed as an eighteenth-century man in knee breeches and a frock, and the fanatical mother of a "musical genius." *Ach du lieber!* None of them spoke English, and none were to be admitted into the rehearsals. So much for my hopes for learning about Bartók's masterpiece.

Back inside the hall, a frail, unassuming woman with a quavering voice entered LB's green room and awaited a bone-crushing hug from the Maestro. Traute von Köppen lived for music. Her life paralleled Germany's history, in a way: her youth brimmed over with the brilliance of pre-war Berlin, and then all was reduced to rubble, save her remarkable children. Music was the one constant, the safest refuge in her long life.

She lived in Frankfurt, so I later shared our travel schedule whenever we changed planes there. Traute ably corralled an electric cart and driver to ferry us around the airport, like an angel shepherding errant souls. The last time I saw her was Christmas Day, 1989, when LB conducted Beethoven's Symphony No. 9 within a stone's throw of the disintegrating Berlin Wall. An electric charge shot through the hall when the baritone declared *Freiheit*, LB's substitution for *Freude*: "freedom" rather than "joy." Traute's head fell against my shoulder, and she wept. In her nearly ninety years, she'd never dared hope to see Germany whole nor its culture a power for healing.

In Munich, Traute escorted us everywhere: a glitter-bedecked party at swishy Kai's Bistro, and to the Hochschule für Musik for LB's investiture as an honorary professor. That ceremony required him to conduct the school's orchestra, so I brought the parts for Robert Schumann's Symphony No. 2, then had to chase after the students who'd stowed those irreplaceable parts in their instrument cases. In *Kinderdeutsch* I shouted, "*Halt! Gib mir zurück die Musik!*" while aerobically running up and down the school's monumental staircase. Harry Kraut had a good laugh.

Adolph Green, connecting with his Hungarian roots, joined us in—as LB always prefaced it—"mad, gay" Budapest. Adolph squired LB on a crawl of the city's colorful nightlife, but it was my last chance for a full night's sleep before another week on the road. I begged off, to my everlasting regret. LB rhapsodized the next day on the otherworldly cimbaloms—the resonant dulcimer that characterizes Hungarian music—and the rowdy singing, the rivers of brandy.

High spirits carried him through a televised rehearsal with the BRFO at Erkel Hall, the site of his 1948 Budapest debut. He reminisced about being "carried through the streets on the shoulders of the audience," a memory all the more remarkable for being true. Hungarian euphoria seeped even into LB's datebook. Where I meticulously penciled in each concert program, LB added the most stultifying encores he could think of: John Cage's *Interiors*, Gounod's 20-minute "Ballet" from *Faust*, the somnolent "Meditation" from Massenet's *Thaïs*. The actual encores were perky movements from LB's *Divertimento for Orchestra*.

The pace didn't let up: a run-through with the brilliant student orchestra at the Liszt Ferenc Academy of Music; a private hour of political debate with Hungarian General Secretary János Kádár; an autograph session at a music store where I helped myself to the scores, all East European reprints in violation of Western copyrights; and finally, a party hosted by the record label Hungaroton, in thanks for allowing the live recording of the BRFO concerts in Budapest. It was a legitimate recording—the territory specified in LB's contract with Deutsche Grammophon stopped short of the Hungarian border.

The morning I packed up the hotel suite—eleven suitcases trucked to Vienna, the rest in our chauffeured car to Zagreb—a friend from my college years came for breakfast with her infant daughter, who kindled LB's latent grandfatherly yearnings. The next knock at the door was the soprano Sylvia Sass, ready for her audition.

In the 1970s, LB had taken Ms. Sass to sing for Maria Callas. Thereafter, she could justifiably claim to be Callas's only protégé. I retrieved a piano/vocal of Verdi's *Don Carlo* from a book bag. LB placed the score on the piano and told me to play. I'd never seen this music before, but it had a vague familiarity.

Fortunately, Ms. Sass knew what she wanted, telling me with her eyes where to pause, where to play. At one complicated passage I sped up, and LB's left hand pressed mightily onto my shoulder as if to say *follow the singer*. Through the rest of the excerpt, I followed Ms. Sass almost without looking at the music, a feat I'd always thought unimaginable. At last, I understood how orchestra musicians played under LB's direction, focused not on the printed music but solely on his gestures and his eyes.

That night in Zagreb, the phone rang in my hotel room around midnight. LB said he couldn't sleep—nothing unusual about that—so he had unpacked all the *Don Carlo* materials: piano/vocal scores in the four-act and five-act versions; the Schiller play in German; the libretto in French, Italian, and English; and volumes of critical studies. Could I help him?

Franco Zeffirelli had proposed filming the opera on location at the Escorial, near Madrid, and LB wanted to prepare. Our *Don Carlo* seminar hurtled me back into LB's teamwork mode, rusting since *A Quiet Place*. We began by reading the Schiller play and sketched out the characters and their motivations. In comparison, the concise libretto by Joseph Méry and Camille du Locle was a breeze. But Verdi had made many alterations to this work, even in rehearsal, mere days before the opera's premiere. LB wanted to understand which version was the most authentic, not merely to piece together the best bits.

Six years later, he continued to ruminate on *Don Carlo*. At a rehearsal conducted by James Levine for the AIDS benefit *Music for Life*, I sat beside LB as Samuel Ramey sang the aria "Elle ne m'aime pas" ("Ella giammai m'amò" in the Italian version). LB said quietly, "She never really loved me," as though he were the character of King Philip II. I must have looked puzzled, because LB followed up. "It's sometimes translated as 'she doesn't love me anymore.'" The *Don Carlo* seminar was still in session.

The Zeffirelli film never came to pass. But that night in Zagreb, when LB allowed me to return to my room at 5 A.M., I had a detailed production schedule in my head. If I'd taken a hit of Dexedrine and stayed up all night, I'd have stage-managed the entire film and blocked all the scenes, relying on my mental map of the Escorial's majestic chambers.

After the concert the next night, the Zagreb crowds dashed off for the last city bus, leaving only two timid university students backstage. LB wanted to go anywhere other than his hotel room, so the students led us to an underground— literally—coffee house, an uncanny recreation of a 1950s beatnik hangout. Our oafish driver, an obvious government spy, disapproved of the place, so I suggested he amuse himself elsewhere and return at closing time, which LB extended by two hours. LB engaged the coffeehouse regulars on his favorite political topic: what makes a society work? Debate! A few students responded gamely, but I could tell they were thinking, *Who is this guy and will we get arrested for listening to him?* Yugoslavia's benevolent dictator Marshal Tito had been dead only three years and life in Zagreb promised no securities.

After the final concert of the tour in Ljubljana, the orchestra hosted a cozy reception where I was all but adopted by the Mauermanns: Erich, the BRFO's soft-spoken general manager, and his physician wife, Jutta. Of all the orchestras and all the managers I'd met in the last two years, the BRFO and the Mauermanns took the prize. The genuine kindness of this family fostered in me a sense of belonging. *This is how to survive on the road*, I thought, *if only I had this support everywhere.* The Mauermanns offered temporary stability, but that may have blinded me to how desperately I needed professional psychological help. Jutta Mauermann must have suspected this, as she gave me a copy of Erich Fromm's little book *The Art of Loving*, in German. In English, I'd once skimmed through it, but in German I studiously clambered over every word.

Onward to Vienna, with a change of planes in Zurich. I hadn't slept well in a while, and hoped to take a revitalizing shower if the first-class lounge in Zurich had one. I had to settle for simply washing my face, but the soap dispenser squirted a peculiarly inert liquid into my hands. It stuck on my face like varnish. Unable to control his laughter, LB pointed out the German word for "shoe polish" on the dispenser. I was too tired to be embarrassed, but I hoped he'd never tell anyone how stupid I was. Scrubbing the shoe polish off my face certainly woke me up.

Back in Vienna's familiar milieu, we headed out to Fritz and Sigrid Willheim's welcoming party. Script conferences with Humphrey Burton filled LB's schedule, and I enjoyed an occasional pub crawl with Jobst and Joachim of the DGG crew. The concerts were the usual drill: Saturday at 3 P.M., 11 A.M. on Sunday. Brahms's Piano Concerto No. 1 launched LB's association with pianist Krystian Zimerman, and Haydn's Symphony No. 88 delighted the crowd in the Musikverein, a delight heightened by an encore. LB repeated the symphony's last movement with his hands stuffed in his pants pockets and conducted solely with his eyebrows. Humphrey Burton ingeniously focused one camera on LB's expressive face. Even the staid Vienna Philharmonic couldn't suppress their smiles.

Cross-purposes developed the next day during the retake sessions. The retakes proposed by the video crew didn't match those from DGG, but LB didn't want to

How to conduct with your eyebrows. LB communicates Haydn's *Allegro con spirito*.

hear a discussion. He wanted his working day to be over. In a fury, he hurled a lit cigarette at the offstage carpet, where it charred a hole that remained for years. LB stomped off to the green room and slammed the door. I followed him meekly.

"Everybody's fired!" he roared, sounding like he meant it. Harry Kraut knocked on the door and LB hollered at him, "Go away, you're fired! You're all fired, the whole lot!"

LB couldn't fire the orchestra, of course, but why not the ten or twelve people involved in recording the concert?

LB lit a cigarette and took a seat. I gingerly toweled his sweaty hair. Harry knocked again but scuttled away when LB bellowed his edict a third time, though he reassuringly pointed out it didn't apply to me. For nearly an hour, we sat there in the green room, two witnesses at a train wreck. LB's silence bothered me, but like an apprentice therapist, I waited and kept mum.

A *pianissimo* knock at the door: it was the solo pianist, Krystian Zimerman. LB said *he* could enter.

"I heard today is your birthday," Krystian said to me. He solemnly shook my hand, kept his blue eyes on me, and avoided LB's. "What can I do for your birthday?" he asked. I was touched. I'd completely forgotten I turned thirty-three that day.

I turned to LB and asked, "May Krystian play something for me, as a birthday present?" and LB grunted. I motioned to the Bösendorfer: "Chopin Mazurkas, starting with opus 59." Krystian nodded and began to play.

That day's drama has remained with me, but Krystian's playing? Vanished, though it was his artistry that salvaged the day. Listening to the same Chopin pieces that I had played during one of his haircuts over a year ago, LB leaned back and his face softened, but slowly took on a fixed resolve. Krystian got to the last notes of Chopin's opus 59, and LB stood. I opened the door and he walked to the stage. After the retakes were completed, we rode back to the hotel and LB mused bitterly, "Why do I have to work so hard?" I thought of his office and household staff, the recording crew, a video company, an orchestra, a sold-out concert hall—those massed troops depending on him—but I said only that in three days we'd be back in New York.

Other than two afternoons at Juilliard with student conductors and composers, and a prayer for peace on New Year's Eve at the Cathedral of St. John the Divine, in New York LB's life reverted to his usual urban social calendar.

But something had shifted. I'd never seen LB as angry as he'd been in Vienna. But hadn't he been that angry when he yelled at me on our first meeting? "You don't talk that way to the *rebbe*!" What had brought this anger back? The unremitting schedule? Or was it something he couldn't share?

LB's Christmas present to me, December 1983: a Cabbage Patch doll. Jamie and Nina darkened the hair and glued on a moustache, thus creating a Charlito clone. I gave the little guy a new name: "Clonito." LB signed the Official Adoption Papers with the date 11 Jan. '84, and added a marginal note: "2 years married." Married? Maestro, let's not get carried away.

26 | How Pleads the Defendant?

AS MUSIC FOR A POLITICAL EVENT, Mahler's Symphony No. 2, the "Resurrection," ranks near the top of the list. At the National Cathedral in Washington, D.C., musicians from the National and the Baltimore Symphony Orchestras voluntarily amassed themselves under LB's direction for one sold-out performance in January 1984, protesting Ronald Reagan's missile installations. All his life, LB ardently supported a global end to nuclear arms.

Political passion made for high-level music-making, with soloists Barbara Hendricks and Jessye Norman, who poured forth "Urlicht" as if in one unbroken breath. Norman Scribner's chorus swelled to a full battalion. I noticed Gilbert Kaplan holding a score in the front row of the tenors. He was the one person in the chorus whose eyes never left LB. As a successful investor, Gil famously funneled his finances into his eccentric passion for the "Resurrection." Less than two years earlier, he had contracted the American Symphony Orchestra so that he could try conducting the work himself. (The performance was for an invited audience, no critics allowed, but one critic published a glowing review.) Eventually, Gil conducted the Mahler "Resurrection" over a hundred times.

Years later, Gil told me that in rehearsal, LB conducted a particular passage in a four-beat pattern, but in performance switched to a larger beat, in two. "We all rose onto our toes, watching him," Gil said. "He took us completely by surprise." So that's how LB seduced the chorus: by changing the beat pattern when they least expected it. LB's subtly subdivided beat, his famous "inner beats," kept all eyes glued on his every gesture.

My D.C. sidekick, George Steel, still at St. Alban's School on the grounds of the Cathedral, bounded up after a rehearsal with a huge ring of keys. "With these, I can open any door in the Cathedral," he boasted. A small group who stayed after the rehearsal followed George up a narrow staircase. A brief jangle of keys, and we entered the Cathedral's cubical central tower, where ten ropes dangled from holes in the ceiling. I recognized the set-up for change-ringing: one person per rope, ringing bells in intricate musical permutations. "Lenny, don't—" George warned, as LB grabbed at a rope that suddenly jerked skyward, nearly pulling LB's arm out of its socket. Far above, a single clang rang out.

At the St. Alban's post-concert reception two days later, the headmaster grilled George Steel. That solitary chime? "Yes, sir, it was a certain maestro who rang that bell, and no, sir, it won't happen again," George confessed. George was also chastised for bringing a visitor—Leonard Bernstein—to the dorm after curfew and bringing alcohol—LB's post-concert scotch—onto the school grounds. Not long after, George transferred to another school, with LB's endorsement.

Back in New York, LB repeated his anti-nuclear "Resurrection" with the Philharmonic, and then I packed seventeen pieces of luggage for a month on the road: Salzburg and Vienna, Austria, and a tour crisscrossing the United States with the Vienna Philharmonic (VPO). In Salzburg for Mozart's birthday, the VPO played with more refinement than ever, their eyes on LB, not on their music stands. That Zen-like state was now something I could comprehend. I'd stepped into that zone myself when I accompanied Sylvia Sass in LB's Budapest hotel suite. But while listening to LB and the VPO rehearse an all-Mozart program, I felt that all the good things in my life had come together. What was it about hearing music played with such clarity? Had my listening ability changed? Or had I finally learned to let go of all the things I couldn't fix?

On my own, I visited Mozart's birthplace, specifically to see the keyboard instruments. LB had once played Mozart's fortepiano and he told me how the lightweight action of the keys allowed his fingers to add ornaments with surprising ease. On my visit, thick Plexiglass protected those keys from claws such as mine. I no longer had a keyboard of any sort, so when we returned to New York many weeks later, I fulfilled a long-deferred dream and commissioned a clavichord, a reproduction of Mozart's own.

After four nights in Salzburg, I took the luggage on the Orient Express to Vienna while LB and Harry traveled in a chauffeured car. This was the way to travel: free from fetching things for the Maestro, I dozed as the wintry Danube glided by. Unpacking at the Hotel Sacher was easier than ever, so I was ready to join LB for dinner with his Viennese friends Fritz and Sigrid Willheim, and Susann Baumgärtel. The next two afternoons, LB rehearsed the last two of Mozart's symphonies. DGG recorded the sessions and pronounced them ready to release. Music-making with the VPO was often that straightforward. A miracle.

With his performance of Mahler's Symphony No. 4 in the *goldener Saal* of Vienna's Musikverein, LB indulged in a little showmanship. Normally, a pause after the third movement allows the solo singer to walk onstage, but LB continued without a break. Suddenly, the head of a boy soprano popped up above the balcony's railing. He'd been there all along, waiting for his cue, and he took the audience completely by surprise. From that high perch, the boy's voice sailed over the orchestra, and enraptured the Musikverein congregation. Afterwards, Christa Ludwig and Gwyneth Jones congratulated the young soloist.

"You sang beautifully," they said.

"I know," he replied, with the cockiness of an eleven-year-old.

This stay in Vienna was the most upbeat by far, until the last few days when the ill-will lurking under the locals' arch charm unnerved me. One morning, the hotel's chambermaid lectured me when I asked for "no starch" in German and used the wrong definite article. Marcel Prawy, septuagenarian dramaturg and critic, had long ago gained LB's favor for translating *West Side Story* into colloquial German, but he then used his access to pester LB with annoying gossip. More than once, Prawy literally stomped across my feet to whisper in LB's ear. Fortunately, Prawy didn't carry much weight.

I asked Christa Ludwig about this Viennese intoxication with intrigue. "Ja, ja," she sighed, echoing the weary Marschallin in *Der Rosenkavalier*. That's the way of the world.

Even Harry Kraut played the Viennese game. The next production of *A Quiet Place* would go into rehearsal at Milano's La Scala opera house in four months, so I met with Harry to go over the upcoming schedule, or so I thought. Instead, he divulged his plan to force LB's European press agent, Dorothee Koehler, to quit. "I'll give her a nervous breakdown," he cackled as he detailed what information he would withhold from her. I hoped that the horror wasn't too obvious on my face.

Dorothee had become a trusted colleague and a personal friend. How could I allow her to walk into this trap? The next day I took her for coffee several blocks from the hotel, and told her as casually as I could that we must work together closely in Milano. She should come to me with any questions, because Harry would be busy with other duties. She patted my arm and said we'd have a good time in Milano. Harry never suspected a thing, and it wasn't Dorothee who fell apart during *A Quiet Place* at La Scala.

VIENNA'S HIGHEST HONOR, the *Ehrenring*, represents the summit of its esteemed artistic heritage—the city's better side. After a morning rehearsal, we headed to the ornate city hall where the mayor presented LB with a chunk of brass that looked to me like the bonus for winning the World Series. It was a huge ring, but it fit one of LB's fingers perfectly, and he wore it during the brief ceremony. As four VPO musicians played the last movement of Mozart's C major string quartet, K. 465, the rest of us stood and listened to that celestial music. I glanced at LB, his face awash in benevolence, more than ever resembling Michelangelo's fatherly creator in the Sistine Chapel. Later, we spoke about music's power to summon the composer's soul, as if Mozart had dropped in on that solemn ceremony to usher LB into Elysium.

To catch the Concorde, we took an Austrian Airlines flight to Paris after the Sunday concert, a taxing day for me. I roused LB, ordered breakfast, got him dressed, did my concert duties, and while packing up the hotel suite, I organized lunch for six people. I'd noticed that Austrian Airlines hadn't indicated at which airport we'd land in Paris. I was concerned it might not be de Gaulle, from which the Concorde departed the next morning. An airline representative assured me over the phone that of course our flight would land at de Gaulle. Oh, those mischievous Austrians. As the flight touched down that evening. I could tell we were just south of Paris. Then I saw "Orly" emblazoned on the terminal. I'd already had a long day and was very weary. My heart sank. How were we going to get to the right airport?

"You'll have to pull a Maestro," I said to LB.

"What do you mean?" he asked.

I kept it simple. "We're at the wrong airport," I said.

Sunday evening. A deserted airport. The perfect place for an aimless stroll. We pounced on an unlucky Air France clerk who recognized LB, immediately turned off his computer and walked us to his Renault. He drove us straight across the city to the hotel at de Gaulle. Refusing compensation—I wrote a letter of commendation later—he also promised that our luggage would be on the Concorde the next morning, which it was. Maestro clout saved the day.

My head barely dented the pillow on my own bed in New York. The next day, the cross-continental VPO tour got under way in Ann Arbor, Michigan, where LB stayed in bed with a bronchial infection. I bought a massive steam inhaler and called a masseur. LB turned cranky, cancelled a reception, and said no thanks to the masseur, who worked on me instead, though I had to leap off the massage table every few minutes to answer the phone.

Two days later in Pasadena, the VPO musicians rented convertibles for a day at Disneyland and showed off their adorable sunburns at the concert that night, on the campus of the Worldwide Church of God. Ultra-conservative rules forbade smoking and alcohol, so to throw our "minders" off, I dragged LB into a toilet stall when he wanted a cigarette and sprayed an air purifier above his head as he puffed. LB's "apple juice" after the concert didn't fool anybody—the peaty tang of Ballantine's permeated the entire backstage. I held my breath when the nonagenarian patriarch of the Worldwide Church hobbled into the green room.

"I don't care what you're doing in here," Pastor Armstrong said, as though he expected to find us playing strip poker. "That was a mighty fine concert."

LB begged off from the pastor's reception, citing his bronchitis, but actually he couldn't wait to get back to the hotel for a drink.

The tour sponsor's corporate jet whisked us to San Francisco right after the next night's concert. As I finished unpacking at four in the morning, LB opened the champagne in the hotel's gift basket and handed me an overflowing glass. None for himself—he didn't like champagne.

"No, thank you," I said.

LB, mimicking Helen Coates's schoolmarm clucking, said, "Mustn't enjoy ourselves, mustn't have any fun." This was too much. I was tired.

"I can't help it if your helpers are all alcoholics," I blurted out, to my instant regret. "I'm going to bed."

As the concert at Davies Hall got under way sixteen hours later, Harry sat me down backstage, looking grave. "Don't talk back to the Maestro," he said. "Lenny said you called all his staff alcoholics."

I burst out laughing.

"Harry, it was four in the morning," I said. "I was worn out and wanted to go to bed, and he handed me a glass of champagne while imitating Helen Coates." I parroted LB's performance. "You got less than half the story," I said. "It won't happen again. I apologized to LB earlier today," I fibbed, but we were both laughing. I was off the hook.

After the next concert in Salt Lake City, the Utah Symphony's music director, Maurice Abravanel, rushed backstage in high spirits. He embraced LB and begged him to stay the night. I was sorry not to spend more time with Maestro Abravanel, whom I never saw again. But the tour sponsor's private jet waited nearby and LB wanted to get going. Off we flew to Chicago in the middle of the night. The lights of western towns glinted far below as the crew served us lobster tails. Despite the late hours, the luxury of this orchestra tour suited me just fine. I indulged in a drink or two, making sure LB noticed that I was enjoying myself.

In Chicago, Harry handed me two tickets for my closest friends from college, Rob and Joanie. The next morning they told me about the fall LB took as he stepped off the podium during the concert's standing ovation.

"It was scary," they said. From stage right, I heard the applause stop on a dime. "He fell flat on his face and didn't move. Two guys hustled onstage and hauled Mr. Bernstein off between the violin stands."

LB was dead white and unable to breathe. An ambulance pulled up to the stage door, and I hailed a taxi to Northwestern University hospital. I reassured the VPO's general secretary, Brigitta Grabner, that we didn't have far to go. Otherwise, neither of us spoke. I tried not to think that this tour was over. Maybe all tours were over.

Doctors determined that when LB tripped over the carpeted steps on the podium and fell forward on his chest, one of LB's lungs collapsed. No broken bones, not even a bruised rib, but the doctors forbade LB from flying to Pittsburgh for the next concert—not until his lung re-inflated.

Was this the lung that collapsed in LB's final year? Was there already a cancer on the pleura, the membrane around his lung? Did LB merely trip, or had he fainted from exhaustion? Was it the beginning of the end? None of us looked beyond that night's immediate setback. Those questions didn't occur to me until four years later, a year before his death, when I heard LB say, "Something isn't right." I didn't know he meant something in his chest.

Sunday morning television all over the country picked up the story of LB's collapse. The phone in my Chicago hotel room rang without a break. My friend Joanie asked if she could bring her infant son, Jeremy, for a visit. "I know where you are," she said over the phone, "thanks to the news on TV." As we slipped into LB's suite, he was laughing on the phone with Lauren Bacall.

"How do you top a standing ovation?" LB chortled. "That old vaudeville stunt: a pratfall." For once, he wasn't smoking during a phone call. When he spotted little Jeremy crawling on the carpet, LB got onto the floor and indulged his grand-fatherly whims for the rest of the afternoon. By the evening his lungs were fully functioning.

The next day at the airport in Pittsburgh, Zubin Mehta waited on the tarmac to "offer any assistance" should LB not feel up to conducting that afternoon. LB couldn't have been more surprised—or irritated.

"I am perfectly capable of conducting my concert," LB replied testily. I greeted Maestro Mehta and asked him to get in the limo with us. On the ride to Heinz Hall, LB turned especially talkative. I acted like everything was normal as I prepared for the concert, and Maestro Mehta returned to the airport and caught a flight to New York before the matinee performance was over. When LB saw that Mehta was gone, he muttered under his breath, "What nerve!"

Once again, we moved on immediately after the concert, heading to Washington, D.C. Normally, the president would come to a concert at the Kennedy Center. That certainly would have been the case if Jimmy Carter had still been president, but we didn't get any word whether Republican Ronald Reagan would attend. After I helped LB change out of his sweat-soaked concert clothes, I ventured into the reception room. Reagan had delegated this concert to his Vice President, George Bush, and his Secretary of State, George Shultz, and their wives.

I introduced myself to the Vice President, who launched into a critique of symphonic form.

"That symphony needs a break in it," he said in his squeaky voice. "It's in four parts just like a football game, so there should be a halftime. When there's a first half and a second half," he ran on, "there should be a break." His wife, Barbara Bush, gave me a bullying glare as if to say, *Don't you dare say anything, you little twerp, or I'll make you pay for it.* I tried to keep a poker face, without much luck.

Out of the corner of my eye, I saw LB sneaking toward his mother and her sisters on a sofa, so I beckoned him over to the politicians. Without shaking any hands, he said curtly, "See that you introduce the Vice President to my mother." Then LB turned his back on the Bushes and retreated into his dressing room.

Five years later, LB refused the National Medal of the Arts, ostensibly to protest the withdrawal of National Endowment funds from an AIDS art exhibit, but his private reason was to avoid the Bush White House. In LB's view, the Bush years were simply an extension of Reagan's worst policies.

After the VPO tour ended at Carnegie Hall, LB made his annual appearance with the New York Philharmonic and conducted three spring-titled works on the first day of spring—his mother Jennie's eighty-eighth birthday. In Stravinsky's *Rite of Spring*, LB got so athletic on the podium that Jamie slyly cautioned her father, "Daddy, if you did that anywhere else in public, you'd be arrested." The Philharmonic brought on a fit of gyrations in LB, and for his savvy New York audience LB always put on a show.

The Philharmonic musicians bestowed an honorary membership on LB, making him inordinately proud. "That's my musical family," he said later. A concept LB stressed with young conductors was the relationship a music director has with an orchestra—and with the larger community. "Think of them all as your family," LB always said.

Apprehensive about the unremitting schedule ahead, I wasn't completely paying attention when Harry put on a patronizing tone to announce, "I've decided to train you to be an orchestra manager." Me? A manager? This came out of nowhere. I should have asked what that training involved, why he thought I was a suitable candidate, or at least flattered him with questions about his own managerial experience.

Instead, I blurted out, "Of all the orchestra managers I've met in the last two years, only three are decent human beings." It was the one time I took Harry by surprise, but for all the wrong reasons. My outburst ended the discussion. As far as Harry was concerned, I'd buried all my future ambitions. Later, a wave of paranoia crept over me. Was he trying to get rid of me? Was it time for a new assistant for the Maestro? Did he regret sharing that wicked plan of his to give Dorothee a breakdown?

It scared me that I could end up completely under Harry's thumb, and the last thing I wanted was to turn into a miniature version of Harry Kraut. But I was serious about the phrase "decent human beings." Thank goodness Harry didn't ask me to name names.

———

IN KEY WEST for two supposedly restorative weeks, we were kept indoors by tornado warnings. I hired a local chef to host dinners for LB's social circle, headed by gregarious Liz Lear, an LB friend who always found him the perfect Key West house. Poet John Malcolm Brinnin brought anagram tiles and tried to cheer me up as I sank into grief over the death of my DGG pal Joachim Niss in Germany, from a syndrome that looked suspiciously like AIDS. After the weather cleared, fashion designer Auro Varani took over LB's social life, and I shifted my focus to Key West's main pastime: drinking.

One afternoon with the eminent theater director Philip Burton, LB asked leading questions about the young man who adopted Mr. Burton's last name, the actor Richard Burton. Was theirs a chaste mentor-protégé relationship? LB didn't think so, aching to pry deeper. I'd never heard LB be so catty. I wanted to return the next afternoon to talk to Mr. Burton on my own, but LB's attitude had left a sour taste in the air.

I hadn't snapped out of my Key West funk when we headed to Philadelphia for the Curtis Institute's sixtieth anniversary gala. It helped me to concentrate on music. I took notes during Susan Starr's solo-piano rehearsal of LB's Symphony No. 2, "The Age of Anxiety," and filled a score with LB's on-the-spot revisions. Later, I passed them on to his publisher, Boosey & Hawkes. Being useful musically fulfilled me more than fretting over Harry's notions for my managerial future. I hoped that option was now a dead issue.

———

WHEN TULIPS BLOOM in Hamburg, Germany, Deutsche Grammophon used to hold a photo opportunity for artists and management, the *Tulpenfest,* at which everyone clutched a single, yellow-for-DGG tulip. At the Hamburg hotel, LB donned his slightly cheesy white suit and headed to Christoph von Eschenbach's house for a *vor-Tulpenfest* cocktail. After setting up the hotel suite, I walked to Eschenbach's lakeside villa. One of his servants said LB and Eschenbach were out sailing and I caught a glimpse of LB out on the lake, but not what I'd call sailing.

He was standing in the water and shoving a dinghy off a mudflat. His pants and shoes were caked with muck. I didn't have a change of clothes with me for LB, so I hoped we could we go back to the hotel before heading to the *Tulpenfest*.

After the dinghy docked, Eschenbach ignored me, as usual, and whisked LB into a car. Suddenly I was on my own. I hadn't seen the *Tulpenfest* invitation, so I had no idea where to go. I flashed back to an evening two years ago, when we'd missed a reception in Berlin because Harry hadn't told me where it was. Now it was Eschenbach. I headed back to the hotel, ready to bring LB a fresh outfit at the *Tulpenfest*, if anyone called.

Three hours later, no one had called. Much later, LB returned, tired and drunk, with Harry on a rampage that I hadn't brought a fresh suit to the *Tulpenfest*. "Obviously, Charlie doesn't care about looking after Lenny," he said belligerently. "I will make my case, and Lenny can decide whether to fire Charlie."

I wasn't ready for this. What had happened? I was now on trial for LB's frolic in the mud and Eschenbach's brush-off. I stood facing LB while Harry ranted. I was trying not to break down. LB wouldn't look at me. This bullying felt like a set-up, carefully planned to leave me defenseless. Why? Revenge for not rejoicing at Harry's offer to put me on the fast track of orchestra management? I realized we were on the hotel's top floor. A jump out the window would quickly end it all.

Harry's rant eventually came to an end, and I laid out fresh clothes for LB as he took a shower. We piled into one car for drinks at Helmut Schmidt's, the former German Chancellor. His wife, Loki, made intelligent small talk with me, but I was still shaking and couldn't speak. She must have thought I was damaged.

On the flights to Israel the next day, we changed planes in Munich, where BRFO manager Erich Mauermann brought his family into the first-class lounge. Erich's wife, Jutta, gave me a stuffed, floral-print hippopotamus with a beguiling smile. I held it to my chest and sobbed, all the way to Tel Aviv. On landing, I forgot to take the hippo with me. El Al said they never found it. Is there anything more forlorn than a forgotten stuffed animal? Yes: a discarded assistant.

27 | Down for the Count

AVI SHOSHANI, MANAGER OF THE Israel Philharmonic Orchestra (IPO), got a hug from me as I stepped off the plane in Tel Aviv. Avi intuited that something had changed because he gave me his home phone number without my asking. My face was probably as red and puffy as a squalling infant's.

On our first week back in Israel, Harry Kraut was off somewhere else, to my relief, so I washed off the residual scum of the *Tulpenfest* with what usually revived me: a plunge into the schedule. Hyper-emotional music by Tchaikovsky was on some of the ten concerts in Israel, and Stravinsky's *Pulcinella*, which I loved. But the selections from Mahler's *Des Knaben Wunderhorn,* which I'd never heard before, comforted me the most and took on special meaning.

The film director George Roy Hill, seated behind me on the El Al flight, ignored my distressed sniffling and introduced himself. Could LB come to a screening of *The Little Drummer Girl*? I'd never watched an unscored film, much less while sitting next to Leonard Bernstein. An interesting challenge, I thought, would be to underline the story's espionage with music. But LB focused on the love interest. Afterwards LB said to Mr. Hill, rather patronizingly, "You want a big romantic love theme. I don't write like that anymore." Mr. Hill thanked LB for his time.

The first weekend in May coincided with Israel's Memorial Day, and LB jumped at an invitation to go sailing on the Mediterranean. In a net suspended beneath the bowsprit, I stretched out and pondered my future. If I could get through the La Scala premiere of *A Quiet Place* in six weeks—around that emotionally freighted day of June 17—I could search for another job afterwards. Or a shrink. Or both.

In Jerusalem for one of the concerts, I called Goldie Feinsilver. She'd taught Hebrew School in Boston decades ago, keeping her eye on one rambunctious pupil, Louis Bernstein—whom everyone called "Lenny." (At sixteen, Louis legally changed his name to Leonard.) Goldie invited me for a walk the next morning, to see what her archeologist friends and colleagues were excavating. Tiny, elegant, bursting with the energy of a natural-born teacher, Goldie led me around the Citadel and the Jewish Quarter. As we looked down into the deep digs, she explained the layers of pre-Roman civilization. Her passion for history and her fastidious scholarship captured my imagination. A love of learning infused everything she said. No wonder LB claimed he "fell in love" with his teachers. When she dropped me off at the King David Hotel, I felt like I'd been away for centuries.

Aaron Stern roomed in the YMCA across the street from the hotel, and on one free day, we rented a car for an excursion to the Dead Sea. Sharing my anxieties with Aaron helped, but I cautiously stopped short of the mock trial in Hamburg. Harry Kraut siphoned gossip from all quarters—but Aaron couldn't talk about something he didn't know. It was better not to tell him. Whom could I confide in about Harry's bullying? My head count came up blank.

The recorded concerts went so well that an hour got trimmed from a Tchaikovsky retake session, putting LB in a mischievous mood. When the IPO's librarian, Marilyn Steiner—several weeks pregnant—returned LB's conducting scores to the green room, LB insisted on predicting the sex of her child. As IPO musicians crowded around, LB eased Marilyn backwards onto the sofa and dangled his wedding ring above her abdomen on a shoelace donated by her husband. "If the ring moves laterally, the baby's a boy," LB said with authority. "If the ring moves the other way, it's a girl." Laughter welled up as the ring orbited in a circle. "It's a boy," said LB, "But with girlish tendencies." Marilyn guffawed as the crowd broke into applause. In due time she gave birth to curly-haired Lorin, every bit a boy and with a sweet disposition.

Having made daily changes to her travel plans for weeks, Shirley Bernstein finally joined her brother in Tel Aviv. LB joked that Israel hadn't witnessed so momentous an arrival since the Queen of Sheba dropped in on King Solomon. Harry Kraut's assistant, Ned Davies, also arrived, to help LB write a script for a video essay, *The Little Drummer Boy*—nothing like *The Drummer Girl* that we'd screened a week earlier. Devoid of love interest or espionage, LB's script explored Gustav Mahler's pervasive sense of guilt, evidenced in the song "Der Tambourg'sell" from *Des Knaben Wunderhorn.*

"What have I done wrong?" LB wailed to the video camera, in the voice of a young boy about to be hanged—an uncomfortable parallel to my recent arraignment in Hamburg, with its similarly unexplained guilt. *What have I done, indeed.*

As Shirley accompanied LB to his dinner invitations, and Ned took Harry's heat off me, I had time to swim in the hotel's enormous salt-water pool and even indulge in a massage. As I half-sat up, the masseur did something I've never experienced before or since: he worked the crown of his head down my spine while pulling back on my shoulders. The force of his head against my vertebra realigned every bone, a boon I felt for weeks. Still, my shoulders carried the weight of dejection. At sunset, I stood on the balcony of my room sixteen floors up and watched the hunky lifeguards swab the salt from the empty swimming pool. As I had fleetingly wondered in Hamburg, I pondered whether a fall would be fatal.

One evening, Jobst from the DGG crew suggested we go to Old Jaffa for dinner. On our leisurely walk along the beach back to the hotel, Jobst invited me to his home in Braunschweig that summer. Another night I called friends who planned to be in Italy in July, and asked if I could join them. We could meet in Milano after the La Scala production of *A Quiet Place*. To make plans, involve other people—this was all new to me.

Mahler's *Des Knaben Wunderhorn* featured Lucia Popp, my one chance to hear that pure voice of hers that seemed to bloom effortlessly from her innate sunshine. My spirits lifted whenever she said my name, and that semblance of happiness enabled me to concentrate on the music. I began to grasp the arc of Mahler's musical thinking, from his song settings to expansive symphonic forms, an aural flowering toward the abundance of sounds in an orchestra. No matter how big the sound, "Mahler is always chamber music," LB said, admonishing the IPO musicians to listen carefully to one another.

To get to Florence, Italy, in time for a Saturday concert as part of the May Festival, we had to leave Israel on a Friday. Could the IPO settle at its destination before Shabbat started at sundown? The Chief Rabbi in Rome—*not* Leonard Bernstein—had to give special dispensation in case of a flight delay, a real cliff-hanger. One by one, the IPO musicians confided to LB, "It doesn't matter to me, it's those others" who wouldn't travel on Shabbat. After the tenth of these confessions, LB waved away their concerns, implying that those strictures existed principally to test how the faithful might dodge around them.

Minutes before a press conference in Florence, LB wrote an essay for the May Festival. His phrase "I don't know anyone who has been given so many gifts as I" was translated by Luciano Berio as "*tanti talenti*"—"I don't know anyone as talented as I," a slight LB could not ignore. "His English is better than that," LB griped. "Luciano did that on purpose." At the press conference, LB barely restrained himself from chastising Berio in public.

LB decided he'd feel less annoyed if he took a nap. What a gift to me: a free hour in Florence. I couldn't go far, but I ventured across the Arno to revisit some Masaccio frescoes that had hypnotized me nine years earlier. As I helped LB dress for the concert that evening, I told him about Masaccio's visceral images and the central position he'd held in the history of painting. LB responded with a professorial rehash of his Harvard inculcation in aesthetics. To me, LB's little lecture revealed the thin comprehension he had of art history. His masterful memory seemed to be completely awash in sound, to the exclusion of all the other arts. (Sound, of course, includes poetry and drama.)

After the concert, DGG producer Hanno Rinke led me to the far raunchier aesthetic of a gay disco, but halfway through a bottle of beer, I opted not to go deaf and headed back to the hotel. The next day I vomited into the toilet all afternoon, so LB told me to stay in bed. Fortunately, the Ricordis were on hand from Milano, so Madina's son Carlo filled in for me during the concert. I never properly thanked him for taking on that backstage duty. Afterwards, LB said he missed me but enjoyed telling Carlo what to do.

The IPO departed from Pisa the next evening. Each musician bade LB goodbye as he boarded a flight on his own, en route to Boston to see Nina, his youngest, graduate from Harvard. Harry Kraut trotted off to the Amalfi coast while I stayed in Florence. All of a sudden I felt much better, well enough to climb all the stairs in the Cathedral's dome, to pop by the Uffizi and Accademia twice, and to walk to the Piazzale Michelangelo for the panorama of the Arno valley. History and art filled my head, and I didn't mind being alone. In a bookstore, I easily read the first page of Elias Canetti's memoir, *La Lingua Salvata*, so I bought it. What better way to improve my Italian vocabulary than with a good book?

In Milano, Dorothee Koehler met me with a van for the luggage. I'd been in touch with her every day, thwarting Harry's nefarious scheme to give her a nervous breakdown. Dorothee had found an entire house for LB, as well as a capable couple to cook and clean. She said that a piano and a stereo system would be delivered soon. When I bought an extension cord and light bulbs, I surprised myself by speaking only Italian. I felt almost at home in Milano, ready for the weeks of working at LB's side on *A Quiet Place* at La Scala.

Madina Ricordi invited me over to meet our driver, the young, aristocratic Nicolò. I almost blurted out Ann Dedman's phrase when she'd first met me in Bloomington: *He's too cute.* Maybe I should have. Shortly after LB met Nicolò, they were found in bed together by Harry Kraut. Harry's laugh was infectious when he told me how the two paramours had sat up and shouted simultaneously, "He made me do it." Even I had to laugh at that.

Jack Gottlieb, who twenty years earlier had been LB's first assistant, arrived to serve as music editor for *A Quiet Place*. Jack, Harry, his assistant Ned Davies, and I boarded in a serviceable residential hotel not far from LB's townhouse and an easy walk in the other direction to La Scala. Somehow I had a free evening to accompany Dorothee to a performance of Mozart's *Lucio Silla*, remembering to wear the beautiful silk tie she'd given me.

Another evening, Madina cooked risotto for a dozen people, the only new face being Susan Sarandon, who arrived on the arm of screenwriter Franco Amurri.

Franco had turned suave and solicitous, an about-face that in no way resembled the petulant houseguest he'd been in Bloomington, Indiana. In the months ahead, he and Susan had a beautiful baby girl, and they named LB as her godfather.

Five days before the dress rehearsal, LB first heard the La Scala orchestra rehearse *A Quiet Place*. For three hours, I sat next to him and took notes—an easy day. The next afternoon, LB and Stephen Wadsworth coached a handful of singers at LB's house, and then we had three long days with the entire cast rehearsing at the opera house. We arrived at 10 A.M. and didn't leave until midnight. Grueling, but under Stephen Wadsworth's detailed direction, the production came together despite some short fuses. One singer yelled at me when I handed him a few notes from LB. I was only doing my job.

Our driver, Nicolò, departed one afternoon for his Olympic fencing trials, so I became the substitute chauffeur. It was midnight when the rehearsal ended and we hadn't eaten since lunch, but Madina Ricordi insisted we stop by to see her. I hoped she'd give us something to eat, maybe LB's favorite *bresaola*, but no. She greeted LB with a wide grin and a tumbler of grappa. On an empty stomach? I wanted to knock the glass from her hand, but LB grabbed it and gulped it down.

Instantly, LB turned incoherent. Madina's son Carlo helped me heave LB into the elevator and then into the back seat of the car. I'd never seen LB so out of control. As I drove the narrow streets back to the house, he kicked the back of my seat, screaming, "You're a fucking maniac," even though we inched along in dense traffic. No doubt LB's head was spinning. I hoped he wouldn't vomit inside the car. Speaking quietly, Carlo held on to LB to calm him.

When I stopped in front of the house, car horns blared behind me. I opened the rear passenger door, but LB wouldn't—or couldn't—budge. The cars behind us honked more insistently, so I drove down the block to the parking garage and stopped in the driveway. Suddenly LB lurched out of the rear door, turned to kick the car as hard as he could, and fell onto his back as the rear fender clattered onto the pavement.

Fortunately, LB landed on a patch of soft grass by the garage's driveway. Carlo bent over LB and tried to get him on his feet. As traffic passed by, I hoped no paparazzi lurked behind those windshields—deep Mississippi Mud. LB lay on his back, looking like death, but breathing. I picked up the fender and said I'd come back after parking.

Inside the garage, it took me a minute to shove the fender into place, and when I returned to the street, Carlo and LB were gone. I headed to the house but there was no sign of them, so I figured Carlo had led LB safely inside. I decided to call it a night. We had a 10 A.M. rehearsal the next day.

No sooner had I taken off my shoes than Harry Kraut knocked on my door. "Are you all right?" he asked, looking at me as though I had just committed murder.

"I'm fine," I said calmly, "But I'm very tired. LB is on a rampage. He kicked the fender off the car, and then he fell on the ground in a drunken stupor. Carlo took him home." Harry said he'd send Ned Davies to the house to find out if LB was all right.

An hour later, another knock at the door. "I went over there, and all the Ricordis were carrying on, laughing, having a good time with LB," Ned said. I had nothing to say and went to bed.

The next morning I told Harry I wanted to quit on July 1, only two weeks away. To my surprise, Harry told me to take off the entire month of July. I immediately called my friends who were coming to Italy. We would meet in Milano and go to Lake Como for a week. Then I'd fly to Germany, stay with Jobst from DGG, and eventually return to New York and make a brief visit to Washington to catch one performance of *A Quiet Place* at the Kennedy Center. I'd be back at the Dakota on August 1.

Alexander Bernstein arrived in time for the opera's La Scala premiere, and LB righted himself. No more grappa.

———

MEANWHILE, LB rehearsed the La Scala orchestra in Mozart's G Minor Symphony and Mahler's Symphony No. 4, several hours of conducting before sitting through a full-length opera that began at 8 P.M. Those orchestra concerts filled the two nights *A Quiet Place* wasn't in performance. But night after night, ticket sales for the opera dwindled. Reviews weren't good and the theater loomed vast and empty. The scant pairs of clapping hands echoed desolately. I sat next to LB in a side box, ready to write down everything he said, but at the end of a performance, my notepad was often blank.

It was time to organize the cast party and settle the bills: the piano, the tuner, the housekeeping couple—who begged to continue with LB in New York, but what would Julia say?—a van to get everything to the airport, including the opera's orchestra parts, the excess baggage fees, and of course floral bouquets for the La Scala staff. LB and Alexander headed to Franco Zeffirelli's villa in Positano before returning to the States.

As I waited in Milano for my friends to arrive, Ned Davies called from Washington. The airline shipping the orchestra parts for *A Quiet Place* had left the trunk on the tarmac during a downpour. The paper in the trunk turned into blocks of pulp. "I'm on vacation," I said. No twinge of guilt in me. The Library of Congress stepped in, freeze-dried the pulp and separated the frozen pages. Then a cohort of music copyists transferred corrections to a new set of parts. I was happy to be four thousand miles away.

A week on Lake Como convinced me I could live in Italy, if only I had the cash. When my friends and I walked back from a restaurant well after midnight and were stopped by the police, I explained in perfect Italian why we were stumbling in the dark without a flashlight. Another evening, I asked directions and fell into a conversation with a charming pair of elderly ladies. Both times, Italian came to me naturally. I even corrected myself now and then. I probably sounded like a pretentious American, but I loved speaking the language.

In Washington, D.C., I stayed with my best friend, John, now in a graduate program at George Washington University. To see how LB was faring, I called the Watergate Hotel and got Harry Kraut's room. Maybe I wasn't on LB's phone list? That afternoon, I entered LB's suite as a friend, and we carried on a riotous free-associative conversation, cracking jokes, playing word games—any topic but *A Quiet Place*. Harry complained later, "I couldn't get a word in," but I heard a note of relief in his voice. In another week, I'd be back on the job.

That afternoon, Harry called to put me in charge of the cast party in Washington, but I'd gone for a walk and my friend John picked up the phone in his apartment.

"How dare you, Mr. Kraut," John said, "Charlie's on vacation. He's not available for another week." John calmly told me this later, but my heart stopped. Did Harry fire me over the phone? Not at all.

"I let Harry have it over the phone," John told me later. "He backed down and somebody else is organizing the cast party." I thanked John and we talked for a while about why I couldn't stand up for myself. I didn't come to any helpful conclusion, other than it seemed I'd worn a target all my life, one that was visible only to others, bearing the command PLEASE BULLY ME.

R. Charlie Harmon
Is no flashy Carmen;
Rather somewhat paler,
Like Micaela.

LB's Insomniads—an insomniac's poetry—usually centered on one insight, couched in disarming levity.

28 | Who's in Charge Here?

WHAT SORT OF INFECTION LB HAD, he wasn't saying, but he began an antibiotic regimen just before his 66th birthday that August. His blood had to be carefully monitored, so three times a week, I drove LB to a medical office in Fairfield, Connecticut. As we detoured one sunny afternoon to buy corn on the cob, black smoke billowed from the hood of the Mercedes. After its most recent tune-up in the city, the mechanics had left the radiator empty. Time to find a better garage, yet again. In a sulk, LB admitted that his beloved Mercedes might be a lemon. Now I was attending to two ailing bodies: the Maestro and his persnickety car.

No way would an antibiotic dent LB's intake of booze, not on his birthday. Twenty friends and family members convened in Connecticut for an all-day party, though no one had fully taken charge in the kitchen, despite a corps of candidates. Julia, intrepid as ever, kept the larder stocked and made breakfast for LB and any number of guests.

That summer of 1984, the aspiring chef was a woman of a certain age, reputedly Hungarian. For LB's birthday, Julia ordered two dozen lobsters, a species unknown in Budapest, I guess, because the Hungarian promptly murdered the whole clutch of crustaceans in a bathtub of tap water. Then she retired upstairs to rest. The cocktail hour swung gaily along until Julia announced that the lobsters were "complete dead." Julia certainly knew how to stop a party. No wonder she always wore black. "No eating a dead lobster," she declared. LB's sister Shirley ventured upstairs and reported, "The cook is too drunk to stand." After a little coaxing, Julia acquiesced and steamed the lobsters anyway—nobody took ill— and I drove one sobbing Hungarian to the train station, making sure she boarded in the right direction.

The next day at JFK airport, I picked up Jobst Eberhardt, who arrived ahead of his DGG colleagues. The year's highest-profile recording was about to get under way: *West Side Story*, with the composer conducting a handpicked cast. Uh, picked by whom? After Neil Shicoff couldn't fit the sessions in his schedule, a hastily convened committee weighed the options. LB had mentioned a tenor he'd heard at Covent Garden—but what was his name? No one bothered to look it up. I joked that if DGG knew what *Mikado* was—and allowed LB to record it—they'd book a perversely Wagnerian cast: *als Yum-Yum ein fabelhafter Sopran, Birgit Nilsson.*

Wasn't it obvious that the singer for Tony, leader of the Jets, had to be American, to nail the accent and the savvy rhythms? But the committee—headed by Harry Kraut—slotted José Carreras, a brilliant but decidedly Spanish tenor, and then didn't send him any music. DGG flew Carreras to New York at the last minute. His luggage ended up who knew where.

West Side Story had opened on Broadway twenty-seven years earlier, and since then, not a single written note had been corrected or coerced toward legibility. As is typical on Broadway, the parts had been copied in a rush. After the successful opening night, those parts were left as they were—extremely messy would be an understatement. Since then, Music Theatre International had rented copies of those parts for amateur productions, and it wasn't unusual for musicians to get lost in the illegible thicket of notes. Even Harry Kraut remembered hearing a trumpeter go haywire during a high school performance. (Harry often boasted that he had no musical memory, so that wayward trumpeter must have been outstanding, but for all the wrong reasons.)

With an eye toward the creation of a critical edition for LB's recording, a crew of music editors pored over the performance materials. They found several hundred discrepancies in the score and many dozens in the orchestra parts. (Years later, when I worked on the first publication of the full score, the number of errors came close to two thousand.) Bearing their list of questions that only the composer could answer, the editorial crew traipsed to the Dakota. LB seated them in his study, plunked ice into a row of tumblers, splashed Ballantine's over the ice—and proceeded to hold forth for two hours without pause. He did not permit a peep from anyone else. So much for all those discrepancies. So much for a critical edition.

LB said that when he was writing the score in the 1950s, as he played the dance numbers at the piano, Jerome Robbins stood behind him. "Eight more bars of that," Robbins would say, pressing his hands onto LB's shoulders. So LB would figure out how to elongate a musical phrase by eight bars, while also keeping judicious proportions within each musical number. Robbins needed enough music to get people across the stage; Bernstein wanted the music to have a shape. Everything came together, but very quickly.

Someone else had conducted in that Broadway pit, nearly thirty years ago. Now LB was looking at the score for the first time as a conductor, re-learning how many bars were in all those extended musical phrases. He studied the work the way he studied every score, as though he'd never seen it before. In this case, he couldn't always make out what was on the page.

Three enormous volumes, a reprint of the hand-copied orchestration, landed on LB's desk. Every page elicited his wrath. A transposed chunk of the "Tonight" duet had never been recopied into the correct key; in the margin LB scrawled, "Thanks a pant load!" (A quote from *A Quiet Place*.) Truthfully, other than supervising Sid Ramin and Irwin Kostal when they orchestrated *West Side Story* in 1957, LB had paid scant attention to the preparation of this music.

On Labor Day, the principal singers—minus Carreras, still in transit—assembled for a piano rehearsal at the Dakota. Dame Kiri Te Kanawa arrived to be coached by the composer in her role of Maria, a session she later told the press was like "working with Mozart." She claimed that to sing Maria had been a goal since she was a teenager.

I took Dame Te Kanawa's fur coat and hung it in the closet by the front door. At an unusual sound, I reopened the closet: excrement oozed from the ceiling and splattered directly onto those pricey pelts. Someone upstairs had flushed a newly installed toilet, unaware of its incomplete hookup. I hotfooted the fur coat into the kitchen and waited until the rehearsal ended to inform Ms. Te Kanawa that insurance would cover the damage. I hoped that was true.

Each day in the old RCA Midtown studio, somebody threw a fit. José Carreras didn't get one more take on his high B flat in "Maria." Dame Te Kanawa, slightly dehydrated after a long flight, justifiably freaked out over the arctic chill of the studio's air conditioning. LB tried to calm her with a tight hug. Later he confided to me how much pleasure he got from pressing her breasts to his chest—but then, he actually did calm her down. In the middle of an otherwise productive session, LB chewed out the editorial crew and then loudly requested producer John McClure not to give Carreras elocution lessons over the sound system: "John, please don't do that." Meanwhile, DGG hadn't booked anyone for the spoken dialogue in "Tonight." Alexander, Nina, and LB himself filled in: the offstage "Maruca!"—Maria's father beckoning his daughter—is Leonard Bernstein, uncredited. Against the back wall, I sat engrossed in a book.

This rocky recording project spawned an unforeseen benefit. Five years later, during discussions prior to recording *Candide*, LB put his foot down: assign all musical preparation to one person—Charlie. By then I could tackle such a test. It helped that I'd seen how much had gone haywire during DGG's *West Side Story*.

Three days later we flew to Pittsburgh for the fortieth anniversary of the premiere of LB's Symphony No. 1, "Jeremiah." Only LB's press agent, Maggie Carson, accompanied us while Harry Kraut globe-trotted off to Japan. A week of rehearsals at 10 A.M., interviews, lunches with the orchestra manager . . . it might have been anywhere, except for the orchestra musicians familiar to me from my student years at Carnegie-Mellon. My mother surprised me by showing up in Pittsburgh, joining me for lunch with my college mentor, Roland Leich. He confided to my mother that of his many students, I was the one who would "make it." She could barely bring herself to share that with me. I guess I was more like my mother than I realized, because I didn't pass Mr. Leich's kind estimation on to LB. What had I made of myself? Not much. I packed bags and answered the phone. Who needs a BFA in music composition to do that?

LB's jaw dropped when he saw that Aaron's parents lived at Amberson Towers. "Why didn't you tell me?" LB asked. Son of amber, progeny of Bernstein, Amberson Inc., Amberson Towers. "Of course there are no accidents," he said. Aaron's mother remembered the dashing conductor she'd seen at the premiere of "Jeremiah" and succumbed to the charm he slathered on forty years later at her dining table. Another no-accident moment. LB knew how to win over his prospective in-laws.

Picking up where she'd left off with LB, ebullient Gail Dubinbaum sang an impassioned "Lamentation" and tossed off a Rossini aria in a program identical to that of 1944, which had featured LB's favorite singer, Jennie Tourel. Nostalgic over his triumph of forty years ago, LB reminisced about his mentor, Fritz Reiner, music director in Pittsburgh at that time. "Reiner never smiled," LB said, "And he used the tiniest stick. From behind, it looked like he was standing stock still," yet he got spectacular musical results. Whether Maestro Reiner reacted to Bernstein's podium antics, LB never said.

After a rehearsal in the Carnegie Institute's music hall, the car drove past what used to be the Hotel Schenley. LB remembered the special treatment he'd received from a bellboy there: a blow job, followed by the greeting, "Welcome to Pittsburgh, sir." LB still thought of himself as a vigorous twenty-six-year-old, "in the prime of his youth," he said—often.

Back in New York for less than a week, I packed twenty bags to see us through two months overseas. Before boarding the Concorde at JFK, I noticed a towering geisha, pretty obviously a man in full Japanese drag. The pop star Boy George? Not about to look up from his crossword puzzle, LB didn't spot the geisha until inside the plane.

"What," he asked loudly, "is that?"

"Sit down and I'll tell you about it," I said, as LB's head swiveled around three times. Mid-flight, Boy George sent his menu to LB for an autograph. "Let's see if he gets it," LB said, writing out the opening of "Glitter and Be Gay"—a reference probably lost on Boy George. As we exited in London, LB stared at the gargantuan geisha gushing at her flock of reporters and photographers. But that's what Boy George wanted: to be stared at.

After a flight to Munich the next afternoon, we caught up with the Mauermann family. Their embrace always buoyed me and kept me on an even keel. Jutta Mauermann replaced my lost toy hippopotamus, and this time it made me smile.

At the end of a chorus rehearsal for Haydn's *Paukenmesse*, LB asked me, "See anything you want?" meaning he had his eye on some cute guy among the singers. I stuttered a little. Honestly, LB never failed to take me by surprise. Checking out the chorus? No, I hadn't even raised my eyes from the score in my lap.

The Amberson office had sent a new set of orchestra parts without noticing that the timpani part, the *Pauken* in the work's title, was missing. Getting up early one morning, I copied the entire part by hand from LB's score but didn't have time to proofread, and I inadvertently omitted one bar. At the first rehearsal, the timpanist asked LB about the missing bar. LB replied, "Let's not tell Charlie, or he'll kill himself."

Harry Kraut returned from Japan and presented me with a cotton kimono that I wore for years as a bathrobe. Had LB told him about Boy George's geisha drag? (No way would I flounce around in white make-up and accessorized wig.) At least it seemed like we were all on good terms.

The next week in London, while LB wrote scripts with Humphrey Burton for upcoming videos, Aaron Stern said, "Let's be tourists for a day." We traipsed from the Tower to Westminster Abbey, and in Harrods, I picked out a present for Jamie Bernstein's forthcoming December wedding. On Yom Kippur, LB atoned at the Marble Arch synagogue, giving me a free day to stay in bed and get over a mild bug, so I was ready for *West Side Story* at Her Majesty's Theater the next night. I'd never seen this musical before, not the film nor a live performance.

LB always talked throughout any performance, but I hadn't expected a private master class.

"This Riff is too sexy, he's stronger than Tony," LB said early on.

But that's the point, I thought to myself.

I caught lyrics even more vernacular than those in *A Quiet Place.*

"Phone'll jingle, door'll knock," sang Tony.

"How did you find music for that?" I asked, but LB was too intent on the pace of "Something's Coming" to hear my question.

"Watch Maria; she puts the plot in motion," LB said during the first bridal shop scene, and then, "I'm so proud of that transition," as the music segued into "The Dance at the Gym." At the "Mambo," LB unconsciously lowered his left hand to slow the tempo, like a car passenger working a phantom brake with his foot. "Trust the music," LB said under his breath, which he repeated afterwards to the conductor backstage.

There wasn't time to bring up the irony of the Jets dancing to a hot Latin *mambo*—LB's comments continued without pause. Under the spoken dialogue in the "Balcony Scene," LB growled along as the bass clarinet outlined *there's a place for us*. "I fell off the piano bench when I discovered how that went together," he said. Two easily recognizable musical lines that happen to fit together, one on top of the other.

Is there any better twentieth-century counterpoint? I asked myself.

Not only was this production spectacularly cast, the dancing reached uncommon heights for a West End revival. Tommy Abbott, Gee-Tar in the original Broadway cast of *West Side Story*, re-created Jerome Robbins's choreography in London. LB greeted him affectionately backstage and posed with the cast for photographs.

The next day, we flew to Vienna to prepare the Vienna Philharmonic (VPO) for a European tour. This time everything ran like clockwork, *obgleich* a fussy Viennese timepiece. The schedule gave us an unusual number of free evenings. During a performance of *Tosca*, starring Sylvia Sass, Marcel Prawy trampled on my feet, as usual, to whisper in LB's ear every five minutes. Another night on the Kärntner Straße we ran into playwright Edward Albee. LB invited him for dinner at the hotel, on an evening that LB had said I should take off. Trying to make me feel left out? It worked.

LB's number one fan from Stuttgart, Ellen Goetz, put her Mercedes at my disposal, so I drove the DGG crew to bucolic Mayerling on a beautiful October afternoon. The crew treated me to lunch and we talked about conductors other than Leonard Bernstein—oh, were there others? A day of true camaraderie.

Two weeks of concerts deepened LB's association with pianist Krystian Zimerman, in the Brahms Piano Concerto No. 2. Then the VPO tour kicked off in Hamburg. Harry Kraut fobbed off on me the requests for concert tickets, about a dozen per concert. Then he took to his bed in Hamburg for a week while we continued to Berlin for appearances on both sides of the Berlin Wall. To cross into East Berlin, a sputtering Trabant, basically a kerosene-fueled lawnmower on a chassis, picked us up three hours before concert time. At Checkpoint Charlie, the East German guards held up our passports one at a time, verifying each facial feature. Eyes? Yes, we had eyes. Nose? Check. Hair? *Jawohl.*

Coming off the stage at the end of the concert in East Berlin, LB looked grim. He said somberly, "These people are starved for music." They were starved in other ways, too. At the reception, a young East German asked me what the little round

My datebook for October 24–25, 1984. The concert in East Berlin at left, the concert in West Berlin at right. The programs are penciled in the middle of each page. Plus: ticket requests by name and number, a reminder to carry visas and invitations, room assignments at the Hotel Kempinski, memos to make phone calls, post-concert receptions, and a note about a Michael Tilson Thomas concert in Brooklyn, lower right.

fruits were. "Kiwis," I said. "But don't eat these, they're moldy." A few years later, an East German visiting Jobst Eberhardt in Braunschweig assumed that a supermarket was simply "a museum for food."

Two more German cities, and then one long travel day that ended in Madrid's Hotel Ritz. LB took the elegant suite favored by Princess Grace of Monaco, and as I unpacked, a charming waiter brought me a drink.

The next morning, I ducked through the hotel's rear garden and ran into the entire Vienna Philharmonic inside the Prado.

"How is Harry?" they asked.

"Better," I said. "He might be at the concert tonight."

In fact, while recuperating in Hamburg, Harry codified his thoughts about me as LB's assistant. In Madrid, he dictated his conclusions. I still have the notepad with my hasty scrawl: *Therapy main thing—rigidity of C[harlie] H[armon]—taking out anger on self rather than letting [it] out.*

Moving his heavy jowls to speak made Harry's chinstrap whiskers look even less appealing. *How long did it take him every morning to trim that scrubby fringe? I wondered.* Harry's pontificating stunned me. This was his thanks for how I managed a tour week unassisted? More likely, payback—for having spurned his bid to forge my future as an orchestra manager.

Before our flight to Barcelona the next day, LB suggested a brief visit to the Prado. I led him to Velazquez's celebrated *Las Meninas* and explained the painting's structure: the Infanta and her attendants, the dwarfs, the dog, the mirrored portrait of the monarchs, the courtier taking his leave in the door—all pinned in place alongside Velazquez himself, at his easel. *Not unlike LB's jumble of helpers*, I thought to myself.

I stopped short of asking the underlying question: who's in charge? The Infanta Margaret Theresa, her ghostly parents in the mirror—or the artist?

29 | Lifetime Achievement = Lifetime Therapy

WELL IN ADVANCE OF ELECTION DAY in 1984, it looked like a landslide for Ronald Reagan, but I still wanted to cast my vote as a contrary Democrat. LB said, "It's not worth making the trip back to New York," and it was too late for me to get an absentee ballot. So we holed up in a suite at the Hotel Ritz in Barcelona for what could have been an upbeat week—if Harry Kraut hadn't unstrung me with his summary of my deficiencies. I should have engaged Harry as my tutor in a constructive plan of self-improvement, and striven toward Eagle Scout status under his expert guidance. But I had never been a Scout, and besides, Harry had already trotted off to some other part of the globe.

I plunged myself into a bathtub of cold water, a shock therapy the nineteenth-century composer Robert Schumann had tried before he committed himself to an asylum. My gargantuan bathroom at the Ritz featured a Hollywood-style roman bath glittering with mosaics, which added an exotic flair to this numbing ritual.

Cold water didn't work. Better were my meandering morning walks to soak up Barcelona's architecture, while LB slept late. After I returned a phone call from a news magazine, LB agreed to a full-day interview, provided the journalist—a personable guy—arranged a car and driver to visit Salvador Dalí. At a café across the street from Dalí's house, the journalist phoned the Master but Dalí's wife said he was too ill to receive visitors. In a little museum nearby, Dalí's childhood scribbles impressed LB no end, but they reminded me of my own preschool doodles. I used to imagine maps imposed on pages of text, the white spaces representing valleys between mountain ranges of text. Exactly what Dalí had done in his schoolbooks, and here they were under glass. Evidence of Dalí's genius was lost on me.

Taking it out on myself. Harry's dictation constantly reverberated in my ears.

During dinner with a couple of LB's venerable Catalan friends, a feeling of complete loss washed over me, as though a rip tide had dragged me out to sea. As I tried to speak, I could hear my voice inside my head, an eerie echo of everything I said. Like a crossed telephone line, my brain had lost its connection to my vocal cords and turned my words into inchoate sounds. I hadn't experienced this since my last bout of severe depression. Was I stuttering? I hadn't stuttered since I was ten.

Across the table that night, LB angrily accosted me. "What is wrong with you?" he said, which made everything worse. Was I going crazy?

I said as little as possible the next day, when a car and driver took us to the holy mountain of Montserrat to hear the boys' choir. First, we were led into the basilica, where the caretaker removed the protective cover from the ancient statue of the black Madonna, the patron saint of Catalonia. LB slobbered all over her face like a happy dog. I kissed a portion of her neck LB's tongue had missed. Our rather intimate veneration promised to protect us against ills of all sorts. Including insanity? And tongue-tied depression?

In the choir room, the boys sang for us, beautifully and simply. The choirmaster wasn't sure who this aged visitor was. He'd never heard of *Chichester Psalms,* which LB had written originally for boys' choir. Later from New York, I sent the score and a recording, but I doubt the Montserrat choir attempted a performance. Hebrew may have been too far afield for them, not to mention LB's peppy seven-beat meter.

Krystian Zimerman, the solo pianist on the Vienna Philharmonic tour, had given LB a magnificent thank-you: an antique wind-up bird in a cage, in working order. LB stayed up all night taking dictation from this chirping automaton. Unlike that of any living bird, this birdsong did not repeat and seemed free of any regular rhythm. The next day LB wound up the mechanical bird and excitedly showed me what he'd written. It looked accurate. He insisted it was a variant of the introductory phrase played on a wooden flute (called a *flabiol*) before a *sardana*, the national dance of Catalonia.

Captive in a fancy hotel, taking dictation from a mechanical toy? Was LB off his rocker? Had we wandered into a surreal play? Maybe we were both crazy.

The last night in Barcelona, LB wanted to go out for dinner. The concierge recommended a place we could walk to, on Las Ramblas. It hadn't occurred to me what we looked like: an elderly man out for a stroll with an obviously gay man half his age. I was oblivious to a posse of male hustlers trailing us until LB stopped to listen to their cocky banter. He said, "They don't know who I am," and turned around to have a chat. A dozen burly men emerged from the shadows.

Certain we were about to be robbed, I did my own bit of hustling and steered LB toward the restaurant. At a table for two, he lapsed into his Therapist of the Universe role, and for once, it may have helped. I hadn't had dinner alone with LB in a long time. I was ready to hear what he had to say, no matter how personal his jibes or preposterous his life-realigning theories. The next day I felt balanced enough to get us to London for some script-writing with Humphrey Burton, and then we finally headed back to New York.

———

BOSTON LATIN SCHOOL named LB "Man of the Year" as part of its fiftieth reunion of the class of 1935. The Harvard Club in Boston hosted the convocation of LB's classmates and surviving professors, who remembered LB as a stellar student—except for his Latin instructor, who'd given LB his lowest mark. LB's mother, Jennie, greeted me at the reception and promised that we'd catch up over dinner. But Phyllis Curtin, as Dean of Boston University's College of Fine Arts, determined the seating that night. I had turned off her video cameras—on Harry Kraut's instructions—during a master class Ms. Curtin had set up for LB at Boston University. To settle the score, she shunted me to the back of the room at the Harvard Club.

I caught Ms. Curtin staring at me to see what I'd do, but I didn't even sit down. At a deli around the corner, I had a sandwich and then caught up on old magazines in the Harvard Club's reading room. LB was angry that I hadn't heard his speech, and he was especially peeved that I hadn't sat next to his mother. "Where were you?" he asked with more than his usual impatience. What could I say? That because of some tiff between Harry and Phyllis Curtin I felt used? I didn't need LB's exasperated scorn, so I kept mum and sank into a despondent melancholy. *Taking it out on myself.*

Back in New York, I asked a gay couple to suggest a psychiatrist and began sessions with an openly gay therapist, but I resisted his penchant for role-playing. We didn't explore my resistance, and by the third session I wasn't willing to say much of anything. When I mentioned this to LB, he said, "What you're doing is merely gay chit-chat." I'd never heard LB indulge in that sort of repartee, but he may have been right.

More productively, over Thanksgiving in Washington, D.C., my friend John—now earning his second graduate degree in psychology—introduced me to his mentor, the chair of a chapter of the national association of psychiatrists. From him I got a list of therapists in New York, my first serious step. One of many I'd put off for too long.

For three months, no airports, no hotels. But no respite, either. The job stayed intense, one week upbeat, the next one a mess. Even the best moments made me wary. On my thirty-fourth birthday, Harry Kraut asked me to meet him at his apartment, where I opened the door to hear LB, Jamie, Alexander, Nina, Ann Dedman, and three of my closest friends shouting, "Surprise!" Involuntarily, I winced, but I hope I showed some gratitude. My state of mind was rapidly deteriorating. Why could I no longer enjoy myself?

That week, LB's octogenarian secretary Helen Coates called me at home around 5:30 every evening, after she'd put away a few glasses—I heard later they were "tankards"—of sherry. Hanging up on Helen wasn't an option; she would have reported me to LB. Over the phone she ranted, "He's beating her, he's beating my mother." It took me a few minutes to grasp that she was talking about her parents, dead long before I was born. When I mentioned these calls to Harry, hoping he'd be discrete, he said, "Get an answering machine." Were Helen's ravings typical of LB's helpers? If this was my future, I dreaded it.

On December 2, LB assumed a new role, father of the bride, when Jamie Anne Maria Bernstein married David Evan Thomas in the Dakota apartment's living room. Nerves, anyone? An itchy rash on his nose kept LB up all night, while Shirley got hives on her hands. I bought a huge tube of cortisone cream and dispensed dollops as needed.

The star-studded evening reception at the Waldorf was an only-in-New York bash. Opera diva Beverly Sills plunked herself in the lobby, forcing everyone to greet her as they got off the elevator. Comedian and distinguished director Mike Nichols toasted the newlyweds with a personalized stand-up routine. LB's brother, Burton, sounded the shofar—the fragile glass one I'd brought from Connecticut and later managed to return intact. LB's toast to Julia Vega raised the roof, though at that moment Julia was enjoying the blessed tranquility of the Dakota from her bathtub. It had been enough for her to attend the morning's wedding ceremony, for once not in her black housekeeper's uniform. At the end of the evening, I wanted to help Lauren Bacall sweep up the bouquets of red roses from the banquet's forty tables, but I had a delicate glass shofar in my hands.

And those itchy rashes? LB and Shirley said they vanished without a trace.

Two mornings later, I carried two cups of coffee into LB's bedroom. LB's exceptionally cute new boyfriend, David (oddly, the same name as Jamie's new husband), sat bolt upright, wide awake.

"When does anybody get any sleep around here?" he whined.

Over LB's loud snores I said, "So he kept you up all night?"

David took the coffee from me and shouted, "Talking!"

I said, "Go home now and sleep. Come back here around five."

LB had a lot more talking in mind, taking *his* David for a short winter break in the Bahamas. Their luggage went astray, a disaster turned into entertainment by David's voluntary nudity for a couple days.

Dear CH:

Let's _always_ do it the lost-luggage way: it makes a perfect vacation.

Love LB

I splurged on my own winter break and took my friend John to Key West for a week, after his first round of chemotherapy for colon cancer had left him drained and disoriented. The chemo had also stripped away layers of his personality, as though peeling an onion left only a flavorless core. But John had now become a professional shrink, and a good one at that. He pointed out signals of psychiatric distress I wasn't able to recognize in myself. During a stressful episode of his own, years ago, John had burst into tears when soap wouldn't wash off his hands. "Exactly," I said. "The littlest things unpredictably become enormous obstacles." John emphasized that I shouldn't put off finding a therapist. It might take a while. He knew I would be picky and that I did not grasp how much was at stake.

I hadn't paid attention to the schedule LB made for himself to see his own shrinks. He coded his appointments in his datebook, usually with an "H," his principal therapist's initial. The appointments always occurred at odd times, say, 6:10 P.M., and LB never asked me to reserve a hired car. He took a taxi. I never caught on to these sessions, though they happened three times a week. In a way, my obliviousness was similar to not having noticed my mother's alcoholism when we lived under the same roof. I sensed LB was hiding something—but I didn't know what. All the while, he badgered me incessantly to find a therapist.

LB's reminder to find a
THER-A-PIST
(be careful how you divide the syllables, Maestro).
The Rapist
by
Chas. Harmon

One morning on my way to Connecticut, I stopped at the Dakota to pick up some books LB wanted, and even before unlocking the kitchen door I knew something was wrong. Steam filled the kitchen, as though a cloud had settled into the apartment. A dishwasher hose had burst, flooding the floor with hot water. I reached under the sink, turned off the water, and ran downstairs to the apartment below. The owner's door was open. He stood at the top of a ladder, swiping the last strokes of paint onto his ceiling.

"You'll see water coming through your ceiling," I said, "But insurance will cover the damage. For now, stop painting." Then I ran back upstairs to mop up the water and everything floating in it, mostly insect carcasses. I called Julia. As always, she said the right things.

"You turn off the water? *Qué lata.* Is good you are there, Charlito. We fix that later," she said. When I described the man painting his ceiling, she let out a low chuckle.

Driving to Connecticut put everything out of my mind. I listened to a new recording of Bach's *Mass in B Minor*, performed by a tiny ensemble, one singer per part, conducted by Joshua Rifkin. On the drive back into the city, I played the tape for LB. The fleetness of "Cum Sancto Spiritu" enthralled him. He listened to it four times on the drive back to New York.

Photographer Andrew French, a protégé of Ruth Orkin's, brought Ms. Orkin's daughter Mary Engel to the Dakota with an album of Orkin's photos of LB's rehearsals at Lewissohn Stadium in the 1940s. Soloists appeared in every photograph: pianist William Kapell, alto Marian Anderson, trumpeter Louis Armstrong, among many others. What a valuable collection, perfect for a classy book. As LB leafed leisurely through the photos, I ran a tape recorder and later transcribed every syllable.

Mary Engel understood that securing Harry Kraut's approval was the first step in a book proposal, so I gave Harry the typed transcription interleaved among the photos, and included the original tape cassette. Harry threw it all away but shifted the blame onto me. He said, "I don't know what you did with that binder of photographs, but it's not here." I kicked myself for not saving a copy and for trusting Harry. *Taking it out on myself.* When would I learn? A project that wasn't Harry's idea, over which he'd have no control? Make it go away by destroying it.

The Recording Academy, popularly known as the Grammys, tapped LB for its Lifetime Achievement Award. LB grumbled, "They think my life is over." He couldn't write "A/C" on this invitation—his "accept and cancel" strategy—but he could still have some fun en route to Los Angeles: how about Mardi Gras in Rio?

In no time, flights were booked for LB and Aaron Stern, a house was rented, and VIP seats were reserved for the parade in Rio. (I stayed in New York and flew directly to Los Angeles later.) I contacted a young musician we'd met in Vienna, Flavio Chamis, now at home in Brazil. He promised to keep an eye on LB. For once, Flavio did not respond with his stock phrase, "No problem." Later, he mentioned one close call, when a gang of street kids waded into the surf behind LB. For them, the shiny medallions hanging from LB's neck would have been easy pickings. Flavio yelled the rudest street slang he knew and the kids scattered.

Ordinarily, LB's idea of shopping was a sweep through an airport's duty-free emporium. But on a Rio street, a fiery warrior angel, an *Ángel de la Guarda,* caught LB's eye. As I helped unpack his luggage in a bungalow at the Beverly Hills Hotel, LB handed me this folk object with a certain reverence.

"When I saw this angel, I said 'Charlito.' It may guide you, or maybe it will protect you," LB said. The hard clay spoke of the fingers that had shaped this rough figure. (To me, this angel is related to Montserrat's Black Madonna and may share her powers.)

With Jamie and Alexander on hand in Los Angeles, LB's behavior was at its most decorous. He was on time for everything, and his rehearsal call for the Grammys got whittled down to a few minutes. That freed him for a music-honcho dinner with Quincy Jones, Wynton Marsalis, and Michael Tilson Thomas. (A year later, Michael Jackson crashed their second get-together.)

Later that night, LB sketched some ideas for trumpet, possibly a concerto for Wynton Marsalis. Then he added a choreographic slant, for Olympic skater John Curry, who had staged an ice ballet of LB's "Allegro Barbaro" from *On the Waterfront*. What a juicy idea, another Bernstein ballet. But the months ahead didn't include any time for composition, and LB's excitement at writing a new piece evaporated.

I'd never been to a rock concert, but I suspected the Grammys would be loud. The polished performances took me by surprise. Hey, these performers were *really good*. I'd brought along a box of earplugs and at the first pause, I scooted down to the front and offered earplugs to LB and his date, the tenor Plácido Domingo. Jamie Bernstein, next to LB, gladly took a pair of earplugs. But the blue-eyed Hollywood bimbo at Jamie's left stared uncomprehendingly at the little box in my outstretched hand. I didn't know who he was. If he didn't want earplugs, bully for him.

My niece chastised me later. She had watched the Grammys on TV and saw me kneeling in front of John Travolta. And I didn't get his autograph? Duh!

LB's brief acceptance speech addressed the conundrum of awards. "I am very happy tonight for music," he said. "And I'll be even happier and maybe even ecstatic if tonight can be a step toward the ultimate marriage of all kinds of music, because they are all one. There is only good and there is bad." There was good Beethoven. There was not-so-good Beethoven. There was good Tina Turner. And not-so-good. (How would he know?) But "all the good music should come together."

Amen.

LB's graphic note on what to do with his dozens of Grammy and Emmy nominations: "Paper" [the] walls of studio bathroom w/ NOMINATIONS

30 | I Should Stay Here and Work

IN THE SPRING OF 1985, LB tried a new tack on his sagging physique: a fitness coach. I bought two thick floor mats and made sure LB was up and caffeinated for his twice-weekly sessions. He yakked through them as though fitness and socializing were the same thing—maybe so, given the spritely personality of his coach. The stretching and grunting kept LB off cigarettes for an hour, but for stamina, LB continued to depend on Dexedrine.

My own discipline focused on my finances. I saved every penny I could. I took my laundry on tour, Julia fed me dinner in the kitchen, and a couple times I helped myself to toilet paper from the Dakota when I ran out at home. When I'd saved a thousand dollars, I commissioned a clavichord from Hugh Gough, a well-known instrument builder and the custodian of historic keyboards at the Metropolitan Museum of Art. A clavichord, the lightweight precursor of the piano, could be toted up the narrow staircase to my apartment. It would never disturb my neighbors. Its faint buzz: quieter than a beehive. Of all keyboard instruments, it's the most personal.

Mr. Gough had enough walnut boards in stock to make one more instrument. As his ninety-ninth clavichord—an exact replica of the keyboard I'd pined for in Salzburg at the Mozart House—took shape without any technical drawings, Mr. Gough explained, "The instrument tells you what its proportions are." I see. More or less what Danny Kaye had said about hamburgers.

To LB, I said, "I'd like to make you dinner so you can see this beautiful instrument. Bring anyone you like." As soon as I said that, I realized I'd made a mistake.

Naturally, LB brought one of those kids—there were many—who crowed, "I must conduct Mahler!" in LB's green room after a concert. To this particular kid, LB said, "Here, tell me what this means," pointing to the tempo marking *Plötzlich langsamer* in his Mahler score. The kid didn't have a clue. But after he spilled his guts about his predator father—which LB repeated to me five minutes later—LB as Therapist of the Universe had felt compelled to take on this ignorant and traumatized lad, an ideal candidate for lifetime mentoring.

That evening, I didn't know that LB had come to my apartment directly from his shrink. He seemed uncommonly subdued. While I put together a simple dinner, LB played a Chopin mazurka on my clavichord, precisely the wrong music for a keyboard with no sustaining mechanism. Still, I could hear the instrument's tranquility, and its resonant low octaves. LB declined to improvise or to try some Mozart.

It was a rarified evening. My new keyboard showed LB that I was serious about music: I had to tune the strings, I had to discipline my fingers to play evenly. A clavichord is all about careful *listening*.

THE PROTRACTED SEARCH for LB's chef continued to drag along, though we lucked out with a temporary chef for Passover. LB had invited only twenty-three people that year. The next chef's perkiness masked a host of demons—she slept on a bench at Penn Station. Then LB's sister, Shirley, dredged up a long-limbed chorus boy transplanted from Las Vegas, personable enough, but at sea in the kitchen. After a famished week in Connecticut, LB begged Julia to make *pastel del choclo*, her immensely satisfying corn casserole. The chorus boy took notes as Julia worked her magic. After he left, Julia found dozens of empty Pepsi bottles and cookie cartons under his bed. Not until summer would a competent chef step into LB's life, when Patti Pulliam steered the kitchen back toward dependable wholesomeness.

The professional association of theater authors, The Dramatists Guild, scheduled a long-anticipated symposium with the authors of *West Side Story*: Bernstein, Stephen Sondheim, Arthur Laurents, and Jerome Robbins, moderated by playwright Terrence McNally. Despite his morning grunts alongside the fitness coach, LB obviously had a case of nerves. We got to the symposium site with twenty minutes to spare. Looking at his watch, he asked, "Is there a place around here to get a drink?" I led him into a bar where I used to put away martinis every Friday with my mentor Dale Kugel, music copyist at Tams-Witmark. Thank goodness the bar was empty. No witnesses to catch LB steeling himself with a drink before facing his collaborators.

We took a booth. Addressing LB's jitters, I asked a therapist's question, "What's the scariest thing about this get-together?"

"Jerry [Jerome Robbins]," LB said, with no hesitation. "What if he takes over the discussion? What if it's all about him?" LB fretted.

"There's a moderator," I said. "And your other colleagues. How likely is it that this will turn into a one-man show?" LB brightened a little. I asked him, "What's your favorite memory of that collaboration?"

Again, no hesitation at all. "When we crammed into a phone booth to make a last-ditch call," LB said, "after we'd been turned down by everyone we knew. Nobody wanted to produce a show that had two dead bodies onstage at the end of the first act." (Riff and Bernardo both die in "The Rumble.")

LB's eyes couldn't have been more focused as he veered into another memory. "But when I saw Justice Hugo Black"—I think that's who LB mentioned—"at the intermission with tears streaming down his face, I knew we had done something right. And real."

We finished our drinks and walked around the corner. LB greeted his colleagues with a big smile.

I HAD MY LAST SESSION with a gay shrink—LB continued to deride those sessions as "gay chit-chat"—and we were off to Europe for six weeks. I had resisted the shrink's role-playing all along and felt more confused than ever, so I resorted to my usual fallback option: immersing myself in work.

In a gesture to help me out, Harry Kraut proposed hiring a second assistant. I'd manage the overseas travel, and another assistant would look after things in New York. Six candidates survived Harry's vetting, but when I saw Phillip Allen's flaming red hair, I knew he'd be Harry's pick. The yearning for his red-haired Boy Scout leader that Harry had harbored from his youth always overruled any resume.

Phillip Allen came to the Dakota to review the to-do list he'd tackle while LB and I would be away: service the two cars, fix the stereo speakers, get the pianos in the living room and the studio tuned, help Julia polish the floors, look after furniture and luggage repairs—so much for the top of the list.

Meanwhile, the luggage I packed for Vienna now included two floor mats and the fitness coach's personalized audio tape. The fitness coach had instructed me to play the tape first thing every other day. I was to get down on a floor mat and follow along with LB's grunts. Soon it was every third day, then every fourth day. If LB made a phone call after getting out of bed, he'd light a cigarette and wave away the exercise tape.

Harry Kraut had struck a deal with the Vienna State Opera: a concert of excerpts from Richard Wagner's *Ring* with the Vienna Philharmonic (VPO) in exchange for staging and recording *A Quiet Place* the next year—though not with the VPO but with the untested Austrian Radio Symphony Orchestra. "You'll get musicians who play a lot of contemporary music," Harry said, attempting to allay LB's doubts.

With these *Ring* excerpts, LB relished the historical irony of Vienna's favorite Jewish celebrity conducting Wagner's music, with the politically reactionary VPO in the city that had rapturously hailed Hitler fifty years earlier.

After LB marked up his score of the *Ring,* a phenomenally proficient copyist worked for three days on the Staatsoper's orchestra materials at a table in the hotel hallway while waiters brought him sandwiches and pots of coffee. My room's desk, an escritoire that offered just enough surface area to address a postcard, was covered with LB's own orchestral parts for Mahler's Symphony No. 9. I spent my nights transferring the marks from LB's score into those parts; his performances with the Concertgebouw in Amsterdam were only two weeks away.

One night, LB noticed the light on in my room. He pulled up a chair and quickly found several errors in the Mahler horn parts. That was as much fun for him as winning at anagrams.

"How can it be that I've never heard these wrong notes?" LB asked.

"The horn players probably figured out the right notes but never fixed their printed parts," I said. Sid Ramin had told me that happened fairly often in a Broadway pit. But these Mahler symphony parts had last been played by the Berlin Philharmonic. How did they know what notes to fix?

Flavio Chamis, continuing his studies in Vienna, reported spending a day on the stage of the Musikverein. Conductor Herbert von Karajan often hired students to sit in the VPO's chairs while he futzed around with camera angles in advance of his concerts.

"I got paid for sitting there two hours, doing nothing," Flavio said.

"I've heard he does that. I'd like to send Herbie a message," LB said, using a nickname for Karajan nobody would dare utter in public.

As usual, Flavio said, "No problem."

Along with a short note on a card, LB handed Flavio the lilies-of-the-valley that a fan had left at the hotel. I wrapped a wet washcloth around the stems, but when Flavio returned the next evening, he said, "The flowers were completely dead, but I gave them to Karajan anyway. He grunted and handed them to his assistant," a man named Papier.

"The perfect name for Karajan's assistant," LB chimed in.

Talk about a toilet-paper job, I thought. Karajan didn't send LB a reply, but LB hadn't expected him to.

Yet another project got shoehorned into that week: a videotape session at Sigmund Freud's house, where LB pretended to consult Dr. Freud about his conflict, if that's what it was, as a Jewish musician conducting the music of anti-Semitic Wagner in reactionary Vienna. Surrounded by books heaped on the replica of Freud's famous couch, LB contended that the printed verbiage on Freud matched the quantity of books on Napoleon and Christ (thus the volume of volumes). But LB hadn't developed his thesis and this "therapy" session with Dr. Freud remained inconclusive. As for the visual aspect in Dr. Freud's study, the camera angles were tight in that confined space. I kept getting in the way; I should have gone for a walk in the May sunshine. That hapless video was never released.

The sun came out in Amsterdam, not only metaphorically. Facing a new orchestra, LB slipped into his seductive mode and turned on his charm. Equally charming Dési Halban attended every rehearsal. Dési had had a magical childhood in Vienna: Klimt drew her portrait, her mother was Mahler's favorite singer. Dési too was a soprano. In New York in 1944, after a horrifying escape from Nazi-occupied Holland, her friend Bruno Walter engaged her for Mahler's Symphony No. 4 with the New York Philharmonic. At a rehearsal, she met the disarming assistant conductor, twenty-six-year-old Leonard Bernstein. Here she was now, forty years later, inviting LB for lunch, along with the Concertgebouw's concertmaster, Jaap van Zweden.

LB insisted I join them, but I had barely begun transferring another round of marks from LB's score to the string parts, my usual post-rehearsal task. I was already smitten with Dési, but getting to know her better would have to wait. I said, "I should stay here and work." LB acknowledged my diligence with a silent nod. That comment of mine changed my life.

After the first performance, LB awaited Queen Beatrix in the spacious green room. We all stood when someone knocked on the door, which I opened to the Deutsche Grammophon (DGG) technician, Jobst Eberhardt.

"We thought you were the Queen," I said.

"Jobst is greater," quipped LB, making Jobst blush.

As per royal protocol, when the Queen arrived, she spoke first. "May I smoke?" she asked LB.

"Thank god," LB said, happily lighting her cigarette and one for himself. They chatted amiably but not about music. Later, LB wondered if she'd comprehended anything about the symphony she'd just heard, or had realized that the composer's name adorned the balcony directly below her seat.

The upbeat week continued in London. The Concertgebouw repeated Mahler No. 9 at the Barbican, where we also caught a gripping *King Richard III*. An auditorium seemed to switch on the performer in LB. At the famous opening lines, "Now is the winter of our discontent / Made glorious summer by this sun of York," LB anticipated the actor onstage by several seconds, and continued to recite, audibly. After a full minute of this, a man in the row ahead turned around and barked, "Will you shut up?"

I was startled. I'd gotten so used to LB talking through performances that I hadn't noticed. I handed LB an Aquafilter to keep his mouth occupied.

A few nights later at the English National Opera, LB's commentary during *Madama Butterfly* provoked a more polite reaction: "Due to some strange acoustical quirk," said a man approaching LB's box at intermission, "sounds emanating from this box are audible throughout the theater." LB interrupted him with a profuse apology. Backstage, conductor John Mauceri introduced the English National Opera's new répétiteur, Justin Brown, whom Harry Kraut invited to Vienna when we returned there in October. A couple years later, Justin's help proved invaluable in preparing *Candide* for the Scottish Opera, and for LB's 1989 recording of the work.

LB's momentum faltered the next week in Rome during *Songfest* with the Accademia Santa Cecilia. Michael Barrett had arrived from New York to be this project's assistant conductor, ostensibly only to rehearse the six singers in *Songfest*. But LB was on a post-Dexedrine slide. After he cancelled the first orchestra rehearsal, LB lapsed into self-indulgence. He stayed up all night and took a sleeping pill at dawn, just before going to bed. I tried to rouse him at 8 A.M., but he covered his face with the sheet. He was in retreat from the world.

"Please tell Michael Barrett to take the rehearsals today," LB said in a distant voice. I didn't sit on the edge of the bed this time. I summoned Harry and stood by while he interrogated the Maestro. In a pique, Harry trotted out the reasons why *Songfest* couldn't be cancelled and reminded LB of his future obligations with this orchestra. Harry managed to get a concession out of LB. He'd lead the afternoon rehearsal with the six singers, and the evening rehearsal with singers and orchestra.

Concerned that the orchestra would mutiny when they faced Michael Barrett instead of the Maestro, Harry left for the concert hall. I stayed in the hotel as LB slept. The phone rang constantly, but between calls I lounged on my room's sunny terrace and read a book. There were worse ways to spend a beautiful day in June. When my mind wandered, I looked out over the domed churches of Rome and tried to remember their names. A bit of escapist exercise.

LB rallied most evenings. The Fendi sisters, purveyors of luxury handbags, hosted two dinners for LB, one including Gian Carlo Menotti before he departed for the Spoleto Festival. My datebook has a reminder to carry extra Tums and Tagamet for LB's indigestion. The other Fendi dinner was family-style, and included LB's friends Alessio Vlad, still unsure whether to conduct or compose music, and Franco Amurri and Susan Sarandon, now the world's most beautiful couple. Franco and Susan invited LB another night to an intimate restaurant near the Pantheon, where I drank too much wine, thereby becoming fluent in Italian. Dorothee Koehler threw a dinner for LB that turned chaotic when the Ricordi family hurled bread at one another across the table. That week, LB's friends descended from all quarters: the Mauermanns from Munich, the Willheims from Vienna. Aaron Stern escorted a wealthy woman friend of his from Illinois. They all seemed to think this was their last chance to see LB alive.

This social schedule seemed to revive LB. He got back into the swing of things, even the rehearsals at 10 A.M. His *Songfest* script had been translated into Italian, so there were also long afternoons in front of a teleprompter to practice his narration.

Meanwhile, many of the singers in "Songfest" had performed together elsewhere, so they made a cheerfully dedicated crew, with one exception. The soprano Clamma Dale, LB's favorite for his setting of "A Julia de Burgos" because she consistently nailed the final high C, locked herself in the women's green room. That forced the other two women—and all three men—into LB's dressing room across the hall. Ms. Dale didn't respond to questions put to her through the closed door, until orchestra manager Francesco Siciliani, a large, rather brutish man, persuaded Ms. Dale to let him in for a chat. Ninety seconds later, she lit out for the stage like a bat out of hell. LB surmised that Siciliani had proposed an old vaudeville coercion: suck or sing.

Gian Carlo Menotti's Spoleto Festival (now the Festival of Two Worlds) had always intrigued LB, so off he went with Madina Ricordi. I followed a day later with Michael Barrett and his partner, Leslie Tomkins. In his well-appointed palazzo, Maestro Menotti served us champagne followed by dinner downstairs in the piazza. It was clear LB had misgivings about this visit. He barely spoke. Conversation limped along until Michael Barrett asked Menotti, "So other than *Amahl*, what have you written that's any good? Ouch!" as Leslie kicked him under the table. At the dress rehearsal of Puccini's *Fanciulla del West*, the cast of cowboys, all handsome young American lads, circled LB like cows around a salt lick. Though flattered, LB chose not to tie up their valuable rehearsal time, and we headed to a hotel for the night.

Back in Rome, the TV news showed Menotti in Spoleto, brandishing a hand in the regal screw-in-the-light bulb wave. LB commented, "Gian Carlo wants to ride in a carriage and wave to his subjects, like a queen going to her coronation." LB's idea for a music festival was something different. Educational, communal, the opposite of imperial.

After our flight to New York, I had seven days to prepare for a Fourth of July concert in Washington, D.C., and a short tour with the National Symphony. Then Tanglewood for two weeks, followed by rehearsals with a youth orchestra in Athens, Greece. When would this ceaseless activity end?

Despite the addition of Phillip Allen as a second assistant, my datebook stayed as overwritten as ever.

31 | The Ends of the Earth

BY JULY 1985, as I stumbled into my fourth summer working for Leonard Bernstein, I'd held onto the job longer than any of my predecessors. Unbelievably, the pace intensified, more activity over greater distances: five orchestras on four continents in only eight weeks. LB gulped down more Dexedrine than ever. How could I keep up?

Friends of LB's who saw him only once a year took me aside, alarmed by his croaky voice, his rundown appearance. "Is he seriously ill?" they asked. Groggy and unable to concentrate, he didn't always catch what was said, and a small glass of scotch—but not until 5 P.M.—affected him more than it used to. His burgeoning gut testified to an overworked liver.

After the Lifetime Achievement Award from the Grammys, an elder-statesman aspect settled onto LB's public persona. It rankled him. "Why do I look like I'm on Mount Rushmore?" he griped of photographs that showed his stonily set jaw. LB's other refrain, "The Maestro said just before he died," cast a chill over many conversations.

How does a Mount Rushmore figurehead celebrate the Fourth of July? Conducting, of course, a program televised live from the Capitol's lawn in Washington, D.C., and afterward hosting a reception inside the Capitol itself. I supplied the guest list of more than a hundred names to the Capitol's security commander. Alexander and Nina were on hand to read the poems in *Songfest*. Their presence helped keep LB in his well-behaved paterfamilias role.

In the division of duties between two assistants, I flew to Washington a day ahead and set up the suite at the Watergate, while Phillip Allen corralled press agent Maggie Carson and manager Harry Kraut onto LB's flight. Every minute was booked. Maggie squeezed in a *New York Times* interview during the brief limo ride to the Watergate hotel.

The Fourth of July concert segued into a short tour with the National Symphony Orchestra, starting at the Jones Beach amphitheater on Long Island. LB's doctor, Kevin Cahill, graciously invited LB to stay overnight at his beach house in Point Lookout, only a ten-minute drive from the amphitheater. I could tag along, too.

"I need a house present for Kevin's wife, Kate—something to make her laugh," LB said.

"Send up those mighty Catholic values," I suggested, aware that Dr. Cahill attended on the Cardinal of New York and an occasional Pope.

How about a garish reproduction of da Vinci's "Last Supper" on a beach towel?

Unwrapping her gift, Kate Cahill said, between guffaws, "This is too good for the beach. This goes up on a wall."

The manager at the Jones Beach amphitheater did what he could to discourage classical music at his rundown venue. Posters of young Elvis and Las Vegas Elvis festooned the stage. That afternoon, Harry Kraut's assistant, Mimsy Gill, industriously whitewashed them all. During the sound check, an overhead light crashed into the second violin section, nearly destroying an instrument. In the middle of the concert, the amphitheater's manager gunned his motorcycle in the parking lot and drowned out everything softer than *mezzo forte*. I never saw Harry backstage that day because he was out front trying to keep things from falling apart.

That concert fell on Alexander's thirtieth birthday, so LB wrote a jazzy birthday number for the six soloists in *Songfest* and I handed out photocopies for an impromptu rehearsal during the intermission. LB's new music added some festive flair to Alex's post-concert party, a far cry from the party three years earlier, when LB had smashed his arm into the Big Mac cake.

The next afternoon, we flew to Chicago to repeat the concert at the suburban Ravinia venue. James Levine, conducting most of that summer season, barged into LB's dressing room right after the music started, his trademark purple towel around his neck.

"Charlie, take the night off. I'll do your job," Maestro Levine commanded. Nothing could have pleased me more. LB got a real surprise at the intermission when he saw Levine handing him a cigarette and a towel—the younger Maestro certainly knew the drill. I stepped in only when the orchestra librarian requested the scores for the concert's second half.

Barely touching down in New York, LB drove to Tanglewood the next day in the Mercedes, taking a favorite route he claimed was a shortcut but that always made the trip longer. When I needed a bathroom break and shuffled into a gas station, LB commented, "Look at you. You're really not well." No kidding.

My eyelids twitched, I looked pinched and wan, and I had no appetite. But I joined LB for dinner with Seiji Ozawa, who chatted about the Tanglewood fellows of note that summer: composers Bright Sheng and Daron Hagen, and conductor Carl St. Clair. Aaron Copland would be on hand for the all-Copland concert with the student orchestra. LB would share the podium duties with three conducting fellows.

Less than a mile from the house on Monument Valley Road, a moderately strenuous trail led up Squaw Mountain. Twice, I got up at sunrise to contemplate the placid Berkshires from the rocky peak where, according to local lore, a native woman had jumped to her death, although that seemed infeasible from those mossy boulders. After a twelve-hour day with LB, I excused myself from dinner and collapsed into bed. It wasn't even dark yet. LB asked Patti Pulliam to set aside her kitchen duties and go to my bedroom door. "Charlie, LB won't eat until you come downstairs," she pleaded. But I was too groggy to eat. Every nerve in my body jangled, my fingertips vibrated, and all I craved was deep sleep. I wasn't up to the job and should have called it quits.

One evening I rallied. When Todd and Helen Perry came for dinner, the eight people around the table matched the number of "fits"—the archaic word for segments of a long poem—in Lewis Carroll's "The Hunting of the Snark." I retrieved LB's copy and we passed it around, each of us reading a "fit" aloud (roughly eighty or so lines). Sure enough, it fell to steady and dependable Todd Perry, the BSO's former manager, to declaim the satirical lines on insurance policies, which pleased LB no end.

"There are no accidents," he said.

The next night, LB took an all-male troupe of composers and conductors to posh Seven Hills. He requisitioned a private dining room and specified "only male waiters, no girls." A woman working in the kitchen that night later asked me, "What was going on with LB?" I had a hunch he'd hoped to repeat an event from the Shark Jacket summer of 1981, when LB got lucky with a Seven Hills waiter. "His erection reached to his navel," LB bragged. I prayed that everyone at Seven Hills was of legal age. I took the night off and slept fourteen hours.

After the all-Copland concert, LB escorted his mentor, Uncle Aaron, onto the stage for a bow. LB said afterward, "First, Aaron asked me, 'Why is the concertmaster a girl?' Then he said, 'I think I know that music.' He wasn't joking—he didn't know where he was and doesn't remember his own music anymore." LB implied that time was running out, maybe for both of them.

After only one night in New York, we were off to Athens for a "Peace Tour" with the European Youth Orchestra and a starry cast: fourteen-year-old Midori Goto in a Mozart violin concerto conducted by Eiji Oue, and soprano Barbara Hendricks and actor-narrator Mendy Wager in LB's Symphony No. 3, "Kaddish," with LB conducting. To supervise the sound systems on tour, Jobst Eberhardt signed on. My steadiest friend on the road, Jobst was better for me than a tank of oxygen.

The best bet for driving to rehearsals in traffic-clogged Athens? A police escort. LB took one look at the lead Greek cop astride his motorcycle, hopped on the back and wrapped his arms around the cop's beefy chest. Off they flew across lanes of traffic, more recklessly than Zeus abducting Ganymede. In the follow-up limo, I prayed to all the gods on Olympus, "Keep LB on that motorcycle—*please*." We reached the arena in less than half the allotted ten minutes.

The cop muscled his motorcycle down the arena's aisle, right up to the stage. The kids in the orchestra whooped, and Jobst almost knocked over a microphone. LB patted his escort and swaggered to the podium, taking Jobst aside. "I touched his balls," LB murmured. Jobst turned beet red. Halfway through the fourteen-hour rehearsal, Jobst asked me for a halfsie of Dexedrine. How else could we get through this schedule?

Actress Melina Mercouri, the bold and brassy goddess of Greek cinema and now Greece's minister of culture, glued herself onto LB like a fly on a fruit bowl and played expertly to a worshipful press corps. LB had only to grin in the right direction. After the concert, Phillip Allen coped with the reception while I headed to the hotel, because all luggage had to be in the lobby by 2 A.M. for our flights to Japan.

During our refueling stop in Anchorage, LB ducked into the duty-free zone and bought me a tiny electric razor (I definitely needed better grooming). But he lost his boarding pass, and the attendant guarding the door to the plane refused to let him reboard. I no longer took any nonsense from anybody. As though speaking to a child, I said calmly, "Very well, don't let him on the plane. He's the sole reason why all these musicians"—who trooped past us, casually vouching for LB's identity—"are on this plane. You make him stay here in Anchorage." She relented.

While LB camped out in Tokyo for one night with Eiji Oue and Phillip Allen, I flew to Osaka with the orchestra and took the bullet train to Hiroshima with Kunihiko Hashimoto. Slightly younger than I, but far more suave, Kuni had served as translator for LB on a previous trip to Japan and happily did so again. With manners as perfect as his English, Kuni's calm settled me enough that I could focus on unpacking in Hiroshima, long after midnight. Kuni quickly became a valued friend. Years later, he translated Bernstein and Sondheim musicals into Japanese. Friends have told me that those translations not only match the syllables to existing vocal lines, but they also nail the lyrics' wit with miraculous idiomatic skill.

LB arrived in Hiroshima the next day, and we piled into a car to visit Eiji Oue's parents in the suburbs, where the driver took me aside. "That tree," he said, indicating with awe the canopy of a venerable pine, "is shaped to show that the Emperor visited here." I thought he was pulling my leg. I hadn't yet grasped the subtlety and reverence that imbues Japanese culture. Eiji said yes, the Emperor had visited his grandfather here.

Even before I'd removed my shoes, Eiji opened the shrine to his ancestors to pray while we seated ourselves in a circle on the tatami mat for tea, elaborately prepared by Eiji's mother. Eiji presented LB with a traditional Japanese *haori*, a short kimono jacket emblazoned on the back with the family crest. It became LB's after-concert robe for the rest of his life.

Before the first rehearsal, for which Maggie Carson had arranged a live broadcast to the United States, we spent an hour at the sobering Hiroshima Peace Memorial Museum. Eiji said that his grandfather never talked about the day an atomic blast had destroyed the city. Now we could see why. A subtle shadow on a stone step was all that remained of someone who had sat there and had been incinerated. It was as though his soul had been photographically etched onto the granite. I touched the stone's surface, which the bomb's heat had liquefied to a surface as smooth as glass.

Before sunrise the next morning, LB and I put on suits, walked to the Peace Ceremony, and took our seats amid ranks of hushed Japanese elders. The other American representatives, the actor Jack Lemmon and his wife, sat directly behind us. What a treat to meet my favorite comic actor, but this wasn't a moment for comedy.

At dawn, the air had felt cool and dry, but the rising sun showed no mercy. Everyone around us produced paper fans from their pockets. Like a thousand fluttering wings, the fans mimicked the origami cranes—symbols of peace—that hung in multitudes around the park. At the commemorative moment, 8:16 A.M., the air was suffocating. I imagined that near where we were sitting now, someone was resting forty years ago on a stone step in the morning heat. Someone looked up at the sun and saw it explode.

Before going to bed for the day, LB said, "Let's have a Japanese breakfast." Pickled vegetables and cold poached fish restored the salts we'd lost in sweat that morning. Until the evening concert, the day was free. LB slept all day. I swam in the hotel's pool, had a phenomenal massage, and then walked through the city. What a perk to be taller than everyone else. Couldn't we stay a week as tourists and shake off the emotional overload? There were gardens to see, there was LB's pal Kunihiko, there might be a sailboat available. I could even catch up on sleep.

Instead, after two concerts bookended by televised interviews and lavish receptions, we headed back around the globe to Europe. LB, Phillip, and Harry took the orchestra and chorus to Budapest for one performance, while Maggie Carson and I flew to Vienna. Maggie insisted that we adjust to the local time—

to which we'd adjusted only a week earlier—by sitting through a schlocky operetta at the Staatsoper. One number was sung in an unrecognizable language. When the tour group in front of us burst into applause, Maggie asked them why. Simple enough: they were from Tokyo and that language was Japanese.

"You'd think we would have known *that*," Maggie said, but what could either of us remember about Japan? That stop was over twelve hours in the past. Besides, my mind churned the whole evening. We had one more Peace concert in Vienna, a week in Schleswig-Holstein to lay the groundwork for a German version of Tanglewood, ten days in Tel Aviv with the Israel Philharmonic, then a tour with the IPO to Japan—another sweep around the globe—for nine concerts there, then on to the United States for three concerts, the last to be in Carnegie Hall in late September. The schedule was more overwhelming than ever. I broke out in a sweat just thinking about it. Could I really do this?

After LB arrived in Vienna from Budapest the next day, I opened the eighteen pieces of luggage in my room at the Sacher and sorted clothes. One pile for overnight laundry and the upcoming IPO tour, another pile for repair, and a small pile for Phillip Allen to take back to New York. I set aside a few items for the trip to Schleswig-Holstein. What a disorganized mess. LB stepped in to ask me something, but after one look at his wardrobe scattered about in untidy heaps, he hit me—hard—as though pain would knock the confusion out of me. I cried at the shock of his blow. I was still unable to speak when Harry Kraut came in a little later.

"Lenny doesn't want you in Schleswig," Harry said. "You'll stay here and get the luggage ready for Israel."

The following day, I handed carry-on bags to the limo driver. LB looked puzzled. "Why aren't you ready?" he asked me, "We're going to the airport now."

"Harry says you don't want me to go," I said, turning away.

LB made his usual gestures of incredulity, his hands open, his arms wide. He began to say something. "But, I mean . . ." he said, but broke off.

Harry sputtered, "Lenny, I understood you to say—"

On that inconclusive dialogue, I closed the limo door.

I got it: just as Harry had plotted a nervous breakdown for Dorothee Koehler, he'd contrived one for me as well. I never saw it coming.

Now what?

32 | C'mon, It'll Be Fun!

AUGUST TURNED SULTRY IN VIENNA. I took lengthy walks that became sweaty tests of endurance. I loathed the place and the people in it, with their veneer of politesse. Dunking myself in a bathtub of cold water helped a little, for a change, as did packing LB's luggage for Israel. But I was so off balance, I didn't speak for two days except to order room service. The day I left for Munich, Fritz Willheim called, but I couldn't cope with a conversation, even with the endearingly sympathetic Fritzl.

At the hotel in Munich, a message from Harry Kraut instructed me to purchase two first-class tickets to Tel Aviv and a ticket to New York for myself. After I telexed Phillip Allen the number of bags to expect in Tel Aviv, I sat on the floor in my hotel room, drained every bottle in the mini-bar, and gave in to uncontrollable bouts of weeping. A televised production of *The Magic Flute* gave me an additional excuse to cry. Pamina threatened to stab herself and Papageno knotted a noose to end his loneliness. That opera is such a comedy. Simple dilemmas face those characters. What was my dilemma? Didn't I want to go home? Why did I feel my life was over? I felt more abandoned than Papageno. Like him, I couldn't figure anything out.

On a four-mile walk, I spotted a slogan on a kid's backpack: *Have a fun-filled life. All you have to do is try.* Exactly what LB's mother had told me! Omens lurked everywhere.

Though I was now a useless supernumerary, I could still check LB's luggage to Tel Aviv. For two intense hours, an agitated official questioned every item in every bag.

"What is this?" he barked, holding up a plain envelope.

"Newspaper reviews—you can open it," I said meekly, my eye on a guard's machine gun. After the last bag cleared, I thought about finding LB and Harry, but that interrogation over the luggage had sapped all my energy—and what if I burst into tears? Neither LB nor Harry would want to see that. In the taxi back to the hotel, I was shaking.

I packed my single suitcase and flew to New York the next day. I took advantage of a Lufthansa business class freebie: a hair-raising helicopter ride into Manhattan. *Let's crash! What have I got to lose?* Everyone else barfed at every bounce. I prayed for a nosedive into the East River.

Before the Israel Philharmonic (IPO) even got to Japan, there was a bomb threat. The Japanese and the IPO took this threat seriously. All the hotels had to be changed. Before every concert, the audience had to pass through security checks. Worse for LB, security concerns forbade anyone backstage after the concerts, so with nothing to do, he returned to his hotel room energized but frustrated. He sent word to me in New York that he missed our rounds of Mental Jotto.

LB had so much free time that Kunihiko—LB's personable translator—said, "Let's walk around Tokyo." Kuni later told me that in the antique district, LB spotted a koto, a plucked stringed instrument that rests on the floor, like an oversize zither. He decided it was the perfect sister instrument for my clavichord, and shipped it air freight to the Dakota. He said later, "I pictured you in a kimono, bent over the koto, plucking exotic melodies of the Orient." *What?* Pretending the instrument was an oriental zither, I wrote a rhyming thank-you note, and LB responded:

Kuni-San Hashimoto
Assured me, con moto,
That this was a KOTO!

I swear by me mither
(Or may me arm wither!)
THIS THANG AIN'T NO ZITHER . . .
Love LB

That was sweet. But what did it mean? I didn't know how to deal with such an outlandish gift.

In a momentous show of trust, Helen Coates gave me a key for Apartment 2DD in the Osborne, the suite LB had kept as a study in the 1950s, when he and his family lived upstairs. For thirty years, Helen had crammed the makeshift shelves and drawers in 2DD with fan mail, photographs, programs and newspaper reviews from every concert—glued into mammoth scrapbooks—and every one of LB's recordings, including ten sets of his landmark New York Philharmonic Mahler symphonies. Helen also asked me to accompany her to the safe deposit boxes where she stashed LB's manuscripts, sorted by size: music, speeches, scripts for young people's concerts, Harvard exam booklets—everything LB ever wrote.

On LB's return to New York, fifty friends welcomed him at the Dakota, a party organized and catered by Patti Pulliam, now permanently, thank god, in the kitchen. I took on the ticket requests for his Carnegie Hall concerts with the IPO, I made his doctor and dental appointments, called the car service, set up some exercise sessions with his coach, got the television cable fixed, carted luggage across town to be repaired, and organized a table for a dozen at a Museum of Broadcasting's black-tie event. My datebook looked as overloaded as always, but my handwriting was larger, more harried-looking. I still hadn't processed my emotional upheaval from the month before.

Halfway through the week, LB said that a weekend escape to Connecticut was mandatory.

"But there's a tropical storm moving up the east coast," I warned LB.

Next thing I knew, Shirley called. "Get some hurricane lamps and flashlights, and extra batteries," she said. "We'll need lots of ice and bottled water. It'll be like camping. C'mon, it'll be fun."

The storm quickly developed into Hurricane Gloria, roaring across Long Island and slamming into Connecticut. Falling trees pulled down power lines, cutting off electricity to a record number of households. When I called the state police, a stern trooper instructed, "Do not drive up here. Dunham Road is closed. There is no electricity. We opened a school as a shelter with showers and toilets." LB and Shirley in a non-smoking shelter, playing anagrams by lamplight? Um, no.

They drove up on Saturday anyway. Sunday morning I took the station wagon to the one restaurant supplier still open, but Long Island restaurants had snatched up every last ice cube. On foot, I traipsed from one hardware store and camping outlet to another, but all flashlights and lanterns had been sold days before— a completely wasted day. Three years before, I'd wasted an entire day cutting up a Christmas tree in the Dakota. Was this how I would spend the rest of my life?

I called Shirley. "We had to show IDs to get to Dunham Road, and there's nothing to eat and no hot water," she said. "Aren't you coming?" She sounded manic. How far did she have to drive for a cup of coffee?

I'd made up my mind. "No," I told her. "I'm staying in the city." At my desk I typed a message to leave on LB's breakfast table. "I resign from the position of assistant, effective October 31," one month's notice. In my datebook, I drew a big box in red pencil around the words "giving notice."

At the Dakota the next day, LB looked drawn and humorless. "You could have made a little effort," he said glumly. I see: if there was something wrong, it was with me, not with the weather. He looked at my note. "If that's what you want to do," he said. "Could you wait until the end of the year?" Three months rather than one, one more stint in Vienna and two more weeks with the New York Philharmonic? I gave in, but December 31 was it. I wouldn't need a datebook after that. Strange, how unemotional I felt.

That same day, LB insisted, "Find a therapist. Don't put it off." I already had a list recommended by my friend John's mentor. I didn't know how to choose one from any other on the list, but what really worried me was the fee. It was bound to be exorbitant.

Long ago, John had said, "When you need it, you'll find the way to pay for it."

I called the guy at the top of the list for an appointment and settled on an hour between a Philharmonic rehearsal and an evening performance on November 14.

One last trip to Vienna. On my final Concorde flight, as LB took his seat, he said, obviously trying to pick a fight, "You've never said anything good about my *Mass.*"

"I've never seen a performance of *Mass,*" I said truthfully. "I know it only from the recording." I tried to steer LB's antagonism toward a constructive dialogue: why the multitude of keyboards, the marching band, the variety of solo singers, the impracticality of dancers on an already-crowded stage? The Celebrant's nervous breakdown struck me as contrived; did it work on stage? LB easily volleyed all my arguing points, except for the Celebrant's breakdown. At that, he kept mum. I should have been flattered that he wanted my opinion on his music, but I wasn't prepared. What an arduous flight. This time, I waved away a third glass of champagne.

We were booked for one night at the Heathrow Airport Sheraton, one of Harry Kraut's money-saving gambits. Yes, it'd be cheaper than the Savoy, but Harry wasn't with us for this experiment in scrimping. I tried hailing a taxi while LB's irritation grew—antagonized about *Mass* or was he being a Maestro?—as each taxi driver shook his head. Finally, a porter explained that taxis were not permitted to carry passengers within the airport, but that a shuttle bus should arrive shortly.

Rain began to fall at midnight, but getting soaked was nothing. I was more concerned that LB might pummel me in front of the bedraggled crowd at the bus stop. LB shouted, "Why are we traveling like guinea pigs?" The crowd stared at him, but just then a bus pulled up to the curb. I shoved our luggage onboard and hoped LB would follow me.

From our cheap hotel rooms, I called Harry and let him have it. "It's not part of the job to be yelled at in public," I said. "Nobody bothers with the details in your organization," I went on, thinking back to the first slip-up, that un-winterized station wagon in Indiana. "If your travel agent can't figure out a simple overnight, I'll do it and charge it to Amberson."

After Harry got to Vienna the next day, he addressed me in a barely audible undertone, his usual "disarming" mode. "You were hysterical on the phone," he said. I exploded a second time. Harry's cluelessness only made me angrier.

———

AFTER LB TOOK TO HIS BED at the Hotel Sacher, I accompanied the porters hefting the music trunks to the Musikverein, where the entire Vienna Philharmonic waited onstage.

"Shostakovich is a modern composer for us, you know," the concertmaster said to me apologetically. "Now we will prepare his symphony number nine, but will you lead us?" I was stunned that the finest orchestra in the world respected me as a musician. They must have thought that I, as LB's assistant, was a budding conductor. Could I lead them through this piece? Well, possibly. The first movement is fairly simple. But what right did I have to stand on the podium occupied by Brahms and Mahler and Bernstein?

"Excuse me, but no," I said. "Here's how it goes," and I sang the opening as I remembered it from LB's 1966 Young People's Concert. The violinists raised their instruments, I gave a downbeat and then took a seat. I was tempted only once to stand and wave my arms to keep them from speeding up, but they played the first movement straight through. For an audience of one.

"We see how it goes, now," the concertmaster said. The rehearsals that week were brilliant.

Following up on Harry's invitation, Justin Brown arrived for a few days and joined LB for dinners and four-hand piano playing. Brilliant at anagrams and musically facile, Justin hadn't yet embarked on a conducting career, but LB recognized Justin's talent and enlisted him in the years ahead to assist with the musical preparation of *Candide*. Justin came along at exactly the right time. He brought a much-needed uplift to LB's tired entourage.

To commemorate a VPO benefit concert, the Sigmund Freud Society printed a caricature of LB sharing Freud's carpet-covered couch: a full-color reminder to find a therapist. LB happily signed copies for each of his New York therapists, and one for my friend John, about to earn his second graduate degree in psychology.

LEONARD BERNSTEIN und die WIENER PHILHARMONIKER geben am 5. November 1985, 19.30 Uhr ein Benefizkonzert im Musikvereinssaal zu Gunsten der SIGMUND-FREUD-GESELLSCHAFT

Leonard Bernstein and the Vienna Philharmonic present on 5 November 1985 at 7:30 a benefit concert in the Musikverein to aid the Sigmund Freud Society.

Back in New York, I let Phillip Allen manage everything. I didn't even unpack LB's luggage. I agreed to work the entire day of Aaron Copland's 85th birthday, November 14—a special date for LB. He'd met Copland on November 14, 1937, and on that same date six years later made his Philharmonic debut.

(November 14 took on an additional association one month after LB's death in 1990: his memorial concert at Carnegie Hall. LB had always said there were no accidents.)

At the mid-day rehearsal on November 14, 1985, LB led the Philharmonic through Copland's "Fanfare for the Common Man." Then I took the signed Freud Gesellschaft posters to LB's therapists on Manhattan's East Side, en route to my first session with my new shrink. I had a hunch this hour might be spent assessing my mental and emotional health, so I arrived a little early to collect my thoughts.

This psychiatrist was authoritative but personable. He efficiently handed me several evaluation exams. I'd seen these standardized forms before. When my friend John learned how to administer psychiatric tests, I had volunteered to be his subject. Back then, I'd been mischievous with my answers, but this time I rapidly checked off my responses, sailing into the third exam when the psychiatrist looked up from exam number one. He said, "Charlie, you need supervised medication. I'm calling my hospital"—his residency at St. Vincent's—"and getting you admitted right now." His voice had an urgent edge.

"I can't go to a hospital," I said, without looking up from exam number three. Was he kidding? "It's Aaron Copland's birthday, and I have to go back to work." I talked as I continued to check off my responses. "There's a concert. I have a job," I said, trying to sound deliberate, purposeful. The therapist wasn't daunted.

"You're suicidal," he said.

"No, I'm not," I said flatly. Wait, was he right?

But no beds were available at St. Vincent's. By the end of his phone call, I had finished the last exam. All those questions had unsettled me. As his diagnosis sank in, I began to feel a tremor, a realization that I would have to put myself into the hands of this doctor. It made me uncomfortable, but I understood how those exams worked. They didn't lie.

Now I was interested in what he had to say. He had my full attention. As he wrote a prescription, he said, "Get this filled today. It's an anti-depressant."

"Okay, but I'll take it only for as long as I continue to see you," I said. "The goal has to be to get off this medication." He nodded. After I finished the rest of the standardized evaluations, I wrote a check for $170.

My bank account now totaled $14.65. My weekly salary—by then raised to $534.60—was no match for this psychiatrist's three sessions per week, plus a prescription. One salary check barely covered my rent. My palms sweated on the bus back to the West Side. How was I going to pay for this?

LB sat at his desk studying. No cocktail hour tonight, not with a Philharmonic concert in a couple of hours.

"How was it?" he asked.

"The therapist said I was suicidal." LB looked up from his desk, his eyes calm and serious. "He wanted to hospitalize me this evening for supervised medication, but there weren't any beds at St. Vincent's, so he gave me this prescription." As I handed it to LB, the color drained from his face. I told him about the evaluation exams and the upcoming three sessions per week. He reached for his checkbook.

"How much was it?" he asked, scratching his pen across a check for twice the amount. "Take the prescription across the street. Put it on my account," LB said, "including all the refills." I hadn't expected this. On my way to the pharmacy across 72nd Street, I rubbed my eyes to stop the tears.

Craig Urquhart agreed to fill the assistant position I was about to vacate. Already friends with Harry Kraut, Craig had met LB years before. Craig had a more serious career in music than I, and I'd run into him a few times but I didn't know him well. He was personable and easy to get along with. At the Dakota, I showed Craig how LB kept his datebook, and the massive Rolodexes, and how to pack for a stint overseas—LB was about to record *A Quiet Place* in Vienna. Craig immediately set limits that enabled him to keep the job even longer than I had. When someone asked for tickets to LB's concerts, I'd always said, "I'll see what I can do." Craig said, "Have you tried the box office?"

Harry asked if I'd undertake an inventory of the contents in Apartment 2DD, LB's old studio in the Osborne. "Lenny says you get along with Helen Coates,"

LB inspects a few of his honorary degrees, among plaques and other framed memorabilia in his old studio in the Osborne. I've lapsed into my "attentive" pose, chin in hand.

Harry said. Nearly chuckling, he added, "You may be the only person who can work with her."

In sifting through LB's saved mail, I had an advantage: I knew virtually all the correspondents. I'd talked with LB about every one of his compositions. In photographs from the present back to the 1950s, I could name almost everyone. I'd even met most of the photographers.

I needed that 1986 datebook, after all.

33 | And Then What Happened? An Epilogue

FAR FROM THE CENTER of the universe—that immense gravitational field, that primordial Big Bang known as Leonard Bernstein—I now orbited like an invisible planet. No more picking up the phone and hearing Betty Comden or Adolph Green. No more waving at Lauren Bacall as she walked her dog. No more opening the door to greet Kiri Te Kanawa or Susan Sarandon or Michael Tilson Thomas. Why would those people remember me, now that I was relegated to the purgatory of "formerly"—*formerly Leonard Bernstein's assistant*.

Then again, I could set my own schedule. I could have dinner with friends whenever I wanted, or see a play, or even subscribe to a series of concerts. I wasn't running around the world anymore.

ON 57TH STREET, the prominence of the Osborne mirrors that of Carnegie Hall. The two bastions of New York's nineteenth century sit diagonally opposite one another. When LB lived in the Osborne and the Philharmonic's home was Carnegie Hall, LB had a short walk to work.

The Osborne's lobby glittered with Byzantine mosaics, but Apartment 2DD was a dingy gray cave. For thirty years, nothing in 2DD had changed, except for the removal of the piano when the Bernsteins relocated to Park Avenue. LB had retained 2DD since then for storage. Beneath the glass tabletop that LB had once used as a desk, photos of family and friends lay exactly where he had placed them decades earlier.

The apartment had seen plenty of activity as LB's studio in the 1950s. One day, a young Stephen Sondheim knocked on the door, sent by Arthur Laurents to find out more about a work-in-progress, *West Side Story*. LB had been trying to write the music and lyrics himself, but he needed help. LB never told me much about that meeting, but when he dropped by 2DD to see how I was doing, he stretched out on the dusty couch and said, "If this sofa could talk."

A week later, Barbara Haws, newly appointed archivist of the New York Philharmonic, and Lou Robbins, the Philharmonic's recently retired librarian, came to take a look.

A pensive moment on the sofa in his old studio in the Osborne.

Barbara said, "Start in one corner, look at each item, write a description. The categories will form themselves."

Lou said, "Always keep this glass tabletop clear, and get another table. You can never have enough working space."

One day, Harry Kraut said, "There's a manuscript appraiser you should meet," and shortly thereafter, George Minkoff sat beside me as we examined music manuscripts, boxes and boxes of letters, thousands of photographs and awards, irreplaceable orchestra materials on loan from the Philharmonic, and recordings by the dozens. What started out looking like an infinite undertaking became a manageable project. George completed his appraisal in three years. At the same time, I had catalogued the entire contents of 2DD. I had created an archive.

Apartment 2DD remained the domain of LB's secretary, Helen Coates, who could materialize at any time from her lair on the ninth floor, ready to reprimand me if I removed something from a wall. Then I'd stay away a few days and figure out some way to flatter Helen. I'd ask her about a photograph or a Harvard exam booklet.

On her good days, she'd confide in me. "I had to tell Lenny to use a deodorant," she said. "He'd come to his piano lesson right after baseball practice."

What? LB played baseball in high school? His team-bonding started young.

"He didn't even change his shirt," Helen said, still affronted a half-century later. What about his piano playing?

"I got him to stop banging and gave him his first serious pieces. He was my best pupil," she clucked. "Here's the plaque to prove it." She pointed to the side of the Steinway in her apartment.

Eventually Helen condoned the heavy-duty shelves I installed in 2DD. She even admired the archival boxes, envelopes, and file folders. Grudgingly, she approved my attention to detail.

During LB's stopovers in New York, I shared with him things I'd found, such as this telegram mixed in with fan mail, sent *during* the radio broadcast of LB's Philharmonic debut:

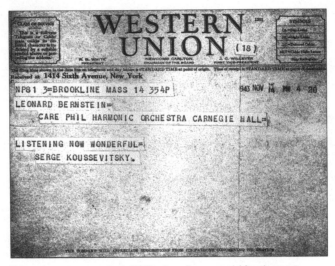

"Listening now wonderful." What audiences said for the next forty-seven years.

Helen had saved everything, thank god, though LB was stumped by a thank-you telegram for an omelet pan, signed "Oedipus de Bergerac." Perhaps someone with a large, uh, proboscis? Forever a mystery.

My working relationship with the Maestro improved, maybe because I saw him so rarely. Helped by my therapist's anti-depressant prescription, my sense of self-worth gradually returned. Time slowed down. Assessing my psychic storage with a psychiatrist took as long as sifting through the contents of Apartment 2DD: 1986–1988, three introspective years.

IN 1988, JOHN MAUCERI put together a version of *Candide* at Scottish Opera in Glasgow, which LB attended and admired. I should have bit the bullet and paid my own way to Glasgow, because plans to record this version—with further changes proposed by LB—developed rapidly. Mindful of the shortcomings leading up to his 1984 recording of *West Side Story*, LB assigned all musical preparation for *Candide* to me. It was his way of acknowledging my improved editorial skills, which had come a long way since 1982, when he'd asked me to make a piano reduction of *AQP's* Act One.

In 1989, computer software for music engraving was not yet adequate for a score as large as *Candide*. I retrieved the original 1956 orchestration pages and filled in the orchestrator's shorthand. On a page that had "*col fl.*" (with the flute) on the staff for the first violins, I copied the notes from the flute staff. I also coordinated the dynamics and articulation—if the flute played *piano*, the violins played *piano*, too—and wrote in all the lyrics. (Orchestrators save time by leaving out the lyrics.) After five months, I had a presentable score. Justin Brown, hired as LB's assistant conductor for this project, flew to New York, and in one high-spirited weekend in LB's Connecticut studio, LB answered my questions as Justin and I turned the pages. I'd never felt so in charge.

Then I made all the orchestra parts and pasted together a piano/vocal. I can't say the entire production went off without a hitch, but the performances were remarkably free of any musical mishaps. The extra dividend was that the recording sealed my friendship with Justin Brown.

After that, I fit easily into the position of LB's music editor. I conferred with Jack Gottlieb on editorial projects at LB's publisher, Boosey & Hawkes. I learned how to plan a publication schedule and how to handle permissions and premieres. As my responsibilities blossomed, I spent less time under Harry Kraut's thumb and more time with conductors, many of them already familiar to me from those summer stints in Los Angeles and Tanglewood. At last, I was capable of meeting the tasks at hand.

I'd never have known that if I hadn't tried.

ON A SUNDAY IN October 1990, less than a year after LB's recording of *Candide* in London, his sometime partner, Aaron Stern, called me at home in New York. He'd had dinner with LB at the Dakota the night before and asked if I'd seen him lately. Without waiting for me to answer, he said, "Go to the Dakota and see him, *right now.*"

It was a sunny autumn day, so I bicycled leisurely up to 72nd Street. Julia stood at her ironing board in the kitchen and smiled. "Charlito, why are you here?" she said coyly. She averted her eyes and said, "The *señor* is in his bedroom. You go in."

I hadn't seen LB in eight weeks, since his final Tanglewood concert. Months before that, he had told me that he'd decided not to continue with chemotherapy. He had seen first-hand how Felicia's chemo had diminished her vitality and stripped away layers of her personality. (I agreed with him. I'd seen that happen to my friend, John.) But I hadn't expected LB to look so frail.

He sat in the upholstered chair by his bedroom door. He had lost weight; his face was almost skeletal. A wheelchair waited by the bathroom door. I hadn't known that he could no longer walk.

"Look at these grapes Zubin sent," he said joyously, offering me a handful. Alexander Bernstein and Mendy Wager left the room through the door to the study, and suddenly LB and I were alone. The alignment of the universe shifted—a moment elemental and sudden—with the realization that I now had to say goodbye. This would take some courage. I knelt on the floor so our faces were level with one another.

Thoughts tumbled around in my head. I must have looked desolate, because before I said anything, LB commanded, "No fond farewells!" My calmness surprised me, but how does anyone begin a valedictory such as this? Oh yes, I know.

I said, "Thank you." That's what I'd been taught as a child, when saying goodbye. Now I really meant it. But what was I thankful for? "You're only the second person I've ever known that I could fight with," I said. The first had been my best friend, John, who so long ago had given me the advice *take your personality with you and put it to work*, a mantra that carried me through my initial job interview with Harry Kraut.

I had another thought. "Arguing isn't the same as confrontation," I said. "When both sides agree to a compromise, a fight deepens a friendship, instead of destroying it."

"Fighting—it's as good as fucking," LB said in his raspy growl.

Oh, the irrepressible Maestro.

Then he took my hand and said, "Please look after my music." I didn't know what to say. He repeated, "Please look after my music."

I said, "Yes," and we simply looked at one another.

From that moment when he shuffled pages of manuscript on his piano in Indiana and handed them to me, from my first attempt to arrange a piano reduction of LB's short score, from his initial admonishments to "be more forceful" with a pencil, LB had been my mentor. I'd immersed myself in his music. I'd followed along in rehearsals, with a score of *Divertimento,* or the "Age of Anxiety," or "Kaddish" on my lap. He had berated me for not appreciating *Mass.* He'd shared with me what made him proud about *1600 Pennsylvania Avenue.* He had explained how *West Side Story* had come together—as he talked over a performance. When we played through a just-finished segment of *A Quiet Place*, he answered my questions as though I had every reason to ask such things. My education had taken nearly eight years.

But what was this new request, to look after his music? How could I do that, without him there? This was more than trusting me with all the works he'd written, he was asking me to secure his legacy. I'd have to make decisions that only LB had made up until then. This was about the future: his future. My future. I could barely comprehend the responsibilities.

In that one phrase, "Please look after my music," LB leveled a charge similar to Dr. Koussevitzky's in that November 14, 1943, telegram: *This role is yours now, my part is done.*

ALEXANDER AND MENDY came back into LB's bedroom. I went to the kitchen to kiss Julia goodbye for now and got back on my bicycle. Such a beautiful afternoon. And LB was really going to die.

It helped me to move around. I bicycled to lower Manhattan and looked out over the harbor: all kinds of boats, sunlight bouncing on the water, a cloudless sky, people walking, jogging, bicycling—but I couldn't focus on anything. My head was empty except for LB's voice. "Look after my music." I returned to my apartment and waited.

At sunset, Julia Vega called and said, "Mr. Bernstein dies." In English, she always spoke in the present tense. At that moment, the present tense sounded absolutely right; her immediacy was comforting. Then she said, "I love you, Charlito," and we hung up.

I would cry later. For now, I thought of all the people around the world who would hear that LB had died, and how we would all share this change in our lives. I thought of his friends, my friends, too, in England, Germany, Israel, and Italy. Japan, Mexico, and Chile. I thought of LB's mother, Jennie. Her grief to me was unimaginable. I cried for Jennie.

An hour later Harry Kraut called to say that LB had died. I asked if I could come to the Dakota, but he said, "No, you don't need to." So I didn't go, though I

A New York City newsstand on October 15, 1990.

had a hunch the apartment was filled with family and friends, which it was. Why did I ever listen to Harry? He said the same thing to Jack Gottlieb, so Jack didn't go to the apartment, either. Jack had felt a more intense sense of duty than I, to sit shiva. He didn't get to fulfill that obligation and remained inconsolable for the rest of his life.

I stayed up late that night, alone in my tiny apartment, thinking of the past, not sure I could imagine the future.

For eight more years, I did what I could to promote LB's musical legacy, starting with the first publication of full scores of *West Side Story* and *Candide*. The first score took ten years, the next one took five. In every bar of music, LB's comments sounded in my ear. Then I picked up the pace. Vocal scores for *Candide, On the Town,* and *Wonderful Town* followed, along with many new productions and recordings, and much gratitude from conductors and orchestra musicians for editions that were correct and legible. The goal: bound volumes of Bernstein's theater works, to be followed by new editions of the concert works. An entire Bernstein shelf in music libraries around the world.

Meanwhile, orchestra librarians wasted their time fixing the hand-copied performance materials for Bernstein's "Serenade," "Jeremiah," and "The Age of Anxiety." Every year I submitted an editorial and publication budget, and every year

Harry Kraut struck two-thirds of those proposals. Harry said, "If there are performances, why do we need a new edition?"

"Because the performances will be better and lead to more recordings," I said, but he wasn't listening.

After ten years of arguing, I gave up. There would never be any compromise in an argument with Harry Kraut. Without planning on it, I quit one afternoon when he said point-blank that someone else should manage the publishing, even though he had no one in mind. The publication pipeline still held nineteen Bernstein works when I walked away from those responsibilities and my eighteen years of serving Leonard Bernstein and his music.

At first I had no regrets. Colleagues in the music business shared with me how Harry had treated them. Contempt seemed to be the norm, especially Harry's scorn for projects that weren't his idea. I'd known about his misogyny and his mistrust of other people's motives, but it startled me to hear about these traits from trusted colleagues. Though most people had been careful not to show it, they'd held Harry at an arm's length for a long time.

But I had betrayed LB's trust in me. There had been no witnesses when LB had asked me to look after his music, but as I shared what LB had said, people believed me. As I thought about LB's request, it seemed that what he had actually asked was for me to figure out some way to deal with Harry Kraut. From that point of view, my departure seemed less like a betrayal of LB's wish than acknowledging my aversion to subterfuge.

Without any effort on my part, LB's music still filled my head. Sometimes I missed working on his music, but conductors continued to call me with questions. Yet, I regretted that there would be a gap in every music library between Beethoven and Brahms, a shelf that should have been filled by Bernstein.

On a visit to LB's grave a year later, I apologized to him aloud. The sound of his voice when he beseeched me to "look after my music" haunted me. I said I'd done what I could. I hoped he forgave me. The soles of my feet burned as I stood on the grassy slope in Green-Wood Cemetery. They still burn whenever I stand on his grave. Maybe that's what Moses felt when the burning bush admonished him to remove his sandals. Talking to the *rebbe* is like that.

⸻

MY CONNECTIONS TO LB's life and music have continued, with conductors, singers, orchestra librarians, opera company managers, pianists, composers—people who dedicate their lives to music, lives Leonard Bernstein illuminated. People still ask me: what was he like? What did he write besides *West Side Story*? Was he gay?

He was formidable in an argument. (What *is* the way to talk to the *rebbe*?) He was a master at asking questions, and he taught me to ask questions, too. But I had to learn something else on my own.

After asking your question, listen.

Be curious, stay eager to learn. Ask all the questions you can think of. And then listen. Carefully, quietly, deeply.

That's the springboard for the rest of my life.

Selected Bibliography

Books by Leonard Bernstein

Bernstein, Leonard. 1959. *The Joy of Music*. New York: Simon & Schuster. New York: Signet Books, The New American Library, 1967.

——. 1961, 1970. *Leonard Bernstein's Young People's Concerts for Reading and Listening*. New York: Simon & Schuster.

——. 1966. *The Infinite Variety of Music*. New York: Simon & Schuster. New York: Plume Books, The New American Library, 1970.

——. 1976, 1981. *The Unanswered Question, Six Talks at Harvard*. Cambridge and London: Harvard University Press.

——. 1982. *Findings*. New York: Simon & Schuster.

Books on Bernstein by Other Authors

Bernstein, Burton. 1982. *Family Matters (Sam, Jennie, and The Kids)*. New York: Simon & Schuster.

—— and Barbara Haws. 2008. *Leonard Bernstein: American Original*. New York: Collins.

Burton, Humphrey. 1994. *Leonard Bernstein*. New York: Doubleday.

Cott, Jonathan. 2013. *Dinner with Lenny*. Oxford University Press.

Gottlieb, Jack. 2010. *Working with Bernstein, a Memoir*. New York: Amadeus Press.

Gradenwitz, Peter. 1984. *Leonard Bernstein, A Biography*. Berg Publishers (distributed by St. Martin's Press, New York).

Gruen, John and Ken Hyman. 1968. *The Private World of Leonard Bernstein*. New York: The Viking Press.

Ledbetter, Steven, ed. 1988. *Sennets & Tuckets, a Bernstein Celebration*. Boston: The Boston Symphony Orchestra in association with David R. Godine.

Peyser, Joan. 1987. *Bernstein, A Biography*. New York: Beech Tree Books/William Morrow.

Rubin, Susan Goldman. 2011. *Music Was IT: Young Leonard Bernstein*. Watertown, MA: Charlesbridge.

Secrest, Meryle. 1994. *Leonard Bernstein: A Life*. New York: Knopf.

Seiler, Thomas R. 1999. *Leonard Bernstein, the Last 10 Years, a Personal Portrait*. Zurich: Edition Stemmle.

Seldes, Barry. 2009. *Leonard Bernstein: The Political Life of an American Musician.* Berkeley: University of California Press.

Shawn, Allen. 2014. *Leonard Bernstein: an American Musician (Jewish Lives).* Yale University Press.

Sherman, Steve J. 2010. *Leonard Bernstein at Work: His Final Years, 1984–1990.* Amadeus Press.

Simeone, Nigel. 2009. *Leonard Bernstein: West Side Story.* Farnham, England: Ashgate.

———, ed. 2013. *The Leonard Bernstein Letters.* Yale University Press.

Selected Discography

For a lengthier discography and a detailed videography, please visit https://leonardbernstein.com/discography

Audio Recordings of Music by Leonard Bernstein

Arias and Barcarolles, Judy Kaye, William Sharp, Michael Barrett, Steven Blier, Koch International Classics 3-7000-2.

Candide, Jerry Hadley, June Anderson, Christa Ludwig, Adolph Green et al., London Symphony Orchestra and Chorus, Leonard Bernstein, Deutsche Grammophon 429 734-2.

Chichester Psalms, Israel Philharmonic Orchestra, Vienna Youth Chorus, Leonard Bernstein, Deutsche Grammophon 415 965.

Divertimento for Orchestra, Israel Philharmonic Orchestra, Leonard Bernstein, Deutsche Grammophon 415 966.

Halil, Jean-Pierre Rampal, Israel Philharmonic Orchestra, Leonard Bernstein, Deutsche Grammophon 415 966.

Mass, Alan Titus et al., The Norman Scribner Choir, The Berkshire Boy Choir, Leonard Bernstein, Sony Classical SM2K 63089.

On the Town, Betty Comden, Adolph Green, Nancy Walker, John Reardon, Chris Alexander, Leonard Bernstein, Sony Classics UPC# 0746 4605 3829.

On the Town, Frederica von Stade, Tyne Daly, Marie McLaughlin, Thomas Hampson, Kurt Ollmann, David Garrison, Samuel Ramey, Evelyn Lear, Cleo Laine, London Voices, London Symphony Orchestra, Michael Tilson Thomas, Deutsche Grammophon 437 516-2.

A Quiet Place, Chester Ludgin, Beverly Morgan, John Brandstetter, Peter Kazaras, Jean Kraft, Theodore Uppmann et al., ORF-Symphonie-Orchester, Leonard Bernstein, Deutsche Grammophon 419 761-2.

Songfest, Rosalind Elias, Donald Gramm, Nancy Williams, Neil Rosenshein, John Reardon, Clamma Dale, National Symphony Orchestra, Leonard Bernstein, Deutsche Grammophon 415 965.

Symphonic Suite from On the Waterfront, New York Philharmonic, Leonard Bernstein, Sony Classics UPC# 8279 6927 2824.

Symphony No. 1, "Jeremiah," Jennie Tourel, New York Philharmonic, Leonard Bernstein, Sony Classical SMK 60697.

Symphony No. 1, "Jeremiah," Christa Ludwig, Israel Philharmonic Orchestra, Leonard Bernstein, Deutsche Grammophon 445 245.

Symphony No. 3, "Kaddish," Montserrat Caballé, Michael Wager, Vienna Boys' Choir, Leonard Bernstein, Deutsche Grammophon 445 245.

Touches, Dag Achatz, BIS CD-352.

Touches, James Tocco, PRO-ARTE.

West Side Story, Kiri Te Kanawa, José Carreras, Tatiana Troyanos, Kurt Ollmann, Marilyn Horne et al., Leonard Bernstein, Deutsche Grammophon 415 253-2.

A White House Cantata, Scenes from *1600 Pennsylvania Avenue*, Thomas Hampson, June Anderson, Barbara Hendricks, Kenneth Tarver, et al., London Voices, London Symphony Orchestra, Kent Nagano, Deutsche Grammophon 289 463 448-2.

Selected Musical Scores by Leonard Bernstein

Visit boosey.com for more information on Leonard Bernstein's music in print.

Arias and Barcarolles, for Mezzo-soprano, Baritone, and Piano Four Hands. Jalni Publications, Inc., Boosey & Hawkes VSB 160.

Candide [Scottish Opera Version], Comic Operetta in Two Acts, Boosey & Hawkes HPS 1180 Study Score, VSB 161 Piano-vocal score.

Chichester Psalms, for mixed chorus, boy soloist and orchestra, Boosey & Hawkes, FSB 467 Full score, HPS 1201 Study score, LCB 214 Vocal score, ENB 264 Reduction for organ, harp and percussion.

Divertimento for Orchestra, Boosey & Hawkes HPS 986 Study score.

Halil, Nocturne for Solo Flute with Piccolo, Alto Flute, Percussion, Harp and Strings, Boosey & Hawkes HPS 972 Study score.

Mass, A Theatre Piece for Singers, Players and Dancers, Boosey & Hawkes VSB 152 Vocal score.

On the Town, Musical Comedy, Boosey & Hawkes VSB 0192 Vocal score.

A Quiet Place, Opera in Three Acts, Boosey & Hawkes VSB 154 Vocal score.

Slava!, A Political Overture for Orchestra, Boosey & Hawkes HPS 980 Study score.

Songfest, A Cycle of American Poems for six singers and orchestra, Boosey & Hawkes VAB 89 Vocal score.

Symphonic Suite from On the Waterfront, Boosey & Hawkes Orchestral Anthology Volume 2 M060 1076s27.

Symphony No. 1, "Jeremiah," for mezzo-soprano and orchestra, Boosey & Hawkes, FSB 597 Full score, SGB 6040 "Lamentation" transcribed for voice and keyboard.

Symphony No. 3, "Kaddish," for mixed chorus, boys' choir, speaker, soprano and orchestra, Boosey & Hawkes FSB 469 Study score, LCB 217 Vocal score.

Touches, Chorale, Eight Variations and Coda [for piano], Boosey & Hawkes PIB 274.

West Side Story, Musical based on a conception of Jerome Robbins, Boosey & Hawkes M051-97020-9 Vocal score, FSB 502 Full score.

Photograph and Other Credits

Page 15: © Copyright 1986 by Henry Grossman

Page 29: © Copyright 1988 by Patti Pulliam

Page 36: © Copyright 1982 by Ann Dedman

Page 39: © Copyright 1990 by Andrew French

Page 42: © Copyright 1990 by Andrew French

Page 45: © Copyright 1983 by Charlie Harmon

Page 61: © Copyright 1986 by Andrew French

Page 69: Courtesy of the Archive of the New York Philharmonic.

Page 80: Courtesy of the Archive of the New York Philharmonic.

Page 93: © Copyright 1984 by Arthur Elgort

Page 95: © Copyright 1939 by Adolph Green

Page 97: © Copyright 1982 by Charlie Harmon

Page 112: © Copyright 1982 by Robert Millard

Page 121: © Copyright 1982 by Thomas Seiler

Page 134: © Copyright 1982 by Henry Grossman

Page 135: © Copyright 1986 by Andrew French

Page 146: © Copyright 1982 by Arthur Elgort

Page 153: © Copyright 1990 by Andrew French

Page 156: © Copyright 1990 by Andrew French

Page 159: © Copyright 1983 by Arthur Elgort

Page 160: © Copyright 1983 by Arthur Elgort

Page 178: © Copyright 1981 by Henry Grossman

Page 186: Screenshots from the video, courtesy of Unitel GmbH & Co.

Page 220: © Copyright 2017 by Charlie Harmon

Page 240: Courtesy of Sigmund-Freud-Gesellschaft, Wien.

Page 242: © Copyright 1986 by Andrew French ·

Page 245: © Copyright 1986 by Andrew French

Page 250: © Copyright 1990 by Andrew French

Page 260: © Copyright 2014 by Linda James

About the Author

CHARLIE HARMON is a music editor and arranger. Sometimes he puts in hours as an orchestra librarian, most recently at the New York Philharmonic, where he is treated like royalty. They still seem to think that when he walks into the hall, Leonard Bernstein must be right behind. He has also worked on special projects in the libraries of the San Francisco Symphony Orchestra, the Boston Symphony Orchestra, the London Symphony Orchestra, and The Royal Opera, Covent Garden. For the estate of Leonard Bernstein, he edited full scores of *West Side Story* and *Candide,* and piano-vocal scores of *On the Town* and *Wonderful Town*, among many other works by Leonard Bernstein. (There are errata lists; nobody's perfect.) As a freelancer, he has edited works by John Adams, Stephen Sondheim, and Christopher Rouse. He assisted Lorin Maazel through the editing and rehearsals of his opera, *1984*, based on the George Orwell novel. He catalogued the archive now known as the Leonard Bernstein Collection in the Music Division of the Library of Congress. He has written program notes and liner notes for recordings, but this memoir is his first book. In words, that is. Words are far more complicated than music.

After many years in New York, he now lives in Florida.

The author points to a warehouse that happens
to have his name on it. Real estate, every
Army brat's fantasy! But it's no relation.